INGÉNUE AMONG THE LIONS

Ingénue among the Lions

The Letters of Emily Clark to Joseph Hergesheimer

EDITED WITH AN INTRODUCTION BY
GERALD LANGFORD

UNIVERSITY OF TEXAS PRESS, AUSTIN

Library of Congress Catalog Card No. 65-11150
Copyright © 1965 by the University of Texas Press
All Rights Reserved
Manufactured in the United States of America
Printed by Printing Division of the University of Texas, Austin
Bound by Universal Bookbindery, Inc., San Antonio

For N. P. L.

ACKNOWLEDGMENTS

For permission to publish the letters in this book grateful acknowledgment is made to the Fidelity-Philadelphia Trust Company, executor of the Will of Mrs. Emily Clark Balch, and also to the University of Virginia as a residuary legatee and devisee named in the Will.

Further acknowledgment is made to the Humanities Research Center of The University of Texas (in which all but the last four letters form part of the large Joseph Hergesheimer Collection), and to the Library of the University of Virginia (where the last four letters are to be found).

Particular appreciation should be expressed to Mrs. James Branch Cabell for her interest in the project and for her generous help with various factual matters.

For permission to quote from works under copyright, acknowledgment and thanks are due the following:

Alfred A. Knopf, Inc., for quotations from *Innocence Abroad,* by Emily Clark (copyright 1931 by Alfred A. Knopf, Inc.), and for quotations from *Prejudices, Second Series,* by H. L. Mencken (copyright 1920 by Alfred A. Knopf, Inc.).

Harcourt, Brace & World, Inc., for quotations from *Between Friends: Letters of James Branch Cabell and Others,* edited by Padraic Colum and Margaret Freeman Cabell, with an Introduction by Carl Van Vechten (copyright 1962 by Harcourt, Brace & World, Inc.).

Mrs. James Branch Cabell for a quotation from *Let Me Lie,* by James Branch Cabell (copyright 1947 by James Branch Cabell, published by Farrar, Straus and Company), and for a quotation from *As I Remember It,* by James Branch Cabell (copyright 1955 by James Branch Cabell, published by The McBride Company).

University of Texas Press for a quotation from *No Place on Earth,* by Louis D. Rubin, Jr. (copyright 1959 by The University of Texas Press).

CONTENTS

INTRODUCTION

"I recall an old definition of a literary clique," Carl Van Vechten recently commented: "ten or a dozen authors who live in the same town and who hate each other cordially. This was not true of our group in the Twenties. . . . Actually it was the nearest approximation to a group that had existed since Hawthorne's day, and certainly there is nothing like it today when occasionally you see a single author struggling with his peers at a cocktail party."[1]

H. L. Mencken, Sinclair Lewis, Theodore Dreiser, F. Scott Fitzgerald, James Branch Cabell, Ellen Glasgow, Louis Untermeyer, Ernest Boyd, Joseph Hergesheimer—these were the most notable of the group of Van Vechten's "friends I frequently broke bread with at Pogliani's or the Hotel Knickerbocker, and with whom I occasionally overdrank illegally."

What drew them together as a conscious group was not geographical proximity, but their zeal for a common cause. In effect they were a guerilla band unwilling to accept America's submission to an enemy labeled by Mencken the "booboisie," that vast army of occupation which divided its headquarters between Boston and the Bible Belt, and which in 1919 had issued a sweeping decree known as the Volstead Act. During the following decade the guerillas scored two particularly gratifying victories. In 1920 the New York Society for the Suppression of Vice induced a grand jury to indict Robert M. McBride & Co. for selling "a certain offensive, lewd, lascivious book" entitled *Jurgen,* by James Branch Cabell. At the conclusion of the trial Louis Untermeyer wrote Cabell: "I was almost expelled

---

[1] Padraic Colum and Margaret Freeman Cabell (eds.), *Between Friends: Letters of James Branch Cabell and Others,* with an Introduction by Carl Van Vechten (New York, Harcourt, Brace & World, Inc., 1962), p. xv.

this morning for rising to my feet when his honor charged the jury (you should have seen those twelve hundred percenters!) to bring in a verdict for Holt, McBride et al."[2] Six years later the Boston Watch and Ward Society had Mencken arrested for publishing and circulating an "immoral" article by Herbert Asbury in *The American Mercury.* "I am going to Boston on Sunday," Mencken wrote Cabell, "to accept responsibility, submit to arrest and go on trial. If I'm convicted, you will have the pleasure of sending me a Bible in jail. If I'm acquitted, half the Methodists of Boston will face suits for damage in the Federal Courts." A week later Mencken reported: "The victory in Boston was sweet and overwhelming. I am now entertaining the Comstocks with a damage suit for $50,000. It is to be argued in the Federal Court on Monday." Again Mencken was victorious; in fact, "the learned Judge delivered an eulogy of *The American Mercury* from the bench and said that he was a charter subscriber and proud of it."[3]

Harrying the enemy was one thing. Forcing it into retreat was another thing entirely, something which none of the literary snipers envisaged as even a possibility. Symptomatically, Hergesheimer appended to one of his letters to Cabell—with whom he felt a special camaraderie—an exercise in what he called "Literary Doggrel [*sic*] of the year two thousand and nineteen":

> Joe and Jim and none beside
> Mark an age that quickly died.
>
> Jim and Joe and none between
> Keep an age's memory green.
>
> Joe and Jim and only they
> Know the spirit from the clay.
>
> Jim and Joe forever are
> With Linda Condon and Ettarre.[4]

It was a brief era indeed—the decade of disillusion and revolt between the November, 1919, slump in Wall Street and that of Oc-

---

[2] *Ibid.,* p. 269. Guy Holt was an editor at McBride & Co., Cabell's publisher.
[3] *Ibid.,* p. 279.
[4] *Ibid.,* p. 112. *Linda Condon* is one of Hergesheimer's novels. Ettarre is one of Cabell's visions of feminine enchantment.

tober, 1929. And even while the spirit of the time lasted, it included a premonitory nostalgia, which has become increasingly poignant in retrospect. Padraic Colum writes:

It seems a long way back to that era, [and] we have a feeling that we are looking back to a happy time. Not in any predictable time will we have another group of writers who can confidently challenge the serious ones of the earth. They are not close enough, these serious ones, to be affected by our discourse, however witty. And those who engage in such discourse . . . are being overawed by men doing top-secret work on space-missiles and the like.[5]

So pervasive was the literary *esprit de corps* of that happy time that even in the hinterland little groups of amateurs began to assert themselves. The most notable of these, in Chicago, spread its influence through the publication of two magazines: Harriet Monroe's *Poetry* and Margaret Anderson and Jane Heap's *The Little Review*. A comparable group came into being in Richmond in November, 1920, when someone said at a party, "Let's start a little magazine." This event was a token of changing times in the South. As recently as 1917 Mencken had published his essay "The Sahara of the Bozart," deploring what had happened to the South since the Civil War. That vast hemorrhage, as he put it, "half exterminated and wholly paralyzed the old aristocracy, and so left the land to the harsh mercies of the poor white trash, now its masters. . . . It would be impossible in all history to match so complete a drying-up of a civilization." Getting down to cases, Mencken wrote:

In all that gargantuan paradise of the fourth-rate there is not a single picture gallery worth going into, or a single orchestra capable of playing the nine symphonies of Beethoven, or a single opera-house, or a single theater devoted to decent plays, or a single public monument that is worth looking at, or a single workshop devoted to the making of beautiful things. Once you have counted James Branch Cabell (a lingering survivor of the *ancien régime*: a scarlet dragon-fly imbedded in opaque amber) you will not find a single Southern prose writer who can actually write. And once you have—but when you come to critics, musical composers, painters, sculptors, architects and the like, you will have to give it up, for there is not even a bad one between the Potomac mud-flats and the Gulf. Nor a his-

[5] *Ibid.*, p. 290.

xiii

torian. Nor a philosopher. Nor a theologian. Nor a scientist. In all these fields the South is an awe-inspiring blank—a brother to Portugal, Serbia and Albania.[6]

Almost by the time Mencken issued his blast, things were changing in the South, and by 1929 the extent of the cultural reawakening was such that Ellen Glasgow was able to make the prophetic prediction: "It is entirely possible that the best writing in the United States will now be done in the South."[7] One of the earliest signs of animation was *The Reviewer,* the publication sportively begun at a party by four unknown young Virginians. The first issue appeared in February, 1921, at just the right time to review Mencken's *Prejudices, Second Series* (the book in which "The Sahara of the Bozart" was collected, along with other essays of the past three or four years). The last issue appeared less than four years later (the rate of publication having slackened from semimonthly to monthly and then to quarterly). Within that short life, though, the magazine had become known and respected in Europe as well as in America.[8]

This feat was contrived during the last three years of the life of Thomas Nelson Page, laureate of a bygone Virginia, who, when he died in 1923, was working on another of his nostalgic romances about the chivalric gentlemen and fair ladies of the Confederacy. Before *The Reviewer* there had been certain indications of the New South to come—for one, the career of Ellen Glasgow, curiously overlooked or dismissed by Mencken. As far back as 1897 she had begun writing novels realistic enough to be deprecated by Page's brother and biographer, who had wondered how a young Virginia gentlewoman could have learned some of the things she knew about the world. In *Barren Ground,* for example, Miss Glasgow was later to write about a betrayed woman who, as she put it, "for once, in Southern fiction . . . would become the victor instead of the victim" —who becomes, in fact, one of the freest and most independent of

[6] H. L. Mencken, *Prejudices, Second Series* (New York, Alfred A. Knopf, Inc., 1920), pp. 136 ff.

[7] Virginius Dabney, "A Prophet of the New South," New York *Herald-Tribune Magazine,* August 25, 1921, p. 6.

[8] Actually the magazine was continued for a fifth and final year by a different group in Chapel Hill, North Carolina. See below.

the New Women of the 1920's. In retrospect, though, as one present-day critic has remarked, the work of this self-styled realist "lies somewhat closer to the same Thomas Nelson Page than to, say, William Faulkner."[9] It is in *The Reviewer* that for the first time one breathes the air of the modern South. "We shan't be surprised," wrote Isabel Patterson, of the New York *Tribune*, "if future historians reckon the beginning of a great Southern literary renaissance from the date of the founding of *The Reviewer*."[10] And some years later James Branch Cabell commented:

When some as yet to be born historian prepares to deal candidly with that which Virginians of the first quarter of the twentieth century thought to be their civilization, then his will be the task to discover through what miracle, or art, or accident, four youngsters caused Richmond-in-Virginia to become a literary center between the February of 1921 and the October of 1924. . . .

In literary columns and in editorials throughout the more or less United States of America, and in Great Britain and her colonies likewise, *The Reviewer* during its short life was discussed as a harbinger and a portent of none knew just what. Freely, however, was *The Reviewer* reviewed "as the beginning of a great Southern literary renaissance." . . . Virginia alone, it must be recorded, did not notice *The Reviewer's* existence. The magazine had few, or rather it had virtually no, subscribers in Virginia. It was glanced over, not without fretfulness, by an exceedingly scant number of Virginians. And Richmond, after having been made somehow a literary center, did not delight in the city's unfamiliar role.[11]

The editor and moving spirit behind the venture, Emily Clark, later wrote her own account, in which she recalled the national as well as the Virginian perspective of the times:

The only book-page carried by a Richmond newspaper at that time had just died, quietly and suddenly. Hunter Stagg and I had assisted at its death-bed. . . . "We will start," someone said, "a fortnightly book-review. Richmond has always been full of writers, and why should not books be re-

[9] Louis D. Rubin, Jr., *No Place on Earth* (Austin, University of Texas Press, 1959), p. 7.

[10] Emily Clark, *Innocence Abroad* (New York, Alfred A. Knopf, Inc., 1931), p. 18.

[11] James Branch Cabell, *Let Me Lie* (New York, Farrar, Straus and Company, 1947), pp. 203 and 215–216.

viewed here?" There was no money available, and to Hunter and me this seemed unimportant. Margaret Freeman immediately reminded us that printers must be paid, although editors and contributors need not be. There was, however, only an instant's thoughtful pause, for Margaret mercifully added that she, personally, would collect enough advertisements from Richmond merchants to support a fortnightly pamphlet for six months. She did. And she resigned this job at the end of six months, after an illness, although remaining longer on the editorial staff of *The Reviewer*. No one, after Margaret's resignation, succeeded in collecting sufficient advertising to make *The Reviewer* a financially independent magazine. Two weeks after the magazine was planned Mary Street joined the self-elected editorial staff, and assisted in the composition of an amazing prospectus sent to possible subscribers in the South and to editors, publishers, and literary critics in New York. Mary, moreover, contributed a necessary two hundred dollars for printing and postage, which Margaret, as a result of the advertisements she had collected, was able to return to her at the end of six months. We asked only a six months' subscription as a trial, reserving the right to stop the magazine at the end of that time if our subscribers were less enthusiastic than ourselves. . . .

The literary scene in the fall of 1920, when *The Reviewer's* prospectus went abroad, was quivering with undeveloped and unexplored potentialities. They had laid Paul Elmer More in his grave and had not yet resurrected him. The post-war insurgence in America and Europe was nascent and exciting. *Jurgen* had been suppressed, but not released. *Main Street* came off the press almost simultaneously with the mailing of our prospectus and was not yet an accepted part of the American language. . . . Stuart Sherman was still in Urbana, Illinois, vigorously fighting for Americanism in American letters, and had not yet shown any symptom of the decadence which overcame him in his later, softer years, after the *Herald Tribune* had summoned him to the easier agreements and compromises of New York. . . . The old *Smart Set* was continuing its cheerfully impertinent experiments under the direction of Mencken-and-Nathan, at that time as inextricably hyphenated as Gilbert-and-Sullivan, or Abercrombie-and-Fitch. The *Little Review* was still in mid career, and *Broom, Secession,* and the *Wave* had not yet lived and died. Harry Hansen had not come East, and Burton Rascoe had just arrived from Chicago, and had not yet begun his upredictable "Bookman's Day Book" on the old New York *Tribune*. . . . There was no Literary Guild and no Book-of-the-Month Club. People who liked books were spontaneous and excited about discovering them for themselves. . . . A boy just out of Princeton had written *This Side of Paradise,* and he and Zelda Fitzgerald between them had just invented flappers. The revolt of youth was serious and intense, and no one dreamed that within ten years the feminine world would go quietly back to long hair, long skirts, curves, and corsets—and like them.[12]

The planning of *The Reviewer* aroused the interest not only of Richmond dilettantes but also of the established literary figures of the state (who later took a dim view of some of the things that were published). Thomas Nelson Page, then ending his term as American Ambassador to Italy, sent Emily thirty pages of advice. He felt strongly that "Richmond and Virginia and the whole South need badly a literary periodical, alive and virile and informed," and he urged that the proposed magazine "should stand for the principles of the Liberal South."[13]

William Cabell Bruce, author of the Pulitzer Prize biography *Benjamin Franklin* and other books, wrote Emily after seeing the first few issues: "Whatever else may be said of *The Reviewer*, it is not dull; and when that can be said Phoebus Apollo will forgive much. Properly financed, and with an occasional good article on political and social topics, *The Reviewer* would be a fine foundation on which to build a really successful Southern magazine."[14]

James Branch Cabell not only gave the undertaking his blessing. As Emily later explained:

a sudden and fortunate fancy seized him to give the world an example of perfect editing as a companion piece to many examples of perfect writing. For three months, October, November, and December, 1921, it must be told for the benefit of Cabell collectors, he edited the magazine single-handed, to show four awed editors just how editing could and should be done. He proved, in addition to brilliant editorial gifts, to be an expert make-up man.[15]

Ellen Glasgow—aloof from the actual planning or editing, as she was from most other involvements in life—wished the venture well in her own way. "With sufficient youth and ignorance to assist you," she wrote Emily, "you *may* accomplish the impossible."[16] And for one of the first issues she contributed an essay, "The Dynamic Past." Likewise Mary Johnston paused long enough in her production of cinematic romances of colonial Virginia to contribute a

---

[12] *Innocence Abroad*, pp. 1–4.
[13] *Ibid.*, p. 12.   [14] *Ibid.*, p. 13.
[15] *Ibid.*, p. 41.   [16] *Ibid.*, p. 55.

sketch, "The Return of Magic," early in the magazine's second year of publication.

Among other literary Virginians who took an interest was one whose name still held a very special glamor—Princess Troubetzkoy, née Amélie Rives. "I had heard all my life of Amélie," Emily wrote later, "as a celebrated beauty and writer of the nineties, as well as a playwright of today. For it has probably never before been granted to any woman to become simultaneously an international beauty and a best-seller." The Princess was one of the very few people by whom Emily was somewhat awed, as her account makes clear:

When Amélie's grandfather ended his two terms as Minister to France and returned to Castle Hill [the family estate in Albemarle County], her grandmother created one French room as a reminiscence. No detail of it has been changed. . . . A signed photograph of Lord Curzon is the single note alien to France, for that "most superior person, who dined at Blenheim once a week," was among Amélie's best friends in England, and was a guest at Castle Hill on his way to Persia in 1890. His letters to her—quite guiltless of superiority—with those of Arthur Balfour and others of his contemporaries, still fill various drawers and cupboards at Castle Hill, which contain also numerous copies of the *Yellow Book,* photographs of the Duchess of Rutland with a baby Diana Manners, other lovely ladies and impressive gentlemen of the London nineties, and, best of all, a first edition of *The Happy Prince,* inscribed: "For Amélie Rives, from her sincere admirer, Oscar Wilde. London—A rose-red July. '89." It was Oscar Wilde who introduced Pierre [Troubetzkoy], just arrived from Paris and Italy to paint portraits in England, to Amélie (then Mrs. John Armstrong Chanler), at a party where the de Reszkes were singing, given by Hamilton Aïde, an indispensable London bachelor of his day, in 1894. They were married at Castle Hill in 1896.[17]

The irresistibly piquant young woman to whose enthusiasm all these writers responded (together with a long list of non-Southerners of considerably wider repute) had been christened Emily Tapscott Clark, a name she abbreviated to an insouciant *ETC* for her stationery letterhead. Her father, a scholarly Episcopal clergyman, had belonged to one of the distinguished families of the state, so that Emily knew everyone of social importance. She was, in fact, something of a snob, with all of the traditional Southern sense of

[17] *Ibid.,* pp. 77–78.

propriety and most of the biases of her time and place. She maintained membership in the Daughters of the American Revolution and the Colonial Dames of America. She reminded Hergesheimer that most of the old homes in Halifax County belonged to relatives of hers, and she did not hesitate to call the first Mrs. Cabell "a common woman." She used the word *ankles* in referring to Ellen Glasgow's legs, because "I wouldn't say *legs* to her." She made snide remarks about the Jewishness of some of the literary people she met in New York. On the other hand, she spoke Mencken's caustic language in writing to him and about him, and she was not out of place in Van Vechten's bohemian circle in New York. All of which is to say she shared the inheritance of Sinclair Lewis's Carol Kennicott and, even more closely, that of an actual young woman named Zelda Sayre, of Montgomery, Alabama.

Emily was too capricious to settle down as a society matron (even if she had not been too tart for the taste of proper young Virginia gentlemen). Instead she became a staff writer for the Richmond *Evening-Journal* in 1919 and for the *News Leader* from 1920 to 1923. Only in 1924, at the age of thirty-one did she surrender the editorship of *The Reviewer* to make a spectacular marriage. Her husband—the sixty-eight-year-old Edwin Swift Balch, wealthy Philadelphia sportsman and author of books about Arctic exploration, who had financed the last few issues of *The Reviewer* edited by Emily—took her back to his palatial home in Philadelphia, but he lived only three more years. At his death he left her a rich woman. In 1927 she published a book of Virginia sketches called *Stuffed Peacocks,* and four years later an account of *The Reviewer* and its most notable benefactors (to which she gave the tongue-in-cheek title *Innocence Abroad*), but gradually she gave up active literary work and adopted the more congenial role of patroness of the arts. For the twenty years preceding her death in 1953, her home in Philadelphia was a salon to which came a succession of well-known writers and artists

Of those who helped make *The Reviewer* what it was, nearly all are now dead. Hergesheimer found, as the Twenties gave way to the Thirties, that he no longer had anything to say, and, even if he had

had, that he no longer commanded an audience. It was a bewildering decline for a writer to whom Emily, with some awe, had once reported Mencken's dictum that *"Cytherea* was the best novel about America, better than Mrs. Wharton or anybody, and that you were a great artist." This was not a surprising evaluation in 1922. As Clifton Fadiman ironically commented in 1933:

> It is a matter for sincere regret that his once large and enthusiastic audience has fallen away from Mr. Hergesheimer; and that vanished are those Cytherean days when reputable critics guaranteed "he need have few fears of rivalry for his position as America's foremost novelist." . . . To the thoughtful reader he must appear one of our most interesting writers. For twenty years Mr. Hergesheimer has written novels, short stories, and even autobiographies about people who do not work for a living. . . . Of all the writers of his time Mr. Hergesheimer has the clearest and most consistent view of the presuppositions of life. He knows on what terms life must be met—profitable terms only. . . . Mr. Hergesheimer's closely knit universe is passing. And because it is passing, Mr. Hergesheimer's pages become of greater and greater value. For these pages are unstirred by the foul intrusion of any breath save the wind blowing through the musical colossus of Mammon. They distil the pure essence of conspicuous waste. Can any of Mr. Hergesheimer's contemporaries present as proud a claim?[18]

Cabell also fell progressively into neglect until his death in 1958, four years after that of Hergesheimer. In 1951, having lost his first wife two years before, Cabell married Margaret Freeman, one of the founders of *The Reviewer* and one of Emily's closest associates. When Emily gave up the editorship in 1924, leaving the magazine to be taken over for one last year by Paul Green at the University of North Carolina, Margaret Freeman turned to her long-standing interest in interior decoration and worked in New York until her marriage. Since her husband's death she has remained in Richmond, and recently she helped edit a volume of letters to and from Cabell.[19]

Van Vechten published a last book in 1932, then gave up writing. Instead of giving up all creative activity, though, he turned his avocational interest in photography into a second career and pro-

[18] "The Best People's Best Novelist," *The Nation,* February 15, 1933.
[19] Colum and Cabell (eds.), *Between Friends.*

duced a succession of famous pictures of people as diverse as Gertrude Stein and Ethel Waters. Unlike Hergesheimer, Van Vechten was always essentially a bohemian. His most characteristic setting remains the one graphically described by Emily:

A June evening in Carl's apartment is especially vivid to me now, with George Gershwin at the piano playing and singing bits from his current musical show to a crowd of people, among whom Theodore Dreiser sat, heavy and brooding, the direct antithesis, almost a contradiction, of all that Gershwin means. And Elinor Wylie sat, aloof and lovely, a contradiction and denial of all that both Dreiser and Gershwin mean. Later some woman danced, and later still Paul Robeson sang. Last of all, James Weldon Johnson recited his "Go Down, Death." And Carl hovered about in doorways, his face, as always on such evenings, benevolent and shining.[20]

Mencken died in 1956, having triumphantly survived the era he loved as well as satirized so stingingly. He seems the one unquestionably permanent figure in the group Emily gathered about herself. And last of all, Ellen Glasgow, who died in 1945. To the end she lived and worked in her stately Victorian home, where one visitor pictured her memorably:

The image that remains is not that of individual novels so much as that of a person, a woman, determined, courageous, who sought to impose upon her art and her times the order of her own personality. It was an unequal struggle, obstinate and foolhardy perhaps, and more than a little heroic, in the old way. The final impression is of the maiden lady in Richmond, regally holding court in her stone manse, determinedly discoursing upon Toynbee, Breasted, Santayana to famous visitors from afar. Beyond the windows the rooming houses and antique shops stretched out in all directions.[21]

It is a happier time that is re-created for us in the series of letters Emily wrote to Hergesheimer, giving him an almost daily account of her precarious and often hilarious stint in the editor's chair. The eminent author of *The Three Black Pennys* and *Java Head* made a week's visit to his friend James Branch Cabell in the spring of 1921, when *The Reviewer* was two months old. Cabell invited the staff to meet his guest, with the suggestion to Emily: "He might possibly

[20] *Innocence Abroad*, p. 144.
[21] Rubin, *No Place*, p. 47.

xxi

take a fancy to the magazine, and if he did, he could do a great deal for it." That remark was all Emily needed. Whether Hergesheimer independently took a fancy to the dubious little publication or whether Emily took a fancy to Hergesheimer, the result was the same. He soon found himself her chief adviser and confidant.

Emily began by inviting him to a hastily called staff meeting at her home, to which he came "cherubically beaming, radiating his special atmosphere of literally boundless vitality," as she later remembered the occasion. "I was warmed, enchanted, by this appreciation. . . . I had found no one else, not even my co-editors, whose enthusiasm quite matched my own. Nor did it seem unnatural that the single person who felt exactly as I did should be one of the most distinguished of American novelists." No doubt Emily's girlish awe (or a good imitation of it) would have sparked the paunchy Hergesheimer's enthusiasm even if he could have guessed what he was letting himself in for. In any event, before the meeting ended, "there burst upon our incredulous but enraptured ears"—according to Emily's arch hyperbole—"the statement from Joe that he not only would contribute a series of articles to the magazine, but would collect for us six other articles by eminent writers of America and England. We had not dreamed of such magnificence. Mr. Galsworthy and Sinclair Lewis were among the names he mentioned."[22]

With Emily's stream of effervescent letters to keep him reminded, Hergesheimer proved almost as good as his word. He sent her a series of autobiographical sketches, which were later republished in the little book *The Presbyterian Child*, and he got her a promise from Sinclair Lewis and an actual manuscript from John Galsworthy. He also brought H. L. Mencken to meet her, suggesting in advance that the prospective guest could "undoubtedly be softened by the cooking," as presumably he himself had been; later he delivered into her hands Carl Van Vechten, who was soon as much concerned as his two friends with the welfare of *The Reviewer*.

The magazine was, of course, dedicated primarily to the cultivation of literary talent in the South, and it harvested a bumper crop. Among the writers whose earliest work Emily accepted and pub-

[22] *Innocence Abroad*, pp. 88–89.

lished were Julia Peterkin, DuBose Heyward, Paul Green, Gerald Johnson, Lynn Riggs, Frances Newman, and Allen Tate; and among its many other Southern contributors were Hervey Allen, John Bennett, Hansel Baugh, Jesse Lee Bennett, Sara Haardt (later Mrs. H. L. Mencken), Josephine Pinckney, Henry Bellamann, Arthur Crew Inman, and George Stevens. All these and others made vivid appearances in Emily's letters as she discovered them and came to know them and their work.

Her editorship was not, however, entirely a regional enterprise. As a bait to attract contributions from gifted Southerners to a magazine which could not pay them (it carried below its masthead the announcement: "The payment for such MSS. as may be found available will be in fame not specie"), Emily contrived to publish their work in the company of a succession of big names. By the end of the first year of publication Amy Lowell was complaining that she was the only important writer she knew who had not been asked to contribute. (She was promptly asked, and obliged with a poem.) Gertrude Stein was represented with an unclassifiable piece called "Indian Boy," which aroused protest on the part of Heywood Broun in the *World,* not to mention several writers of irate letters to the *Times.* In addition to Hergesheimer, Van Vechten, and Cabell, others lured into making freewill offerings to the cause included John Galsworthy, Arthur Machen, Ronald Firbank, Aleister Crowley, Douglas Goldring, Edwin Björkman, Robert Nathan, Edwin Muir, Achmed Abdullah, Louis Untermeyer, Babette Deutsch, Burton Rascoe, Ernest Boyd, Maxwell Bodenheim, and Robert Hillyer.

It is with these writers and others encountered along the way that Emily's correspondence with Hergesheimer is principally concerned. Thus the letters throw varied sidelights on the literary world of the Twenties. Emily's chitchat about the foibles or the wives or the table talk of the great and the near-great is not only unfailingly amusing. Often it reveals new aspects of the familiar, as when she writes that Mencken "is really splendid and I like him lots, but he bursts out now and then with something that seems to terrify him, and then he walks on eggshells for awhile, and it amuses me. . . .

He's so big and knows so much about everything, and yet, in a way, is so innocent."

Emily's own personality is not the least of the attractions in her letters, and it emerges as provocatively as if the printed page were scented with her perfume. She tells Hergesheimer she "can hardly wait for you to see my makeup and my hair. I wash it every six days now, and am almost as dizzy a blonde as the Capertons."[23] Laid up after an automobile accident, she tells of receiving from a woman friend a pair of stockings "with gold clocks that shine and a message saying 'Lest you forget that your legs are as much admired as your brains'." And she demurely quotes another woman friend who had said that "if I live with nineteen men—which she doesn't advocate —I will not be sophisticated at the end. And that I will ask the nineteenth man just as amazing questions as I did the first, and they will never feel they have got anything stale or shopworn."

The reader of these letters will not feel that way, either.

GERALD LANGFORD

The University of Texas
Austin, Texas

[23] Richmond debutantes, mentioned several times in the letters.

INGÉNUE AMONG THE LIONS

1008 Park Avenue
[Richmond, Virginia]
[April 26, 1921]

Dear Mr. Hergesheimer,

You are making me break all my precedents. I never go to the Writers' Club,[1] and I went. Neither do I answer letters the day they come—until today. I ought to say I'm so sorry things haven't gone well since you left Richmond, but I'm not, because now perhaps you will come back sooner. I can have lots of tea parties—much nicer than the other, because that was a meeting. And at a real party the guests can be more carefully selected. You were more reckless than you know in making such a lavish offer of assistance and advice, because I'm considered quite accomplished in finding things for people to do. But even I hesitate to put great artists to base uses. I may go to New York in a week or two for a few days. I wonder if it would be at all possible for you to be there too. It would be extremely nice. Shall I tell John [Powell][2] what you say? He will quite rightly consider you a gentleman and a sportsman, because of course he *did* talk nonsense. I might have told him this evening, because I've just, by telephone, warded off a visit from him. It would have meant an all-night séance, you know. So instead, I'm writing to you. About books—you are wonderfully kind. Was your heart wrung by what I told you about the price of soap and powder making books prohibitive? First, as many as possible by Mr. Hergesheimer (is that impertinent?), or Mr. Mencken, or "Youth and the Bright Medusa"[3]—I haven't read this one, or any of Miss Cather's books yet—

[1] The Writers' Club of Richmond, some two years old at the time, had been established by a group who wished to entice Cabell into active participation in the literary life of the city. He served as president at first but gradually withdrew from anything but token membership.

[2] John Powell was a Richmond pianist, soon to become a nationally known concert performer and composer.

[3] Willa Cather had most recently published *My Antonia* (1918), *Youth and the Bright Medusa* (1920), and *One of Ours* (1922).

and if you haven't these I'll think of others. My Mother[4] says I won't know for twenty years how extraordinary a book "Linda Condon"[5] is, but I do. Oh, and of course "Jurgen."[6] I forgot that! Mr. Holt[7] has sent me "Taboo,"[8] and (would you believe it?) Mr. Cabell is just a trifle sulky about it.

Very sincerely yours,
Emily Clark.

[4] Emily's own mother and her father were dead. Alice Clark was her stepmother and lifelong companion.

[5] Hergesheimer's novel, published in 1919.

[6] Cabell's novel, published in 1919, revised in 1921.

[7] Guy Holt. See Introduction.

[8] *Taboo: A Legend Retold from the Dirghic of Saevius Nicanor, with Prolegomena, Notes, and a Preliminary Memoir,* by James Branch Cabell (1921).

1008 Park Avenue
[May 26, 1921]

[2]

Dear Mr. Hergesheimer,

I'm so sorry things are "dark and difficult." You must be having a trying time and I hope it won't last. Thanks so much for your advice, although evidently Mr. Cabell didn't ask you exactly what I told him to. I wanted to know what I must tell Mr. Liveright[1] to pay me for reading a book (because he was suddenly moved to write and ask me for my bill—he usually sends what he sees fit—and I don't know how to make out a bill!) It's a pity Mr. Knopf[2] went abroad—I think he would be more satisfactory. I gave Margaret[3]

[1] The well-known publisher, partner in the firm of Boni and Liveright.

[2] Alfred A. Knopf, whose firm published the work of Hergesheimer, Mencken, Van Vechten, and others of their circle.

[3] Margaret Freeman (later to become James Branch Cabell's second wife) had helped found *The Reviewer.*

her manuscript the day it came. It is *very* charming, and the rest of us, too, are deeply grateful for it. Mr. Pinckney[4] insisted on my having a talk with Mr. Thomas Nelson Page[5] last week. I had to cope with him single-handed. He is just back from the Riviera, and in spite of all these years of being ambassador at Rome is as hopelessly Virginian as ever. Aren't fat old men depressing? Mr. Mencken recently sent The Reviewer a terrific article on his pet topic, the poor dear South, from his Baltimore paper, with no comment this time on us, but a few encouraging words for The Double Dealer.[6] The other three took it in subdued silence, but I lost my temper and wrote him a horrid, impudent letter. He answered it the day it came, with a wonderful, long, overwhelmingly gracious letter, full of advice, and promises of favorable notices for The Reviewer and an article by himself. Mr. Cabell said it was quite extraordinary, considering the source. He also said he would like to come down at once, and would, as soon as possible. I hope he doesn't look like his picture in Vanity Fair. Does he? You will be glad to know Mr. Cabell has resigned entirely from the Writers' Club. He is also changing visibly—progressing, I mean, and acquiring the human touch you said was needed. It must all be due to you. Hunter Stagg[7] and I are giving a party next week just to him, with no one else at all invited, unless, of course, you will come down for it. The Country Club is nice now—more men than in the early spring, and the Dorothy Perkins roses are in bloom.

Very sincerely yours,
Emily Clark.

[4] Cotesworth Pinckney, a Richmond friend. For the Pinckneys of Charleston, see Letter 21, n. 8.

[5] The eminent author of such novels as *Red Rock* (1898), such volumes of short stories as *In Ole Virginia* (1887), and such other works as *The Old South* (1892) and *Robert E. Lee: Man and Soldier* (1911).

[6] A little magazine published in New Orleans, beginning in 1921.

[7] Hunter Stagg, one of the founders of *The Reviewer,* was a Richmond amateur of letters. He later conducted a book-review section in each issue of the magazine.

1008 Park Avenue
[June 7, 1921]

Dear Mr. Hergesheimer,

It was nice to hear what you are doing and are going to do, and very nice indeed to know you are sending me some of your books—only I wish they were all to be autographed, instead of "mostly." But I suppose I musn't be grasping. I think you told me that "one must always be the little gentleman." That, however, was apropos of fits, and poor Hunter. Mr. Cabell says there is a little book about you, put together by Mr. Knopf. I'd like to see it if I may. It was at dinner at Reveille[1] yesterday evening—the old house on the way to Tuckahoe[2] that I wanted to show you, when you wouldn't get out and be introduced. Mr. Cabell was there, and he and I talked of you. As you know, he admires you greatly, and says more than he usually says. When we were leaving, Mrs. Stuart Reynolds, who looks like a movie actress and is very obviously dangerous and sophisticated, reproached Mr. Cabell for being "vamped" by me. When he said I hadn't been doing it she replied that of course he didn't realize it, for it was the "most insidious kind, being disguised by an ingénue manner." He looked rather queer, and said that if it was vamping it was an entirely new and unrecognizable variety, and that he would have called it anything but that. Then I realized for the first time, from his expression, that I hadn't said a *word* about him, but had just made him talk about you—which wasn't by way of being fascinating, was it? But he had been quite sweet and patient through it all. Do you notice that I'm using dashes now instead of parentheses?

[1] One of the oldest houses around Richmond, Reveille is located on Cary Street Road. According to tradition, its military name originated during the Revolution, but the earliest surviving record is dated 1791. After changing hands frequently, it passed in the 1870's into the hands of Dr. R. A. Patterson and then to his descendants.

[2] Said to have been built somewhere between 1674 and 1725, Tuckahoe (located thirteen miles west of Richmond) was originally the home of Thomas Randolph, and it remained in the Randolph family until 1830. After two changes of hands, it was bought in 1898 by J. Randolph Coolidge, of Boston, the great-grandson of the original owner, and so it was again Randolph family property when Emily visited it.

That's in honor of you. . . . I went to the Ellett commencement today, and—what do you think?—Miss Jennie[3] used in her little speech some of the things you said in her apartment! Princess Troubetzkoy (Amélie Rives)[4] wants me to come to Castle Hill[5] for a week-end soon, and I think I'll go. I'd like for her and Prince Troubetzkoy to be really interested in the Reviewer. She has something in the next issue, with John Powell, but it isn't worth anything. Mr. Mencken has written Mr. Cabell that he feels quite pleased with us since I wrote him, and is going to write something about the Reviewer for the August Smart Set.[6] We had a meeting today and I'm a wreck. I hate things that aren't smooth. Do you think when I'm editor[7] I'll be able to keep them so? Hunter and I are having Mr. Cabell to tea to talk to us at the end of the week—did you know he had a beautiful time at your picnic?—and I wish you were here. But I forgot, you wouldn't come because you don't approve of that sort of party. No one has helped the Reviewer as much as you, and Mary[8] has been in a wonderful mood because you liked her sketch. The book review in this (June 1) issue that has no initials signed is

[3] Virginia Randolph Ellett ran a girls' preparatory school in Richmond. Originally the school—begun in the 1890's—had been for both boys and girls, and one of Miss Jennie's early pupils had been James Branch Cabell.

[4] Amélie Rives (married to a fashionable Russian portrait painter, Prince Pierre Troubetzkoy) was one of Virginia's internationally celebrated women. Daughter of one of the first families of the state (and, incidentally, a cousin of both Thomas Nelson Page and James Branch Cabell), she had spent much of her life in Europe, where she had been a friend of Oscar Wilde and of almost everyone else of importance in both literary and social circles. Noted for her beauty and charm, she also became a popular novelist during the 1890's (e.g., *The Quick and the Dead, A Brother to Dragons, The Man of the Golden Fillet*). Later in life she wrote several plays which were successfully produced on Broadway.

[5] Located in Albemarle County, the estate of Castle Hill was part of a grant made by King George II to the Meriwether family. The present house was finished in 1764, and passed into the Rives family in 1819 when Amélie's grandmother married William Cabell Rives.

[6] The magazine edited by H. L. Mencken and George Jean Nathan from 1914 to 1924, when Mencken founded *The American Mercury*.

[7] Emily did not take over as sole editor until the end of 1921. The last three issues of the year were edited by Cabell.

[8] Mary Street was one of the founders of *The Reviewer* and was now listed in the masthead as coeditor.

Margaret's. She should have signed it because we promised we would, but she says she forgot.

I've missed you since you left, and when you have time to write I am very glad. There is no one so easy to talk to. It is unusual to find anyone who thinks as I do in many ways—and very pleasant.

Very sincerely yours,
Emily Clark.

[4] 1008 Park Avenue
[June 18, 1921]

The books have come, and you know how glad I am to have them. I began in the middle of San Cristobal[1] at an accidental sentence and read all the morning when I should have been doing something else. It is very beautiful, and I know now why you said what you did about Frederick O'Brien's book.[2] But they aren't autographed, and you said you were truthful. I don't understand. Mr. Cabell is jeering at me because his are. He came to bring me a magazine, not to a party—I didn't have the party. Unless I hear from you in the next two days, saying you are away or have writer's cramp, I'll mail them all to you to sign your name in. Of course you'll have to send them back at once, but I understand on good authority, that celebrated writers are accustomed to doing this, even for persons they have never seen, so I can find no reason why you shouldn't do it for me. I even saw you docilely autographing books at the Writers' Club. Please be very careful with them and return them safely and promptly. Did you get the Reviewers which, at the

[1] Hergesheimer's book *San Cristóbal de la Habana* (1920).
[2] Frederick O'Brien was the author of *Mystic Isles of the South Seas* (1921).

request of your secretary, I sent you—and eight or ten more? You have vanished into space, leaving not even a reassuring countenance like the Cheshire Cat, so I feel really nervous about sending the books on so problematical a journey. But I shall do it, unless I hear at once that you are not there or ill. There is an important Reviewer question I must ask you if you are there. Margaret has been sick and Mary in Philadelphia, so Hunter and I are quite busy. I haven't gone to Castle Hill yet, but probably shall in a week or so. The Troubetzkoys are really interested, and have just written again. The Reviewer has had some quite discriminating and distinguished attention lately which I would tell you about if I were certain you are anywhere at all. The books will reach you soon. Was *Beauty—and Mary Blair*[3] all right?

> Very sincerely yours,
> Emily Clark.

I'm *ever* so grateful, but I still don't see why you didn't sign them. You shake my faith in promises, and I've always been so serene and undisturbed—it's a pity. Mrs. Cabell has just come back, and she's sort of edgy, like Dame Lisa in *Jurgen.* She was *so* put out with him. He looks very stubborn.

> E. T. C.

[3] One of Emily's articles in *The Reviewer.*

CASTLE HILL
Cobham, Albemarle County
[5]   *Virginia*   [July 4, 1921]

I've several things to ask you and tell you, and I shall do it now instead of writing you I "might have done it," hoping you will think that I'm behaving like a reasonable Pennsylvanian instead of an unreasonable Virginian. But you needn't have been so cross, because I thought I'd written you an extraordinarily nice letter, filled with gratitude and all sorts of complimentary expressions. If anyone sent me a package of Reviewers to sign I'd feel very much gratified, if a trifle harassed. And *don't* speak to me again of "gestures" and "duties." Where did you learn such abominable words? They are even worse than "sense," which I've abolished. The first part of this letter is business and would have been written anyway. The last part is social, because I've been wanting to tell you about this place ever since I came. When that part begins I'll tell you. Part I. These are my questions. I'll number them like Mr. Mencken. (1) Do you think it will make a bad impression if, in August, when we take new subscriptions for the monthly Reviewer, beginning October 1, we take them for another six months instead of a year? As we aren't going to ask for outside money yet—because of Southern financial conditions—Mary's money will have to carry it, and we don't know how long it will last. Then perhaps we can get money from other sources later. We don't want to fail before the subscribers' terms are out, like some of the Greenwich Village magazines, and this way seems honest. But we don't want to look queer either. (2) Do you think, as this magazine is quite informal and different, we could make it a nine months' affair instead of a year, eventually? It would cost the subscribers less, and save me from editing it in summer, and the others too. But I'd rather run it all summer than seem unbusinesslike and silly. (3) One of us—not me—has suggested inviting two contributing editors to come in for a stated term, on condition that they pay several hundred apiece. They would also contribute every month, so I wouldn't have to collect so much outside stuff. But we might not like what they write, and even if their connection with the magazine were limited they would certainly feel they had a voice in it if they had money in it, don't you think so? Wouldn't it be safer not to have any more editors and just use Mary's money? She is doing it for herself, you know, because it gives her pleasure, and I have no fear of her wanting to take charge of it on that account. (4) Do you think we can last another six months without paying for contributions? Because we won't be able to pay. If you can get us six, as you said, it would be an enormous help. And you owe me a manuscript of your own, too, "Cape Jessamine." You know I gave you that name and you said you were going to sell it to the Post. But you've already sold my other article, "Ju-Ju,"[1] to the Post and I don't see how you could find it in your heart to do it again. Besides I can give you any quantities of other Southern flower names for the Post. "Souvenir de Malmaison" is a lovely name, and there's "Sweet Betsy" and "citron alys" and ever so many more. (5) I sent Mr. Liveright a bill for twenty-five dollars, a week ago, and he hasn't answered. Until now he has always answered the day my letter reached him. Shall I send him another bill? Mr. Mencken is taking a hectic interest in The Reviewer, and averages a letter a week of advice—whether I answer or not. Last week, on the heels of two letters which I hadn't had time to answer, came a note, written instead of typed—the first time I'd realized he was a human being—enclosing the Reviewer article from the August Smart Set, with a command not to let it out of my hands before July 12. I've shown it to no one but Mr. Cabell, because he told me, the day it came, not to answer it till he told me what to say. But of course I said something quite different. I wish I had another to send you. Mr. Cabell says he means it to be extremely nice, but it isn't fulsome. Why does he think the South is controlled by Baptist and Methodist ministers? I've never even met one of either. And Margaret is the only person I know socially who is a Methodist—I've always thought it a queer dreadful skeleton in her family. Virginia is fearfully Episcopalian. But of course it's wonderful publicity for us. I realize I'm taking a great deal for granted in asking you all these questions, but you told me you were "very dependable" in some sorts of engagements which you didn't specify, so perhaps you meant Reviewer business. But if you could tell me all these things soon I'd be so grateful. Part II. I feel much more cheerful than when I wrote before. Alice[2] was sick then and everybody I like best had left town. It's still outrageously hot, and we've put the rooms all in white and keep them half dark, and put mint into everything

---

[1] Published in *The Saturday Evening Post,* July 30, 1921.
[2] Alice Clark, Emily's stepmother.

we drink—the mint bed is still at the back gate. And when you get a whiff of it and hear ice rattle, sometimes, if you have temperament, you can pretend it's the Virginia that used to be. Things were rather horrid, so quite suddenly I bought a perfectly darling new dress and came up here, where I met with gratifying appreciation. I'm going home Wednesday, but I'm so glad I came. Castle Hill, you know, is one of the two or three loveliest places in Virginia, and to me it is the most lovable. I like it better than the James River places, and the box is unequalled. It has the air of quite unattainable aristocracy and seclusion that you like, can't be seen at all from the road, and there is a placard up outside warning the public when the family is at home, so that nobody will come near! That's why I'm writing you a book now. The questions had to be asked anyway, but ever since I came here I've been wanting you to know the rest of this, because you must come, and you'll adore it. Part of the house is two hundred and fifty years old and the new part is more than a hundred and the same family has had it always. The box-bordered drive that leads to it is so tall (the box, I mean, not the drive) that it makes the way dark, with the nicest sharp clean scent. The Troubetzkoys are delightful, and they've said more really discriminating things to me than anybody since you left Richmond, and began talking to me about "duties" and "gestures" and "enormous debts" from Pennsylvania. And they knew right away that my new dress looked exactly like a certain kind of sherbet. Of course the Princess's books have been just popular ones, but she knows that and doesn't take herself seriously. She's just read me a play of hers that Ethel Barrymore is considering, and she and the Prince had such a funny letter from John Barrymore the other day, signed "Mad love, Jack." You will like her because she is charming and has obviously been lovely. She's frightfully made-up now. All my life I've heard of her, because she's a legend with the men of Father's generation—most of them were in love with her. But she hasn't been in Richmond for fifteen years and I didn't know her till now. She is said to have had more beaux than any woman in Virginia, even Nancy Astor. And that makes her tremendously interesting to me. And she is different from

Lady Astor in the way you said in "Charlotte Russe."[3] She was born with certain things, and the other achieved much of hers, which makes Amélie Rives more picturesque, I think. The Prince is a darling. He paints portraits, you know, mostly of pretty women, and they have to live in New York in winter. They've both lived everywhere and know nearly everybody. Oscar Wilde introduced them to each other in London, and she was the only American member of "The Souls," that Wilde and Mr. Arthur Balfour and Margot Termant (Asquith) belonged to. There's a verse about her by Lord Curzon in Margot's Autobiography. And she was a great success in London in the time of the Yellow Book. She has stayed with Lord Curzon, and still writes to him and to Mr. Balfour. There is an Italian named Minetti staying here too. He is sweet, with white hair and white clothes and very bright eyes. He lives next to the Troubetzkoys on Lago Maggiore. You know Miss Amélie's grandfather was twice Minister to France, and the drawing-room is full of things that her grandmother brought back. It has a bare, polished floor, huge mirrors and darling stiff chairs around the walls. There are French paintings and funny French gift books, and the most delicious faded green and gold curtains, on carved brass rods, brought from Paris in the time of Eugénie, which have never been replaced and clocks and vases under glass—nothing is changed. All over the rest of the house France and Italy are mixed with Colonial Virginia in the most startling way. My room, where I'm writing now at an ungodly hour, is in the oldest part of the house, with the sweetest white-paneled walls and fans over the doors. But the furniture is modern, all pink and white. It looks like something very good to eat, but it isn't interesting like some of the others. It has a bath of its own though, and all of the other rooms haven't, so there are compensations for its newness. She won't have electric light put in, but uses lamps and candles. The lawn is one of the most beautiful I know, like England with views of the mountains everywhere, enclosed in box, and there is a terraced garden on the other side of a

[3] A sketch by Hergesheimer published in the August, 1921, issue of *The Reviewer.*

high box wall. It is all so shut-in that it looks unreal. And the white columns in front extend throughout the east and west wings, as well as the porch. To me there's more atmosphere about this place than many of the others, because, though it hasn't bullet marks and all that, so many charming people had a wonderful time here. She has just given me her last book, which is unimportant, and also Jurgen, which is not unimportant, and should make you feel badly! They had three copies and said they were waiting for someone they really liked to give the first one to. Wasn't that a proper spirit? Now *this* is the important part of the letter. They love your books and have most of them but Linda,[4] which I shall send them when I go home. I told them about the studio party where Pleydon met her, and Prince Troubetzkoy told me to ask you if it was Ben Ali Haggin's.[5] They knew about you years ago through English friends before you were so celebrated, and they were much pleased at your writing for The Reviewer and have been asking lots of questions about you. They wanted to know if you had ever been a painter because you wrote like one.[6] They think you are very wonderful and that you write better than anyone over here, and they knew you liked old houses and lived in one. They want you to come here ever so much and have told me several times to tell you. They think October is probably the nicest time, but if summer suits you better it suits them. They've also asked me for the same time, and want me to explain to you that the next time you come to Virginia you must come here. Then, if you will tell me what time is convenient, she (she makes me call her Amélie, and it's hard to remember, because she's Father's age) will write you a perfectly proper note about it. But not having met you she wants an explanation given you before she writes! Mr. Cabell tells me that you may go to Rockbridge Alum[7] with them, but I thought you were going to Canada. You spoke of going to Fairfax County in September to get atmosphere,

[4] Hergesheimer's novel *Linda Condon* (1919).

[5] A fashionable artist who had a studio in New York.

[6] A shrewd observation, for Hergesheimer had begun by studying art at the Pennsylvania Academy of Fine Arts. He had turned to writing only after several years' study had convinced him he could never become a significant painter.

[7] A vacation resort in the Virginia mountains.

14

and I hope you will, because there's plenty of it, but there's much more here. I think you'll find it useful. If you come to Virginia soon I'll keep the books for you, but if you don't I'll have to send them to you, because you might be wrecked or something on the way to England without signing them. I'm alarmed at myself when I regard the number of pages I've written, and fear for my own balance, but I shan't apologize because I think Castle Hill and the people in it are an interesting subject. Her ex-husband, brother of your Mr. Bob Chanler, has his place, "Merry Mills," within a stone's throw of this, but it doesn't seem to bother her a bit, and she is still good friends with the other Chanlers. She has remarkable poise. You'll have to take the afternoon off to read this instead of playing golf, but it will be cooler anyway. Please remember to tell me the things I have to know. They say not to bother about Mr. Mencken. I told them some of the things he said, and they think it would be absurd for us to fight and scream, and "expose" people. That's what he says I must do to people like poor old Mr. Tom Page, and Mr. Armistead Gordon,[8] who have known me since I was born. Don't you think it's better for us just to ignore them and not ever let them contribute? Your "Georgette crêpe and silk stockings" would be torn to shreds in the sort of riot Mr. Mencken wants.

Very sincerely,
Emily Clark.

Monday, July Fourth (It has turned into July Fifth, I forgot, and there's a gorgeous storm going on that's making it very cool). She has the best cigarettes of anybody at all, but you have to send to New York for them and they are horridly expensive. I'm depressed at discovering them.

[8] Armistead Churchill Gordon was a Virginia lawyer and writer. He served two separate terms as rector of the University of Virginia, and he published such books as *Befo' de War* (1881), *Jefferson Davis* (1918) and *Virginian Portraits* (1924).

1008 Park Avenue
[July, 1921]

I'm sorry to be a bother or to make The Reviewer one, but it can't be helped. A letter came to me yesterday from Mr. Edward Bierstadt,[1] who frequently writes and says what he thinks of The Reviewer. I'm enclosing a copy of the last paragraph and of the article which provoked it. Do you agree with Mr. Bierstadt? I haven't read Back to Methuselah, but Hunter's article didn't sound childish to me. We've had him write a number of reviews, because he has plenty of time and likes to do it—and because most people here like his work—especially Mr. Cabell. Mr. Cabell was here Thursday and talked to me several hours about the fall, and seemed to think Hunter entirely qualified to take care of the books, which of course is a large department. He also said he (Mr. Cabell) was coming back here the first of September and help me make up the October issue. I'm glad, of course, that he's so interested, but I don't know whether I'm sufficiently interested myself to be back here then! He thinks I ought to. He said he was arranging his work so he could give a good deal of time to The Reviewer, which is nice of him. Please tell me what you think of this article, and of Hunter's work. I know your criticism isn't affected by the way people impress you personally. Sometimes I think Mr. Cabell's is. Of course Hunter is needed, and I hope this letter is just one man's opinion. So what do you think? It will be quite all right if you answer this and the Reviewer questions I sent you from Castle Hill secretarially. I don't want to take up your time. The things Princess Troubetzkoy told me to ask you can wait. I stayed there longer than I had intended —it's such a perfectly darling place—and sent them Linda Condon this week. Margaret has resigned as business manager and wants to run a dramatic department, and as Mary is away and hasn't consented yet; I don't know what will be done, or very much care if only it is settled amicably. No matter who attends to the money, it

---

[1] Edward Hale Bierstadt had published *Dunsany the Dramatist* (1917) and was later to publish such books as *The Great Betrayal: A Survey of the Near East Problem* (1924), *Enter Murderers! Eight Studies in Murder* (1934).

won't be me, so I'm not deeply concerned! Mr. Cabell is trying to get Mr. Mencken to write something for October, as he thinks that issue specially important. And please, if you can, get us something nice for the same issue. Charlotte Russe comes out August 1 to put people in a hopeful mood for the fall. I put Miss Montague[2] in the present number (we had to use her because one of them asked her in the winter) so she needn't appear with you. Mr. Cabell seems to be expecting you to go away with him the last of this month and write The Bright Shawl.[3] I saw Nellie Tompkins[4] the other day and she says you are wonderfully kindhearted, which encouraged me about The Reviewer. I hope she speaks authoritatively. I like so much your Aiken paper[5] in Vanity Fair—who is the man who sang? But never mind answering that, because I mustn't distract you from the main issue. What do you think?—Mr. Liveright wrote yesterday that he had *lost* my bill and wants me to send another. I'm horribly irritated with him. Mr. Cabell has just written an introduction to go in his Modern Library,[6] and I think it was silly of him. His letter was *very* polite, but sounded untrue.

Very sincerely,
Emily Clark.

Saturday

[2] Elizabeth Mary Montague, author of such books as *Beside a Southern Sea* (novel, 1905) and *Southern Songs, Rhymes and Jingles* (1916).

[3] Hergesheimer's novel, published in 1922.

[4] Nellie and Delia Tompkins, two unmarried sisters living with their mother, were second cousins of James Branch Cabell. Nellie had literary interests and had published several stories.

[5] "An Aiken Paper: How the Characters of a Novel, as Yet Unwritten, Came into Being," *Vanity Fair*, July, 1921.

[6] Cabell's book *Beyond Life* (1919) was to be included in Boni and Liveright's Modern Library in 1923.

These are the proofs of the circular The Reviewer will issue in September. They made a mistake and put the Atlanta and Richmond notices in the beginning, but I've told them to change it to the end. I think Douglas Freeman's[1] editorial, which I extracted from him two weeks ago, is a good ending, don't you?—and will calm those who are infuriated by Mencken. What do you think of these notices? Don't you think they make a better circular than personal things— the sort we sent out at the beginning? I did *not* tell Dr. Freeman that you and Mr. Cabell were "coaching" us. He must have decided that, himself, because I've quoted you both to him whenever he couldn't understand what we were doing. I used his name, instead of just the Leader, as a reward to him for always doing what I ask him to. Mr. Mencken has joyfully agreed to write for the October issue and needed no urging or manipulation. He's also offered to write book reviews now and then, and says he venerates you. Mr. Liveright paid me what you told me to charge him, with a very polite letter saying he had been out of town, and that's why it hadn't been done before. Do you think perhaps he's more honest than you had supposed? Alice and I are here in Halifax, visiting Cousin Grace Clark at my great-uncle's old house. It's name is Hoveloke —Indian, of course, but the station and post-office are named Clarkton after him. It's an adorable place—very quiet, and we motor a lot and go to bed early. They both think it's very good for me on account of date hours and various irregularities since The Reviewer started. I think they are afraid I may get queer on account of it, you see. I *sewed* in the library for an hour this afternoon after the large midday dinner which we have here. Some of the furniture is darling—the old things at home came from here and all the rest are still here where they belong. There are two four-post beds in my room and one in Alice's, and there are fire-screens and ottomans that

[1] Dr. Douglas Southall Freeman, then editor of the Richmond *News Leader,* later gained eminence as the biographer of Robert E. Lee and George Washington.

my grand-mother worked in cross-stitch, like samplers, and a portrait of my great-uncle, painted at fourteen, holding a book of *Latin verse*. So I feel very correct here. There's a lot of box, too. You'd like the house, but I don't know if you'd like Cousin Grace. She's quite fat and has very decided opinions—I never smoke here—but her saving grace is that she was brought up partly abroad and partly in New Orleans, and because of the latter, thinks that everyone ought to sleep several hours summer afternoons. So I'm supposed to be asleep now. Alice wants very much to see you. She was out last time you came. She likes Java Head next to Linda, but I like the Three Black Pennys next.[2] We are going home Friday, and she's going to the Virginia mountains in a day or two, and I'm going North. I'll pass through Philadelphia and join Elizabeth Preston —you've met her at Mary Tompkins'[3]—for a little while at Chelsea. There are several quite serious and important things about The Reviewer that I want to ask you. An *alarming* situation has developed since you were down here last time, and I didn't use all of the time profitably, anyway, by asking you all of the questions I might have. I was with Mrs. Tompkins and Mary[4] just before I left home and they told me so many things about you, that I didn't know, that my mind was all confused. But they also said, just as Nellie did, that you were extremely kind and helpful, so please put your mind on The Reviewer for awhile when I tell you all that is happening. They said that if they went anywhere they would join me in Chelsea if I could find them a place, but they didn't think they'd go away on account of Mary's health. I don't think it was polite of you not to write me, when you went back, because I was extremely nice to you. Do you realize how nice? Do you like the circular, and have we published too much?

Emily Clark.

[2] *Java Head* (1919) and *The Three Black Pennys* (1917) are two of Hergesheimer's best novels.

[3] The mother of Nellie and Delia Tompkins.

[4] Mary Street.

Chelsea, Atlantic City
3305 Pacific Avenue
[8]   [August 29, 1921]

I came here today and the weather looks very depressing. The place seems to be swarming with people from Virginia, but Mrs. Tompkins and Mary have decided not to go away at all—I haven't seen any of the people, but Elizabeth says there are some at the Chelsea—not any that we like very much though. I remembered, after I mailed my note to you Saturday, that it might reach you in the middle of the night and infuriate you. A special delivery that needn't have been sent waked me at one o'clock not long ago and I was very angry indeed. I mailed it (my note) at Bristol, the first place that had a mail box, with such a pretty little street by the river, and such dreadful looking people at large on it. You can either write me here, Care of Mrs. Merrill, or telephone me here this evening about a quarter after seven, or tomorrow morning about half-past nine,— the number is 1813. I'm enclosing a Reviewer circular. Jim Allison[1] has given us an office, but we can't use it until nearly October, so the address won't be changed till the new magazines come out.

Sincerely yours,
Emily Clark.

[1] A Richmond friend and patron of *The Reviewer*.

1008 Park Avenue
[9]   [September 13, 1921]

This is the carbon copy of the thing I wrote to account for The Reviewer in the October issue. It won't have to go to press till Friday and I'd be glad if you'd return it by special delivery so I can use your suggestions. Mr. Cabell has the press copy, and is going over it, but I'd rather have your corrections than his. He's already said that the Arabian Nights quotation should be cut to five lines but I'm not touching the copy I'm sending you. I think the subject is far too trivial to take so much space, but Mr. Cabell insisted on having it long. I don't think it's much good, because I didn't have time to give it a thought those last two days in Chelsea when I'd intended to write it, and I had to write it in a great hurry Sunday morning here, without a single re-writing. But that, after all, is the way I write everything. It makes me so very nervous and impatient and depressed to go carefully over even a single sentence. I wrote what you suggested—quite informally, as you see—just how it began and how it had let us in for more than we realized, and a more serious statement of our intentions at the end. Do you think it at all adequate and fairly easy to read? Mary has used your corrections and I'm ever so grateful to you for taking the job from me. I'm extremely glad I came home instead of going to the Green Spring Valley because I feel much more cheerful about the magazine than I did. That silly Leader[1] article was written by Dr. Eckenrode, the dreadful looking man in big spectacles that you met at Mr. Cabell's, and that Mrs. Cabell made Jim and me take home. You know, it was he and another man who wanted to join us when we started The Reviewer, and put money into it, and we turned them down flat. It made them quite angry and they have been very jealous of The Reviewer—but as it has mercifully relieved me of his periodical visits I haven't cared—until he burst into print about us. It was me that he came to see about coming into The Reviewer. Douglas Freeman has been spending some time at Mr. Stewart Bryan's[2] camp in New Hampshire, and Dr. Eckenrode wrote the editorials for him. If Dr. Freeman and Mr. Bryan had been here it never could have happened, and I think they are very much ashamed of it—because of course he very stupidly gave Mr. Mencken just what he wanted, the satisfaction of getting a rise out of the Richmond press. As for his calling us unconventional—everyone thinks that's absurd, although of

[1] The Richmond News Leader.
[2] John Stewart Bryan was the publisher of the News Leader.

course it must seem to him the height—or depth—of unconvention-
ality to refuse both men and money. No one here takes it at all seriously, except that Mr. Cabell, who now considers himself part of
the staff, is very much peeved at being called a young lady even
though a gifted one. Hunter knows Dr. Eckenrode well and says that
he ignored his existence from sheer spite![3] Mr. Cabell is being a perfect lamb. I was out there this afternoon and I'm so much relieved
by Mr. Mencken's article, "A Morning Song in—something. I forgot what—Major."[4] I shan't quote it to you, as we said, because
there's nothing in it to make trouble. It's extremely well written—
not a bit of his slam-bang style, and Mr. Cabell says he could have
sold it to any magazine at all. He's going to take the first issue[5] to
press for me, and he'd counted all the words and got everything in
order before I came. He's going to run his "Lichfield Lineage,"[6]
which is coming out in January, serially in the first three issues of
The Reviewer, and he's written to Burton Rascoe[7] and several others
for articles. He asked me to ask you please to have your third article
here before the middle of October for the November issue, and to
ask if you will be responsible for the next three issues, just as he is
for these three. Really, will you get us some articles soon? I'm so
afraid English papers can't get here in time for this six months.
Could you get some American articles? They might not be as good,
but they'd be better than those I could collect—anybody that you
think would be interesting. What about Llewellyn Jones[8] and Hey-

[3] The Eckenrode article had been an unfavorable estimate of *The Reviewer*.
Eckenrode had been unaware that Cabell was associated with the magazine, and
had failed to mention Hunter Stagg as a member of the staff.

[4] "Morning Song in C Major," an appraisal of the Southern literary reawakening, published in *The Reviewer*, October, 1921.

[5] From February to October, 1921, *The Reviewer* had been a fortnightly pamphlet. Emily refers to the enlarged, monthly publication as if it were the first issue
of a new magazine.

[6] Cabell's new novel, published in 1922.

[7] Burton Rascoe, to whom Cabell had dedicated his novel *Jurgen*, was literary
editor of the New York *Tribune* at this time. He later wrote such books as *Theodore Dreiser* (1925), *A Bookman's Daybook* (1929), and *Titans of Literature*
(1932).

[8] Author of *Joseph Hergesheimer: The Man and His Books* (1920). Jones was
literary editor of the Chicago *Evening Post*.

wood Broun,[9] or any others that you or Mr. Knopf know? I'm terrified by the number of pages that have to be filled. Mr. Mencken is quite crazy about your idea of writing on Sensitiveness, but I want most of all something beautiful like Charlotte Russe. I think that's quite the loveliest thing I've seen in a long time. So does Mr. Cabell. He's improving wonderfully, and is quite a different person from what he was a year ago. The Provincetown Players are going to use his Little Theatre League play.[10] He says he's been buying the Red Book every month to find The Bright Shawl. I'm not infuriated now, though you did say perfectly *dreadful* things to me that didn't quite sink in until after you'd gone. But what you write is much too beautiful to stay cross with. I haven't seen Margaret's dramatic stuff yet because it isn't ready—I hope it's all right. Mr. Cabell says I mustn't ask Mr. Mencken for a book review yet. Do you agree with that? Hunter wrote him about something last week and thought he was a little curt, but my letter today was wonderful and he seemed in a perfectly good humor. Please send me back my copy right away and say anything you please about it. I'm quite honest and unsensitive about writing—you know I didn't mind when you said my Frederick O'Brien review was very bad. Do you think I've made The Reviewer sound so silly and accidental that nobody will take it seriously or want to subscribe to it? I thought it would be more interesting if I told the truth. Mr. Cabell says I used "didn't" and "wasn't" more than was necessary, and that I caught it from you. It will be an enormous help for you to tell me about it.

Very sincerely,
Emily Clark.

They've quoted one of my reviews in Atlanta with my name on it!

[9] Broun's well-known column, 'It Seems to Me," had appeared in the New York *Tribune* until 1921, when he moved over to the *World*. He had written such books as *A. E. F.: With General Pershing and the American Forces* (1918), *Seeing Things at Night* (1921), *Pieces of Hate* (1922), and the novel *The Boy Grew Older* (1922).

[10] *The Jewel Merchants* (1921), a one-act play, first published in *Smart Set*, July, 1921.

How do you like this issue—and Hunter's book article? I used all of your suggestions except "pleasure" instead of "fun." It's really more fun than pleasure, and you said I had always to be honest. I've marked on the cover the fillers Mr. Cabell wrote and signed with other names. There were people here last night who stayed until twelve, and when they'd gone I read Linda for two hours, and wondered how I'd dared to be so irritating and impertinent, and to send the silly thing of Mr. Mencken's to a very great artist. The next time I see you I shan't talk about myself at all—I'll just sit at your feet very quietly and listen. I feel insignificant beyond words and disgusted with myself. Amélie arrives in town tonight—I suppose she sent you the same cryptic and frantic letter she sent me, but I gather from her relations here that the trouble pertains to her teeth. She's probably broken them or something, and she's very serious about her appearance, poor dear, so don't tell her when you go there that I said anything about it. She wishes to be very beautiful for you and she is really sweet. I'll see her this week if she'll let me and find out all about it. She has written me that no one must know she's here as she will see no one, so I haven't told. She wrote me to explain to Mr. Cabell about coming a little later too, as she'd asked him for sometime next week. Alice is so pleased with the Lemon Verbena[1] story in the Post, but I thought you were going to call it Citronalis, because it's prettier, and it's all the same thing. Are you still cross with me the way you were last time I saw you? The suspense is bad for me and I think you might relieve it.

E. T. C.

Mr. Mencken wrote me that this [issue] interests him much more than the Double Dealer. We'll have our office address next month.

Mr. Hergesheimer Mr. Cabell changed all my "didn't"'s and "couldn't"'s into did nots and could nots when the proof came back to him.

---

[1] "A Sprig of Lemon Verbena," *The Saturday Evening Post*, September 17, 1921.

24

1008 Park Avenue
[October 3, 1921]

I'm sending you the other stamps which I should have put on your Reviewer today. I sealed it and put only one stamp, which was quite wrong—and it will either come back to me or you'll have to pay postage. I put a note in, too, and that is illegal, so it may not reach you at all. It was a very nice note, telling about Amélie, and asking you not to tell her when you see her, and asking if you are still cross with me, and saying what a very great man you are and that I'm overcome by my own insignificance. So I hope you get it, and that it isn't lost. I also marked everything Mr. Cabell wrote and explained about mine and asked about Hunter's. So it is more interesting than your official copy. Have you been paying extra postage on all the other Reviewers I've been sending you? Because I think I sealed them all. Do you think this is a good number? Are you cross?

Emily Clark.

We have no business manager whatever, because neither Margaret nor Mary will be it. Burton Rascoe is coming to see Mr. Cabell and is going to write us something. I wrote Mr. Van Vechten[1] and he sent something very nice. Thanks so much.

[1] Carl Van Vechten, in 1921, had published half a dozen books of music criticism and was preparing to publish his first novel (*Peter Whiffle*, 1922). He appeared in practically every issue of *The Reviewer* from November, 1921, to early 1923, and occasionally thereafter, most often under the heading "Pastiches et Pistaches" (collections of random observations).

1008 Park Avenue

I've seen Amélie and I hope you'll go to Castle Hill. She's going back tomorrow and she especially wants you. She has had a very bad time with vertigo and her teeth and really couldn't have been presentable to anyone—she has been invisible much of the time here. She has had the blinds painted and the hedges clipped in your honor, and is giving you her nicest room—so she'll be fearfully disappointed if you don't come. She will be at Castle Hill steadily until December, and said she was writing (or had written) you to set your own time for coming, so it wouldn't interfere with Tol'able David[1]—and that anytime would suit her. Fall is really the best time there. She's enormously interested in you. I really like her more than ever—she's a darling, and I think I know why Linda[2] bothers her, though she thinks it's beautiful. You see, she's been beautiful herself. She's less made up than in the summer, and sometimes, at moments, she's lovely—and always very much of a real person. I believe she's quite crazy about Prince Troubetzkoy too, which is interesting, at her age. And wonderfully honest in every way. I thing she will entertain you a good deal. She likes Java Head the best of your books and the Three Black Pennys next, and said, from what she'd heard, she expected to like San Cristobal best of all. She has most of the others, and I would have lent her that, but you said you might give it to her. Mr. Cabell has brought me Domnei.[3] Your preface is very beautiful. He brought me his book about you too,[4] and I like it, but he said you didn't when it was in the Bookman. Amélie is angry with him for editing her little thing in the last Reviewer. She stamped her foot and said "Damn," and said the editor of the Fortnightly Review cabled her before he changed a word of her last

---

[1] *Tol'able David* was the movie version (1921) of a short story of the same title which had appeared in *The Saturday Evening Post,* July 14, 1917, and which was included in the collection *The Happy End* (1919).

[2] *Linda Condon.*

[3] Cabell's novel, originally published in 1913 under the title *The Soul of Melicent,* revised under the new title in 1920, with a preface by Hergesheimer.

[4] *Joseph Hergesheimer: An Essay in Interpretation* (1921).

26

contribution. She admires her cousin James,[5] but says he has "vertige des sommets," since Jurgen. But I don't think he has. She's brought the most adorable maid with her, Marewska, from Prague, who looks like a stage servant—she'll be at Castle Hill. The magazines have all begun celebrating the Dante anniversary, so I'm writing for November on What Dante Does Not Mean to Me. Babette Deutsch[6] is mad with Mr. Cabell for editing her poems, and has written a letter about it. I'm glad you aren't going to write a critical paper for The Reviewer, but a lovely one. Let me know when you can go to Castle Hill.

Emily Clark.

Amélie has been worried for fear you wouldn't understand about this week. She has the most wonderful pearl pin, with each pearl a different shade, from mauve to white.

[5] James Branch Cabell.
[6] At this time Babette Deutsch had published only one book of poems, *Banners* (1919).

[October 26, 1921]
1008 Park Avenue

[13]

I'd like to talk to you—there's nobody here intelligent enough to talk to. Why don't you come down to Castle Hill?—it's nicer there at this time of year than here, although it's wonderful weather everywhere in Virginia now. I want to tell you about Mr. Cabell and some other things and I want very much to have you see the house and Amélie—and perhaps write a story about it. Has Tol'able David ever opened? I haven't seen any notice of it. Mr. Cabell is being arbitrary about The Reviewer, but his régime only lasts through the

December issue. He edits our things and changes our proof, and he has made me say "sonorous balderdash" in my November article—a phrase I would never have used in a thousand years. Don't tell *anybody* I said all this. I like much better the way you correct things, but you write more Beautifully than anyone. I think what Mr. Cabell wrote about Linda Condon was very lovely, but I don't see why he had to worry about your future just because people read your books and like them. They like Conrad's[1] too, and it hasn't hurt him. I wasted twenty-five cents on a Red Book because you said The Bright Shawl would be in it, and it wasn't. Miss Frances Newman,[2]—you know she has written us several articles—is passing through on her way to New York and came to a Reviewer meeting here yesterday. She said that Mariana in the Three Black Pennys was the most attractive woman in American literature and the best dressed. But she likes that better than Linda Condon because she likes the woman better, and I think that's silly. I grew hoarse at a Country Club tea the other day trying to explain that Linda isn't really a woman at all in the sense they mean. People are so stupid, aren't they? You usually know what I'm talking about. Miss Newman is clever, of course, but so silly for a woman of her age. She drawls and coos and says your books and everybody's that she likes are "darling" and "sweet." I hope if I got that way at her age somebody who really likes me will kill me with a club. I don't like her writing as much as Mr. Cabell does, do you? It's so fearfully erudite and full of shop. Mr. Cabell is putting something of hers into The Reviewer that says something impertinent about you and him. Don't you think he's being rather high-handed? Do you think he has "vertige" as Amélie said? Miss Newman has been corresponding with Mr. Mencken about her work, and they've made an appointment for lunch in New York this week. I think he's going to be badly jarred when he sees her. Mary was in Philadelphia and Margaret came late to the meet-

---

[1] Joseph Conrad, whose most recent novel had been *The Rescue* (1920).

[2] Frances Newman, who worked in the Atlanta public library and wrote features for the Atlanta *Constitution,* later published such books as *The Hard-Boiled Virgin* (1926), *Dead Lovers Are Faithful Lovers* (1928), and *Six Moral Tales from La Forgue* (1928).

ing, and she literally turned her back on Hunter and me and slopped all over Mr. Cabell. It became so absurd that we had to go out in the pantry and sit on the floor, and we laughed until we were hysterical. I believe Mr. Cabell saw that she was funny too. Of course I *am* grateful to him for putting aside his book for The Reviewer, and I know I don't sound so, but I want very much to tell you all about it. Do you remember The Cords of Vanity?[3] He said yesterday that Robert Townsend—in that book—was a study of a typical artist. Do you believe it? It makes me ill to think it. Mary and Margaret are getting on better than I'd even hoped they could, and I feel as young and carefree as I did before The Reviewer started, and I'm quite fond of them. It's so nice to have things serene—they are ever so much better than when I was in Chelsea, so of course I'm in a better humor. I've had some wonderful letters about the magazine, especially Louis Untermeyer's,[4] who wrote on the most dreadful scalloped paper. Isn't it queer that talent shouldn't give him good taste or make him a gentleman? I can't understand it. He says he's coming here in February, and he's probably perfectly impossible. You know, you promised to bring Mr. Mencken some time. Alice has been spending several days in Norfolk and I've given two parties and had all the people she doesn't like. She specially wants to be present at the next one for you though. Elizabeth Preston came home yesterday—she's been paying visits in the North ever since I left her— and told the Tompkins you thought The Circle[5] was a foolish play. Nellie was shocked, because she liked it, just as we did, and just as Heywood Broun does. Why do you think it isn't good? The Reviewer office walls have just been painted red and black by the people who lease the building. It looks exactly like hell fire, especially at night—I had to go there last night—and everyone is stunned when it glares at them from the end of the hall. It looks as

[3] Cabell's novel, originally published in 1909, revised in 1920.

[4] In 1922 Untermeyer had published two books of poems, *Challenge* (1914) and *These Times* (1917), as well as a critical book, *The New Era in American Poetry* (1919). He was preparing the first edition of his long-lived anthology *American Poetry Since 1900* (1923).

[5] Somerset Maugham's play, produced and published in the United States in 1921.

if something sinister emanated from it, instead of something black and white and blameless like The Reviewer, and is very bad for my hair. I've been reading The Lay Anthony[6] again, and it's quite lovely. You must have been an extraordinarily wise young man to have thought of exactly that. The person in The Cords of Vanity *isn't* typical, is he? I can't help it if you are bored with all this—I wanted to talk to you, so I did. I think you said you didn't read long letters. Mrs. Cabell left for New York last night without Mr. Cabell. She thought until the very last minute that he was going, just as she did last spring when you came down, but he got in the same stubborn fit and stayed behind. She's furious. He's implicated in a vortex of parties, as Grace Shepherd[7] is a debutante. They are giving a big dance for her in a few weeks, and I wait with interest to see if he really will stand in a line and receive with his wife and family. I know he'll crawl out of it, don't you? I wish you'd hurry and come down here. You could go to Amélie for a week-end if not for a week, and she'd understand. The place is really adorable and they aren't going to New York until after Christmas. I bought a new dress, that I like better than anything I've had in three years, to take there and it's getting quite worn out already. Please don't ever tell that I talked about Mr. Cabell to you because I wouldn't do it here. Do you think Mr. Knopf would advertise in The Reviewer if I got Frank West to write him? I sent him a special copy and I think the October issue was good don't you? Be sure to come soon.

Emily Clark.

Will your picture[8] come here soon, or will it still be in New York when I go there later?

---

[6] Hergesheimer's first novel, originally published by Mitchell Kennerley in 1914, and in 1919 reissued by Knopf, who by then had become Hergesheimer's publisher.
[7] Cabell's stepdaughter. Her mother had been Mrs. Emmett A. Shepherd, a widow with five children, whom Cabell married in 1913.
[8] *Tol'able David*.

1008 Park Avenue

I think the Scots Grandfather[1] is very delightful—the sketch, I mean, not him. Episcopal clergymen, really, aren't nearly so extreme. Please send the others soon, because I want to read them, I'd rather have these for The Reviewer than anything else. But I'd like the manuscript of Juju too. And anyway, you promised it to me last April, almost as soon as I met you. I do like these better, but that has nothing to do with the other. I think personal recollections of yours would make us noticed, too. I do think you write better than anyone. Isn't that Lichfield Lineage[2] irritating? The New York Evening Post has had an article about us and quoted Mr. Mencken. And last Sunday the Times noticed us and quoted no one but me—Mr. Mencken and Mr. Cabell weren't mentioned and I was so glad. I hope Mr. Mencken saw it. I called up Mr. Cabell and told him and he said their opinion was worth nothing, which of course it isn't! He's just given me the Line of Love[2] with Mr. Mencken's preface and is going to give me Chivalry[2] next week. Miss Newman wrote me today and she's at your Algonquin, which seems to be Mr. Mencken's too. According to her he's "darling" too—there seems nothing in the North to chill her exuberance. She says he's very excited about your bringing him to Virginia, and asked dozens of questions. Mr. Cabell doesn't think he's really coming. Amélie wrote me today that water was running again and she hoped very much that you were coming, and so do I. Perhaps you could go there before or after you come here—it's so near. You must really be sure to go. I wrote you as I did because I hadn't heard from her then and though she was waiting to hear from you, because she said

---

[1] The first of Hergesheimer's "Tintypes," which were a series of autobiographical sketches contributed to The Reviewer ("A Scots Grandfather," "An Absentee Father," "A Cabinet Photograph," and "The Presbyterian Child"). Together with "An Aunt in Jet," published earlier in The Forum, these sketches were collected in a small book entitled The Presbyterian Child (1923).

[2] The Lineage of Lichfield (1922), The Line of Love (1905, revised 1921), and Chivalry (1909, revised 1921) are three of Cabell's novels which are components of the continuing Biography of Dom Manuel.

when she left here that she wanted you right away. I didn't think of the water situation. It's been bad at Dumbarton[3] and always worse, of course, in the mountains. I went to a country house once to stay a week, and found the water dried up and had myself telegraphed for in two days. It was horrid. But I hope you'll go soon now, before another accident occurs! Please say something about *The Reviewer*. I've just seen Mary Tompkins and she talked about you incessantly, and explained you to me very carefully, because, she said, she didn't think people who had just met you were apt to understand you as she did. I said, "Probably not."

Emily Clark.

[3] Dumbarton was a country suburb of Richmond, where Cabell lived at this time. He called his home Dumbarton Grange.

[15]   1008 Park Avenue
                                        [November 20, 1921]

We are so glad you can come to dinner. Mr. Mencken accepted at once and said he would be here at seven, but I think half-past seven would be safer. We could make it a quarter of eight if you like, but I don't think that will be necessary. And if Mr. Cabell comes I suppose he'd like it as early as possible. He doesn't want to go to his party at all. Ida has come to Richmond for a few weeks, as Taylor[1] is in Mexico, so I'm having her instead of Mrs. Trigg[2]—she wants to see you. You know she had a baby in July, and she's much too fat I think, but she's very attractive. It's so queer to see her with a baby. She's a few years older than I am and she's been married

[1] Ida and Taylor Burke, Richmond friends.
[2] Emma Gray Trigg (Mrs. William R. Trigg, Jr.), a prominent Richmond woman who contributed poetry to *The Reviewer* and other little magazines.

ever so long, and I'd got so used to her without one that I never dreamed it would happen. She belongs more than anyone here, I think, to the South that Mr. Mencken says is destroyed, as practically everyone on the Washington monument is her ancestor! I think your second paper is beautiful. I may use two together if many more are coming. The manuscript hasn't come yet, nor Juju either. Do you think you could get me another really distinguished paper for January? We shall use that issue for advertising purposes—to send sample copies to get more circulation, and I want one more name to go with yours, just as we had Mr. Cabell and Mr. Mencken together in October.[3] Please think about this, because it's very important. We are going to have a number printed extra, so I need another really desirable paper by December tenth. Dr. Tucker[4] has talked to me a good deal lately and he wants The Reviewer to try to get money at once to run another year, and to enlarge its circulation in January. I've grown quite fond of him—he's tremendously interested and has found a new advertising man. He thinks publishers should advertise and I hope you and Mr. Mencken will make Mr. Knopf do it. I'll probably go to New York in January. But I wish Dr. Tucker didn't want to contribute. He is really sweet and seems to have the magazine on his mind—and is far more useful than Mr. Pinckney ever was. He's going to take a share in it if people take stock, and he says he will give me any spare time he has. I'm sending a clipping from last week's Evening Post. They don't mention us as often as the Times. And the Times quoted the same poem today. Mr. Nathan,[5] I think, really owes us a great deal. Please give Mr. Mencken a cocktail at the Jefferson. We have only enough to cook with and use in ice-cream—it improves food very much, don't you think? Are you still determined to go to the party? Mr. Mencken writes that he doesn't want to, and that he hasn't danced since the minuet and the

[3] Mencken's article was "Morning Song in C Major"; Cabell's contribution was the first installment of *The Lineage of Lichfield.*

[4] Dr. Beverly Randolph Tucker was a Richmond neurologist whose hobby was Southern folklore.

[5] Robert Nathan, who had published several sketches in *The Reviewer,* was at this time known for the novels *Peter Kindred* (1919), *Autumn* (1921), and *The Puppet Master* (announced for publication in 1922).

varsovienne went out. Mrs. Sale wants you and him to come to Tuckahoe Saturday afternoon. She is very fond of you and she wants to enlighten Mr. Mencken. I wish he could see Westover,[6] but it's closed. John Powell has just had a wonderful write-up of his recent New York concert in the Evening Post. Their critic says that the mantle of Paderewski has descended upon him, and that it marks a new era in his career—also that the audience crowded up on the stage to seize his hands—isn't it annoying? I'm so low and contemptible that I'm not glad. He won't be endurable at all and I dread seeing him. Don't ever tell anyone that. I'm glad you think my letters are wonderful—yours are not—you don't tell anything. Why don't you try to imitate my style if you admire it? I shan't write an article in The Reviewer and say that it's really me and not Henry James, if you do, so it would be quite safe. Mrs. Cabell took Mr. Cabell to a debutante party Friday night and he was very cross. Mr. Holt[7] says she really has herring for breakfast every morning instead of eggs, like the woman in The Cream of the Jest.[8] I don't see how he could have published it, though. I'll be glad to see you. Let me know if you want to come at half-past seven or later.

Emily Clark.

I hope you aren't bored with The Reviewer. Don't bother about the things I asked you if you are—but you are wonderful about it and I really don't see how you *could* be bored. I think it's perfectly entrancing to talk about. There's a great deal more that I could tell, but I'll wait until you come.

E. T. C.

---

[6] The home built about 1730 by William Byrd II on the planatation his father had bought in 1688. In Emily's time the estate had recently been bought by Richard Crane.

[7] Guy Holt.

[8] Cabell's novel, published in 1917, revised in 1922.

1008 Park Avenue
[December 5, 1921]

The January Reviewer goes to press Saturday, and it is the number we shall use for advertising purposes, so we want Mr. Galsworthy and you in it. May I use one, or both—either you like—of your Tintypes in that issue, and the others later? Dr. Tucker says he doesn't think we ought to wait any longer than January to try to enlarge the circulation, so it's very important to make that one really distinguished. Either one, or two, of yours would be quite all right. Please let me know right away if I may do this. Prince Troubetzkoy is back here again to paint Mrs. Jacquelin Taylor's portrait. Ida said after that night here that he was the most thoroughly aristocratic person she had ever seen. Do you think that? I like Mr. Mencken much better than I did at first. He has written such nice letters and said he was coming back, and asked to be friends. So I said I would. He sent Emma Gray and me Pistols for Two[1] just after he left, and now he's sent me the first Prejudices and Prefaces and another book about Man and Men that I can't make out very well, something about Socialism—and says he's going to send me the second Prejudices[2] next week, and the others in January—and write something else for The Reviewer very soon. I've never read any of his books before. He writes nicer inscriptions than you and Mr. Cabell. I think it's dreadful you haven't written, but I have to know about the Tintypes. I wish you weren't so cross and horrid. Hunter says that everyone says my figure is better than anyone's else, here, and he didn't believe there were lots in New York that were better. It was comforting after all the discouragement I had. Everyone here, nearly, is mad with me, and I'm very depressed. But some of them have cause, and I've done nothing whatever to you except make you talk on the way to Cobham. Several people, here, are displeased with me all at once, and when I told Alice about it she wouldn't sympa-

[1] *Pistols for Two*, by O. Hatteras (a pseudonym for Mencken and George Jean Nathan), had been published in 1917.
[2] The Mencken books referred to are *Prejudices: First Series* (1919), *A Book of Prefaces* (1917), *Men Versus the Man* (in collaboration with R. R. Lamotte, 1910), and *Prejudices: Second Series* (1920).

thize, and merely said that I'd been trying to drive four-in-hand when I hadn't the years or the brains to do it. I don't know what she means and she won't discuss it. She's going to the country Wednesday and leave me alone for ten days because she's harassed. She's usually so serene and now she's just as you were, in the train, impossible to please. She said yesterday that she might just as well live in the house with a fish or an oyster or a Linda Condon, and I don't know what she means by that either, because I'm always very affectionate to her. I'm quite crazy about her, really, and would rather have her than anyone's else mother. She's always said she didn't want me to marry, because she thought it wouldn't be nice for the man, but now she says she wants me to marry a well-off, nerveless person who is stupid enough to be pleased by a soft voice and a flattering manner, and that's really the last straw. Because somehow I don't seem to have that necessary quality of steel in my make-up that Ida and Emma Gray have, and that really fits you for living—because I turn quite sick when at close quarters with that proposition, and they don't seem to. They are very soothing to me, though, and are rarely ever cross with me like some of my friends who are unmarried and a few years younger. They are nearly always tolerant. The world has been looking almost as black to me as it does to you and Mr. Mencken and Mr. Cabell and François Villon. I feel only slightly better today because I went to two parties yesterday and everyone liked my new black hat—it's the most expensive one I ever had, so I was very much interested in it—and today I had lunch with Jim Allison and he gave me the first really kind words I've had for some time. But he was a little cross because he'd wanted to come to dinner with you and Mr. Mencken. Margaret and Mary are annoyed with me too. Mr. Bierstadt wrote me another horrid letter a few days ago. He'd just learned from Mr. Cabell that I'd shown the first letter to him, and said I must be secretly trying to injure him! He talked as if I were Lucrezia Borgia or Margot Asquith. As if I'd dream of going about secretly annihilating literary young men, when I need them in my business. Did you ever hear anything so absurd? I'd never answered the first letter, but I answered that at once, and told him that I was often indiscreet but never malicious and that I'd adore being subtle and dangerous if I knew how, but was, unfortunately, entirely transparent and shallow. He sent me an abject apology by special delivery, literally abased himself, and said my friendship was very, very important to him, and he didn't deserve to see me when I came to New York in January, but that if he were locked up, as he ought to be, I might find it entertaining to come and throw nuts through the bars at him. Wasn't that nice of him? I don't see what more I could expect of any man. Amélie sent me today a letter she had written him—pages of scathing reproof—that she wanted Mr. Cabell and me to read first—but Mr. Cabell made me write and stop her at once, for fear he might throw himself into the East River, he said. So that's that, and I don't think he'll dream of being impertinent again. Mr. Mencken says you are insane. Why? The Troubetzkoys were charmed with you, even though I was not. You were very kind and sensible in many ways and I'm ever so grateful for it and the wonderful manuscripts for The Reviewer, but I can't see why you were cross with me unless you didn't want to go to Castle Hill and I let you in for it. But it didn't last long and you did like the other people I arranged for you to meet here. So anyway it was unreasonable. I wish you'd seen the garden. You might have felt better. I wish we could be friends politely and nicely. It would be such a comfort, because you know so much more than anyone else I know. Alice says you talk more brilliantly than anyone she has ever met. And I wish you'd stop being peevish, because so many people here are, and I'm naturally very amiable indeed. Amélie says Mr. Cabell lives in an ivory tower, and Alice says he's the only person she's ever seen who has achieved complete detachment like the people in India. Swamis, aren't they? But he's really very human about the little magazine. He even helped take the December issue to the post-office, and ran up and downstairs over and over again, carrying it. We, and the Lichfield Lineage, are in the Nation this week. Mrs. Cabell says you told her you didn't like anybody in Richmond any more, and that you were never coming back again. I think it very unkind of you—and to her, of all people—and several persons' feelings are hurt. Please let me know right away about your articles, and *please* let me use one in January with Galsworthy, be-

37

cause it would enormously help our most important issue. Mr. Cabell is coming here tomorrow to help me make up the magazine, but we'll leave that part open. You *are* good to The Reviewer, and it is very dependent on you. Did you say those dreadful things to Mrs. Cabell? Another one of my best friends has just had a baby. I was at Ida's Saturday afternoon and hers cried all the time, so that conversation was impossible.

Very sincerely yours,
Emily Clark.

1008 Park Avenue

[17]   [December 21, 1921]

    I think John Partins[1] is wonderful, and that your Philadelphia audience is wonderfully stupid to have taken you literally. It is much the most distinguished paper The Reviewer has had, and that's why I'm not splitting it. It was very, very kind of you to give it to The Reviewer. I used the second paper with the paragraphs and Mr. Cabell has just taken the other one home to read. I haven't thanked you for it because I've been sick—an impossible time of the year to be knocked out, I've really forgotten it's Christmas—but I'm out again now, though rather wobbly. The Reviewer proof is coming in three times this week and I'm perfectly dizzy with it. It's the first issue I've made up without Mr. Cabell. We thought we'd better try

---

[1] "A Note on John Partins," published in *The Reviewer*, January, 1922. Concerning this discussion of an imaginary writer and his novel *The Alabaster Saint*, Hergesheimer wrote to Emily: "The Partins affair was a paper I read before something like two thousand people in the Academy of Music in Philadelphia. No one seemed to discover that I had made him up, there was a large local demand for books by John Partins, and in consequence of this there is a certain buzzing demand for my account of him" (*Innocence Abroad*, by Emily Clark, p. 96).

38

one alone. I correct the proof because I can spell and punctuate and Mary does the other part because she can count. So I hope this issue will be presentable. You have really made it, with your paper and Mr. Galsworthy's,[2] and the Knopf advertisement. We were a page short of advertising, so it came just in time to save us. I'll be so glad to send Miss Hoopes the fifty Reviewers—we've never had so many on sale in one place before. I'll use Mr. Goldring[3] in February. We have engaged Mr. Winfree, at Dr. Tucker's suggestion, as business manager, and his name will be in the February issue. He is young and very businesslike and quite crazy about The Reviewer, and Margaret doesn't like it any more, and I don't know whether or not she'll stay with it. Don't tell anybody this. But she is really cross when nice things happen to it, and she's very half-hearted about getting advertising. Mr. Winfree says we could get more. I can't understand what's the matter with her. I haven't seen her for nearly six weeks, and work entirely with Hunter and Mary. She really likes Mary now better than me, though she didn't like her half so well when The Reviewer started. The other two are very amiable and Hunter will always do anything I ask him. Of course I'm going to ask Margaret to stay with the magazine, as editor, as long as it lives. But I think we'd better have a man, who is interested, for the business. I had a legal document from Mr. John Hemphill[4] the other day, asking for copyright assignments for the "stories" you "sold" to The Reviewer. I was shocked at such appalling ignorance about the magazine. Why don't you explain it to him? Mr. Cabell dictated what he said was the correct form over the telephone, and I sent it to him. I shouldn't think he'd need to worry about your rights where The Reviewer is concerned. Mr. Carl Van Vechten has written some extremely nice letters about the magazine, and so have lots of other

[2] Galsworthy's two-page essay was entitled "Burning Leaves—A Meditation." It was the featured contribution for January, 1922.

[3] Douglas Goldring was the author of *Streets: A Book of London Verses* (1912), *On the Road: A Book of Travel Songs* (1916), *The Fight for Freedom* (a play, 1920), *Reputations: Essays in Criticism* (1920), and *James Elroy Flecker* (1922).

[4] John Hemphill, Hergesheimer's brother-in-law, was his legal adviser in his dealings with publishers and movie producers.

people lately. A wonderful thing happened today. Mr. Cabell Bruce[5] wrote me from Baltimore and said that if we ever wanted to sell the magazine he believed he could find a purchaser. I think he means himself. I'm so excited about having made something that somebody wants to buy. Were you, the first time you sold a story? Though of course that's quite different. Margaret thought we were too free and easy for him, and that he wanted us to be like the Atlantic, and she especially disapproves of my articles. And he said he thought the whole magazine was distinctive and piquant, but he liked my papers best of all. But of course I shan't tell her that. You know I met him last summer at his country place before I went North and he was such a funny old gentleman and disapproved of my writing to Mr. Mencken. But he must have learned lots since then, because he urged that we have semi-social affairs for The Reviewer, at which you and Mr. Mencken and Mr. Cabell and his brother-in-law, Mr. Tom Page,[6] would speak, and "other literary stars," he said. Did you ever hear anything so screamingly funny? —Because Mr. Mencken would run about and bite everybody in such an assemblage. But he has millions of money, like old Mr. Page, and I'm going to print a rotten poem of his. Because he may help. George Sterling[7] likes The Reviewer too. He's been writing me about it, and today he sent me his new book of verse, all nicely inscribed. I think it was really sweet of him. It's encouraging, isn't it, for such different sorts of people to like it? I don't believe such an improbable group was ever got together before. Several people have written me lately and said they liked my papers, and perhaps I shall begin to take myself seriously and behave like a literary person. Do you think it would be a good thing? You said in New Jersey that I didn't work enough and Amélie said at Castle Hill that I played too much, but I've worked fearfully hard lately, and before I was sick I gave up everything else for several days. I was asked to a party "to

---

[5] William Cabell Bruce, United States senator from Maryland and author of the Pulitzer Prize biography *Benjamin Franklin* (1917).

[6] Thomas Nelson Page was Bruce's brother-in-law, not Cabell's.

[7] Author of such books of poetry as *Beyond the Breakers* (1914), *The Binding of the Beast* (1917), and *The Last Island* (1921).

amuse John Powell," but replied that I was clearly intended for a higher purpose than to amuse him or any other man. In spite of Nietzsche and Mr. Mencken, for the present I shall devote myself to war, not to the recreation of the warrior, and perhaps I shan't go to parties during Christmas. I feel perfectly rotten anyway, but perhaps it won't last long—it never does, with me. Prince Troubetzkoy came yesterday to paint Miss Jennie's portrait, and was here today. He really *is* too nice to be an artist, but I don't believe I'm a bit too nice to be one. I have everything except the gifts. It was nice of you to get Mr. Knopf to send me the check, because the advertising isn't my job, and I like to have something tangible, like a check, to send Margaret—because she thinks I'm no good for that, I know. John says if I go to New York the latter part of January he will introduce me to some people who can help, but I don't know yet when I'll go. Emma Gray says he is a really great artist. Do you believe that? Will Cytherea[8] be out early in the month? Because I've ordered it for someone for a Christmas present, and I'd like it to come as soon after Christmas as possible. Mr. Mencken continues to write me about unknown Southern authors, but I shan't encourage them unless they are rolling in money. If The Reviewer ever gets on its feet, though, I shall become like John Partins and refuse to be either threatened or bought. He really is a tremendously interesting person and I'm very proud of having the paper. I met a very attractive Englishman at a tea this afternoon, Francis Hirst, editor of the London Economist, who is rumored to be the Gentleman with a Duster.[9] I wanted to ask him for a paper, but refrained for fear of being turned down, on such short acquaintance. And I've grown superstitious about it—so far I haven't been refused and if I should be I'd feel quite certain the luck had turned. You are wonderfully good to The Reviewer. I'm sending this special delivery because I haven't been able to thank you before. . . . May we use two Tintypes one month and two or three the next? Do you think we can go another year without paying for manuscript? Mr. Cabell does, but I don't

[8] Hergesheimer's new novel, published in 1922.
[9] *The Glass of Fashion: Some Social Reflections, By a Gentleman with a Duster* (London, 1921). The author was Harold Begbie, not Francis Hirst.

41

know. I'd rather have your things than anyone's. I liked having the Lichfield Lineage, but no one here will read it. I'm glad you didn't say those things to Mrs. Cabell—she's a very common woman and it's better not to forget it.

Sincerely,
Emily Clark.

Please answer these questions.

[18]   [December, 1921]

This came today. It's an extremely good advertisement. Who wrote it? I hadn't remembered the date of publication of Cytherea,[1] or I wouldn't have asked you. It comes so soon after Christmas that it's quite all right for me to send it. Miss Coombs[2] wanted me to see about the spacing—Is this the way you want it? If it's not, let me know, and I can change it next week. The Reviewer is out next Thursday. So if it needs correction it must be done as soon as possible. I don't think blank spaces matter at the bottoms of pages, do you? Mr. Cabell thinks I shouldn't have left any. Prince Troubetzkoy has finished Miss Jennie's portrait and he's got her exactly. You must see it sometime.

E. T. C.

I've had another letter from Mr. Hemphill. He says I must go and swear to everything before a notary. I'll do it next week. Please explain to him about The Reviewer. How many extra copies could

[1] Knopf took a full-page advertisement for Hergesheimer's novel in the January, 1922, issue of *The Reviewer*.
[2] Hergesheimer's secretary.

we send Mr. Galsworthy, and hadn't you better send them? And I
think it would be nice to send Mr. Walpole[3] one.

[3] Hugh Walpole, who at Hergesheimer's instigation, kept intending to contribute to *The Reviewer*.

[19]   1008 Park Avenue
                                                             [January 2, 1922]

   I sat up nearly all night with Cytherea. It is, I think, the most
interesting of all your books—it goes so fast. And I suppose it is the
most tragic. A wonderful ending though—a serene not a tragic one
—when you think about it. Happy certainly for Savina, and happier
for Lee than anyone had a right to expect. I didn't look ahead as I
usually do, and I kept wondering what you'd do with them. Because
there would have been absolutely nothing for her when she was old,
and she was nearly old when the book began. It was the first time it
had occurred to me that a woman over forty could be like that, and
I was tremendously interested. With men, of course, it's quite different. They don't seem old until they are really old—Lee was
young—but I've always thought of middle-aged women as just utili-
tarian people; or mothers; or pathetically trying to seem what they
aren't—or just a part of the background. How did you find out
about her? Are there many like that? Alice has always said that most
women of that age were hopeless—she likes them my age and
younger, or really old. And she says she is different because she
skipped middle age and went from youth to extreme old age. And
I think she did. She just looks on, and reads a great deal. The other
women of that age I know are so absorbed in details that they forget
what the details are attached to, and the men aren't a bit like that.

43

Young women and old ones are often, as John Partins thought them, "inherently profound." But don't you think the others mostly become so violently engaged with clothes and servants and houses and how to keep this and what they do to their hair, that they never stop to think what it is all about? And it's so boring, because though I adore clothes, all the point is lost when they are considered that way. And their parties aren't much good because they think them so important. And I didn't dream that any women of that age wanted really important things badly, or would take them if they did. I thought, as I said in the December Reviewer, that only young ones ever did as they pleased. But a woman like Savina must be wonderful. Because if only a middle aged woman's mind wasn't atrophied she'd naturally be far more attractive than a young one. I can't get the book out of my mind. Probably it will often, as you say, be misunderstood but it ought to sell because it's such a good story. Even people who don't know what it's about will think that. But I can't see Lee as a business man because his mind worked like an artist. Are you sure that is all there is to it, and it's the best that anybody can do? But it probably is, because they were really more fortunate than most people and rather to be envied. How does Lillian Gish[1] like being in it, and has she ever caused such damage? I'll probably know more exactly what I think of it when I'm a little way off from it. It's more real to me than any of your books—I don't know whether that's because it's better or because it's modern. But I know it's a wonderful and very disturbing book. Do you suppose that's really as close as anyone comes to Cytherea, and why was there any hint of her in Anette? But perhaps only a man could see that. Tol'able David opened here today at the Broadway, and will be here all the week. I'll see it soon. I heard it was quite lovely and that there was a double line of people outside. I'm enclosing the advance notice that Mrs. Channing Ward,[2] who writes theatres and music for the Leader, wrote. Do you like this Reviewer? Let me know how

---

[1] The character Mina Raff in *Cytherea* was modeled on Hergesheimer's friend Lillian Gish, who, however, did not appear in the movie version when it was produced in 1924.

[2] For further information about Mrs. Ward see Letter 48.

44

many you want for yourself and Mr. Galsworthy. A comma was left out of your paper in some of them and put in, in others. And in mine, two lines were misplaced. And it was all right in the proof too. But the same thing happened when Mr. Cabell was making it up, so I don't suppose it can be helped. I used the subject you said —the young man's letter. Tell me something to write about in February. The magazine goes to press January tenth. Shall I use one, or two Tintypes? Please write me as soon as possible when you think you and Mrs. Hergesheimer are coming, if you come, because I shall probably go to New York the latter part of the month—but I won't go at the time you come. Emma Gray Trigg may go with me. Mr. Cabell has given me The Jewel Merchants. I've never liked it as a play. Have you seen it? If Alice had a success with Mr. Mencken I should think he'd mention her. He's written several letters and sent polite messages to Mrs. Sale and Emma Gray and Mrs. Crutchfield, but never to Alice. And I don't think it's quite polite. I don't see how he finds time to do so many things—Reviewer letters and polite letters and Christmas letters and books and magazines. A few days ago it was the Congressional Record, where he had recently been quoted by a senator. If the South becomes literary and Congress uses him as an authority he'll soon have nothing left to scold about, and then he would be compelled in honor to commit hari-kari, I suppose. Write me as soon as possible about your coming here—I hope you are. I want to ask you lots about The Reviewer too—we didn't do anything about it the last time. Is your long trip to England?

Very sincerely,
Emily Clark.

I'm using the two Tintypes in the February Reviewer, so I want the others as soon as you can send them. Tol'able David is lovely —the clipping is from the Leader. Shall we send some magazines to Mr. Galsworthy, and do you think it would be nice to send some to Mr. Walpole? He liked the October number. Do you want any more? Mr. Mencken wrote that he was going to spend Sunday with you, so don't tell him what I said about sending messages—it was silly. Mr. Knopf hasn't sent Cytherea to The Reviewer, although it's on sale here. But it's being reviewed for February anyway. You didn't tell me anything to write about and I don't know anything— can't you think of something? I've another manuscript from Hansell Baugh[1] that is probably very clever, but I can't understand it. I'd send it to you except that you may come. He writes like Miss Newman, and Mr. Mencken and Mr. Rascoe and Mr. Van Vechten are crazy about him, but I get horribly balled up. Wasn't it queer for Mr. Starrett[2] to think those people wrote like Mr. Cabell? I don't see how they ever extricate themselves from their sentences. And yet in a way I'd like to be brilliant and complicated and I think I *could* be a little more so, but Mr. Cabell says it's better for me not to bother. Do you think that? Didn't you think Adam and Little Eva[3] was foolish and shopworn? I did. He accepted that early in the fall. But I have something splendid from the same young man for February. Don't tell Mr. Mencken I talked to you about him. When are you coming here?

Emily Clark.

---

[1] Later known as a scholar (e.g., editor of *General Semantics*, Papers from the First American Congress for General Semantics, 1938).

[2] Vincent Starrett, who at this time edited *The Wave*, a little magazine published in Chicago. He had written facetiously to *The Reviewer*, surmising that most of the contents were written by Cabell under a variety of pseudonyms.

[3] A sketch by Gene Donald in *The Reviewer*, January, 1922.

The February Reviewer has just been put together and I used the first Tintype, and Mr. Goldring's article second. I decided to use the Tintypes one every other month—another in April, you see, and then you'll give me the other three that you first promised, for the summer numbers, won't you? You said there might be no more. Surely you meant only for this winter, didn't you? Because I want them very badly, and had expected four or five. I'd rather have them than anything at all for The Reviewer. If I use these two in February and April there'll be plenty of time for you to write another for June. It's wonderful that you are going West, but I'm sorry it happens just now, because you can't come here and you won't be in New York when I'm there. Are you going to write papers about the West for the Post, as Julian Street[1] did for Collier's? You were so unsatisfactory with that blue paper letter and no information except just Mr. Lorimer.[2] It sounds terribly impressive though. Please tell me what it is you are going for, and I'll read the Post. I'm trying to think, as you told me, of everything that should be said or asked. (1) *Please* don't stop the Tintypes, and I can't see any reason why you should, because you can finish when you come back—write one here in April. You see, they are different from anything else we could have, possibly, and quite valuable. (2) Where is my other Tintype manuscript? (3) Please send Douglas Goldring's other article and the two English subscriptions you spoke of before you leave. I'm frightened about getting enough good material, because you are going away, and Mr. Cabell was responsible only for the first three months. (4) Please get something in the West if you can, from Zona Gale[3] or Ben Hecht[4] or somebody. Will you go to Chi-

---

[1] The most recent publications of this well-known essayist and novelist were *Mysterious Japan* (1921) and *Rita Coventry* (a novel, 1922).

[2] George Horace Lorimer was editor of *The Saturday Evening Post* and a close friend of Hergesheimer's.

[3] Zona Gale's most recent successes had been *Birth* (1918) and *The Secret Way* (1921).

[4] Known in 1922 as the author of *Erik Dorn* (1921) and *Gargoyles* (1922).

cago? Vincent Starrett sent us something three months ago, and later wrote a letter, and I didn't answer either until last Sunday and I'm afraid he's mad. (5) The special reason I want to go to New York now is to be certain of at least one or two good articles a month for The Reviewer. Mr. Mencken's Southern talk is all very well, but it won't fill the magazine—with much but slush. Whenever we grow really Southern we are stupid. We are using Dr. Tucker and Frank Beirne[5] in February, and they are both dreadful. Mr. Cabell thinks if I talked to a few people it would be more useful than writing to them, and he is going to write Mr. Holt and Mr. Rascoe and Robert Nathan and some others, and tell them to be sure and give me some papers when I see them. Will you tell Mr. Van Vechten and Mr. Knopf and anyone else you think would help, and tell them what I want, and that they must do it? Mr. Van Vechten sent something yesterday, but I'd like several more from him. (6) Can you get some more English articles later, and would Mr. Walpole like The Reviewer? That's all I can think of just now, except why did Lee Randon drive a Ford sedan when you hate them even on country roads and were cross when the Troubetzkoys used one? And why did Fanny[6] rub vaseline into her nails at night? I never heard of that before and I think it a loathsome habit. And Alice wants to know why Jasper Penny[7] was in love with Susan Brundon.[7] The Partins article is wonderful. Many people have said it is better than any magazine article they have seen, and it made that issue much the best we've had. Several Philadelphia book shops have written for it, and one of them wants Reviewers every month, and likes it very much. Mr. Van Vechten said you had done nothing better, and that "all the world would speak of it." He enclosed an article from the New York Globe, quoting your paragraph about English lecturers and saying this was an unusually interesting number of The Reviewer. Prince Troubetzkoy was here yesterday—he has come back

[5] A writer on the staff of the Baltimore *Evening Sun,* husband of Emily's friend Rosamund Beirne.
[6] Characters in Hergesheimer's novel *Cytherea.*
[7] Characters in Hergesheimer's novel *The Three Black Pennys.*

48

for an exhibition of his portraits—and said he and Amélie thought
your paper one of the most brilliant things they had read. She has
been sick, and hasn't written about the book I sent her either. They
like San Cristobal better than any but Java Head, he says. She has
written one good story about Castle Hill. Would you like to read it?
I wish you'd write a story about Virginia even if Mrs. Tompkins did
tell you not to. When you go to Charleston would you like me to tell
the Pinckneys?[8] (7) Another question that I forgot—if I want to
know anything do you mean it should be telegraphed? (8) Do you
think I'll have difficulty in getting material for a year ahead without
paying for it? Mr. Cabell and Mr. Mencken seem to think not.
When terrible things appear, you'll know it's because they are
Southern and we must, if we want Southerners to put money in it.
Won't you see The Reviewer while you are away? I've written something very nice for February—an editorial against progress and in
favor of race suicide, with a slight leaning to the Roman Church, for
aesthetic reasons. Mr. Cabell has just given me The Cords of Vanity. It isn't at all nice, is it? I've heard such an interesting and authentic story about him, but I can't write it—it happened a long time
ago. I think it's splendid you are going away for Mr. Lorimer, but
I do feel frightened about The Reviewer being left to itself entirely
just now, and I wish it wasn't going to be so long. The magazine
could die between now and April, but it won't if I can help it.
Prince Troubetzkoy says I must talk to Mr. Henry Anderson[9] about
this—the one who went to Romania with the Red Cross, you know,
and became so involved with the Queen. Please write me all these
things and don't be cross because I asked them when you are busy
because you told me to, and I have to know. You are wonderful to
The Reviewer and I hope you have a very nice trip indeed. I'm

[8] Of the well-known Pinckney family of Charleston, Josephine was the most
conspicuous member in her generation. She was one of the founders of the seminal
Poetry Society of South Carolina, and her own verse appeared in Poetry and other
magazines. In later years she was to write several novels: Hilton Head (1941),
Three O'Clock Dinner (1945), Great Mischief (1948), and My Son and Foe
(1952).

[9] See Emily's further identification in Letter 23.

sorry you can't come now. The blots and scratches are because I'm sleepy.

Very sincerely yours,
Emily Clark.

[22]   1008 Park Avenue
[February 27, 1922]

I'm going to write you a regular letter in a day or two because there's lots to tell you about The Reviewer—this is just to explain the enclosure. Though writing to you is like dropping things down a well and wondering if they've reached anywhere, and that isn't interesting. Because I often don't know whether you get them or not. You had almost become a myth when I heard from you in St. Louis—but of course I know you are busy. I'm sending this through Mr. Hemphill, because it's important. This paper came to us from New York when I was away, and it's just been turned over to me. The others and Mr. Cabell thought it was clever and that it might be interesting to use, just as we used the Ben Ray Redman[1] thing about Mr. Cabell. It has several misspelt words and the beginning of it irritated me, but the end is clever, I think, and rather an original compliment—the "distaste," I mean, "for what he was proclaiming." Some of it is silly, but whether we use it or not depends on whether or not you care for it. It makes no difference to me. Mr. Cabell, as you know, adores literary arguments. I've been a little out of patience with him lately. *Why* does he adore Guy Holt so? I can't understand it. Do other people take him as seriously as Mr. Cabell does? I enclose some of your publicity from the rural

---

[1] A poet and critic who later published *Masquerade,* a book of poems (1923), *Edwin Arlington Robinson,* a critical study (1926), and translations of several French plays and novels.

districts of Virginia, showing that they sometimes mention the author. Please send this back as soon as possible and say what you think. Read it very carefully, please, because it's apt to be deceptive at first glance. It made me mad until I read it the second time. How do you think the "Booboisie" would take it? Did you get the Reviewer I sent? I'm using Mr. Goldring's other article for March. Shall I send his copies to Dower House,[2] or will you give me his address? I'll write you about the Tintypes this week. The April Reviewer goes to press March 10, so let me know as soon as you can. We have incorporated and have just sent out letters asking people to take stock. We haven't had time to hear from them yet. I'm all alone here, as Alice has gone to a hospital for two weeks—I'm not allowed to see her, but she's not seriously ill. Mr. Benét[3] was asked to two teas for me in New York, but couldn't come, so I went in to thank him for noticing us so often. He was amazed to know we didn't pay, and asked about the English papers. I told him you got them for us. He thought it was wonderful and mentioned it the next time. It's marked near the bottom of this clipping.

Emily Clark.

The Tintype was quoted in the Herald.

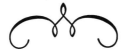

[March 12, 1922]
1008 Park Avenue

[23]

We aren't using Mr. Eddy's[1] paper. I think it's quite superfluous, and doesn't get anywhere. He is crazy about The Reviewer.

[2] Hergesheimer's home in West Chester, Pennsylvania.
[3] William Rose Benét, who since 1921 had been on the staff of *The Literary Review* of the New York *Evening Post*. He published several books of poetry, most recently *Moons of Grandeur* (1920).
[1] Frederick B. Eddy—who appeared in the June, 1922, issue with a review of

He subscribed only two months ago, but he has taken fifty dollars of stock and is going to send me some advertisements. He lives in New York. It was so nice to hear from you, and you must be so glad to have left the Middle West for the Far West. I suppose it's unfair, but because of the dreadful books the Young Intellectuals write about the middle part I've developed an unreasoning horror of it. And Scott Fitzgerald's sophisticated people are as common as Mr. Lewis' and Mr. Anderson's and Mr. Dell's[2] village people, don't you think so? And in New York they all told me that Sherwood Anderson was a great writer, and perhaps I'd think so if I could read what he says, but I can't. The Björkmans[3] asked me to meet Floyd Dell, but I couldn't go that day. But the Far West must be wonderful—I envy you. Alice adores it, but I've never been there. But I'd like some papers from the Y. I.'s, if they are not too melancholy. Can you get me any? It's angelic of you to take so much stock, and we are all tremendously grateful. It will make you quite an influential person because it is four shares. We have seventeen hundred and fifty dollars now, and we want five thousand. One of the useful things I've been able to do for The Reviewer lately is to get Henry Anderson as a director. They are, of course, only nominal, but their advice is useful and they are expected to help. I asked him just before I went to New York, not really thinking he would, because he's so crowded already, but he was lovely about it and said he'd like it. I don't know yet what he is going to do, but he wrote me a few days ago and asked me to have a directors' meeting soon. He is quite the most distinguished lawyer in Virginia, and was head of the Red Cross in Romania, you know, and ran for Republican vice-president! He has to be in New York a lot, but I think he'll be useful because he's much the most broad-minded person here. Prince Troubetskoy had dinner with him alone not long ago, and said he

Arthur Machen's novel *The Secret Glory*—was identified in that issue as a New Yorker who "is, we gather, a business man, though apparently not tired."

[2] Floyd Dell had published such novels as *Moon Calf* (1920) and *The Briary-Bush* (1921), and was soon to publish *Janet March* (1923).

[3] Edwin Björkman was a well-known journalist, critic, and translator. It was he who introduced American readers to the work of Strindberg, Björnson, and Schnitzler.

was more satisfactory to talk to than any American he'd met except you and Mr. Mencken. He always dresses for dinner, too, of which you'll approve. Dr. Tucker is another director. They seem to think we can get enough money to go on. I'm very busy now because Mary Street has gone down to Charleston for a week or so. And I have to have the first director's meeting while she's away. I'm horribly frightened because she is supposed to take charge of it. I'll send Ralph Van Vechten[4] the two Reviewers. Those two are almost impossible to get, but Mary and I are each giving him one of our own. Carl Van Vechten has just completed his file too. If his brother is like him he must be wonderfully nice. He said you promised to bring him down here, but brought Mr. Mencken instead. He says you'll probably bring him later though, and I hope you will. I had lunch with him and he wanted to give me a party in his apartment the next week, but I couldn't stay. They were upset at the time, because Fania Marinoff[5] was just opening in a revue, Frank Fay's[6] Fables. He took me back in her dressing-room the first night, and I think she's charming. Philip Moeller[7] was there too, and she was embracing him frantically. I met him again afterwards and he promised me a one-act play for The Reviewer. I hope he does it. Mr. Van Vechten is writing me a paper a month—one on Jeritza[8] for April. The March number is dull except for him and Mr. Goldring —the worst except December, I think. I'll use the next Tintype in May—please try to give me another in the summer, so we can use them at intervals. Mr. Mencken sent me In Defense of Women[9] yesterday, and said he had reason to believe you had been killed by the Indians after crossing the Mississippi, and to tell you, if I knew your address, that he was praying you would break your leg. He is

[4] Carl Van Vechten's older brother, a Chicago banker.
[5] The actress Fania Marinoff is Mrs. Carl Van Vechten.
[6] The actor Frank Fay wrote, produced, and acted in Frank Fay's Fables in 1922. In later life he made a tremendous hit in Harvey, which ran from 1944 to 1946.
[7] Author of such plays as Two Blind Beggars (1918), Five Somewhat Historical Plays (1918), and Sophie (1919).
[8] Maria Jeritza had recently (1921) joined the Metropolitan Opera Company.
[9] Published by Mencken in 1918.

reviewing Chrome Yellow[10] for us. He is so queer in some ways. Mr. Van Vechten and Louis Untermeyer knew what I meant about him. They said he was a real aristocrat with men, but that he was afraid of women, except a certain kind. He is really splendid and I like him lots, but he bursts out now and then with something that seems to terrify him, and then he walks on eggshells (I've just found I've no more letter paper) for awhile, and it amuses me. He forgets and walks on the inside of the street too. Mr. Van Vechten says he has never known any kind of women well except the Broadway kind and middle-aged intellectual ones likes Edna Ferber[11] and Zoë Akins[12]—if they are intellectual—and Mr. Untermeyer says that people he can't classify upset him. He says Mr. Mencken doesn't get Mr. Cabell and that Mr. Cabell was kidding him when he talked to him about immortality. Mr. Van Vechten said he believed Mr. Cabell had his tongue in his cheek most of the time, and that on account of his inheritance he was born tired and sophisticated, without doing anything to get that way, but that Mr. Mencken was ingenuous and full of gusto. But I'm not sure that Mr. Cabell was kidding on that occasion, are you? The Untermeyers asked me to tea with Glenn Frank,[13] but I didn't get there until he had gone. Mr. Nathan[14] is very good-looking, I think, and has rather an appealing manner. He looks as if he were born tired too. Someone said he looked twenty-six, but he doesn't. He looks as if he had become mummied at twenty-six. But he's small, I think, in every way. He said you and Mr. Cabell and Mr. Mencken were mistaken in thinking he wouldn't write anything for me, because he was going to this spring, but I don't know if he will. He has influenza now. He says he thinks he understands The Reviewers better than Mr. Mencken does. But I like Mr. Mencken lots better. He's so big

[10] The novel by Aldous Huxley, the American edition of which was published in 1922.
[11] Edna Ferber's most recent books were *The Girls* (1921) and *Gigolo* (1922).
[12] Most recently Zoë Akins had published *Cake upon the Waters* (1919), and was to publish *Déclassée* in 1923.
[13] Author of *Stakes of the War* (with T. L. Stoddard, 1918) and *The Politics of Industry* (1919). In 1923 he was to publish *An American Looks at His World.*
[14] George Jean Nathan.

54

and knows so much about everything, and yet, in a way, is so innocent. Do you think that? We've just had a clipping from a Memphis
paper with something nice that he wrote the editors about the Reviewer. I like Burton Rascoe too. I don't like Robert Nathan much,
though he's quite picturesque. He says he's coming down here. He's
just been divorced, and he poses all the time. Once when I had tea
in his apartment he took a rose out of a vase and walked around with
it. Wasn't that perfectly dreadful? I ran into Miss Coombs one
afternoon. I didn't know her, but she recognized me and stopped.
She looked lonesome and I took her to tea. She seems to consider
you a most estimable and superior person. You ought to hold on to
her when you get back. She's so nice and quaint, I think. She said
she belonged to something in West Chester called the Home Circle
Literary Club! This clipping is from the March Bookman. I met
John Farrar[15] at the Björkmans' and I didn't dream he'd publish the
silly things I said. And I don't even remember saying that none of
our contributors were clever. Mr. Farrar is so insignificant and book-
ish looking. Mrs. Cabell went to New York when I did, but I saw
her only that time. Mr. Mencken, who came up the same week,
didn't look her up, although I told him she was there, and I don't
think she liked it! Mr. Mencken and Mr. Van Vechten both adore
you, but I don't think they like each other. This month is a strain,
because The Reviewer is still unsettled. It would quite break my
heart if it didn't go on, but I think it must, don't you? John Powell
was in New York when I was there, and had to have a medical
examination. He called me up after midnight to say he had only
five months to live, and I was so cross and I don't believe it. He's
still going about Richmond. He says he wants to have a very good
time during these months. I suppose it's a good card to have up
your sleeve when you are bored and not very happy, but I'm not a
bit impressed. Emma Gray couldn't go to New York with me because her nurse left at that time, so I went alone and stayed in Mary
Taylor's apartment. You know Emma Gray has a three-year old son.
And at Ida's it wasn't nearly as nice since she has a daughter. Did I
write you that Mr. Mencken sent me a valentine there to send his

15 Editor of The *Bookman*.

little niece, so she wouldn't know where it came from? It really was wonderful—hardly anyone I know would have thought of it. He must be crazy about his family. Alice has come home, but is still resting and getting flowers and things. She asked if you inquired about her when you wrote, and was cross when you didn't. I wish you didn't have to stay West so long. I want to see you and I need your advice. Did you speak to Ben Hecht and Zona Gale for me? You are so good to us—The Reviewer couldn't live without you. Mr. Cabell has been quite useless for two weeks. He's revising Gallantry,[16] to come out in the spring. Are you going to write anything about the Mormons? Alice says the women in Salt Lake City were terrible when she was there, to look at, I mean. Mary Street has written such a surprising poem. She must have a complex. I hear everywhere that Cytherea is selling enormously. I wish you'd write soon.

Emily Clark.

[16] Originally published in 1907.

THE REVIEWER
Richmond, Virginia   1008 Park Avenue
[24]   [April 22, 1922]

This is The Reviewer paper. Do you like it? Please do something for me. Write Mr. Cabell before long and tell him you think we are doing very well with The Reviewer, but *don't* let him think you wrote for that reason, or say I asked you to. He was here yesterday, and he gets nervous because I edit differently from the way he did. I'd like him to know that you and Mr. Mencken really like The Reviewer, that you don't merely tell me so. This will be a real help to me if you will do it. Mr. Cabell said you hadn't written him for ages anyway, and I said you hadn't to me. And Mr. Mencken wrote him yesterday and said you wouldn't write him. He has spoken to me about it several times. He is spreading dreadful stories about you.

56

He says you have been killed by Indians and that you have lost all
your money shooting craps and that you were in a fight in St. Louis
and that you had been poisoned in Denver by wood alcohol. I think it
outrageous of you not to write, to me at least, because I sent you two
Reviewers. I don't believe you have it on your mind at all. I shall use
the next Tintype for May. I had such a nice letter from Ralph Van
Vechten the other day. He is so glad to have the two Reviewers, and
he asked me to send him some stock subscription blanks, because he
might be able to interest some of the members of the Caxton Club in
taking stock. I think that was wonderful of a Chicago man and I'm
ever so grateful to you for talking to him about it. Mr. Mencken says
he is going abroad for two months this summer. He is a great help
and thinks of lots of people to write articles. He said that W. L.
George[1] had told him he was going to write us a paper and he
thought you had spoken to him about it, but I think Mr. George has
gone home and he's never sent it. I think it very strange that he never
comes to Virginia. Mr. Walpole is coming back next fall. In a letter
from Burton Rascoe last week with a paper he told me he wanted
Hunter to write some book reviews for him in the New York Tribune. Did you know that Mr. Rascoe has just left McCall's and has
taken Heywood Broun's place on the Tribune? Hunter has done
Peter Whiffle[2] for him to use tomorrow, and will write one or two a
week. I took some New England people to Tuckahoe last Sunday.
You ought to see it in April—they were entranced with it. There
was tea in the garden and the whole place was drenched with lilacs.
The iris is in bloom too. You know there's a long walk with thick,
purple borders of it. Mrs. Sale has had a baby. It came in February and everyone was amazed. No one knew—I don't think even
Mr. Sale did, and she was receiving at the new governor's wife's reception—Mrs. Trinkle—only a week before. The Trinkles are
dreadful—from Southwest Virginia. The baby isn't seen or heard at
Tuckahoe and they never mention it. It was written up in Town

[1] The British novelist, author of such books as *The City of Light* (1912),
A Bed of Roses (1919), *The Intelligence of Woman* (1920), and *Ursula Trent*
(1921).
[2] Van Vechten's first novel, published in 1922.

Topics because it was so funny. Emma Gray thinks she adopted it—
I had lunch with her today. She has been helping Mrs. Archer Jones
put on a play for the Woman's Club. It was Mr. Cabell's story,
"Simon's Hour," from Gallantry, dramatized as the Little Theatre
League did the first one last year. Douglas Freeman was the most
important person in it and was remarkably good—a debauched English vicar and loathsome beyond words. John Powell was asked to be
in it and refused. It was a better play than the one the Little Theatre
gave. I don't know whether Mr. Cabell liked it or not. He sat in the
front row and looked perfectly phlegmatic. You know I wrote you
I was so mad with Miss Margaret Montague because she said my
head was turned by New York—but I'm not now, because she made
a speech about The Reviewer at the Woman's Club this week. I
never go there but the others heard it and she said that it showed "all
things were possible to youth, gallantry and talent"—and there was
tremendous applause! Wasn't it funny? I don't know why she did it
after being so hateful—except that after I heard what she said first I
went to see her and talked to her about The Reviewer because I
thought it so unfair of her to make up her mind about it and me.
Dr. Tucker is really sweet. You know I disagreed with you about
him last summer but I don't now. He works hard about The Reviewer, and he's gone crazy now about the influence of glands on
personality instead of Freud and Havelock Ellis. I've never read a
line of any of them so I can't talk to him about it. Did I tell you the
Tompkins had sold the house in Linden Row? But they won't move
for some time and they don't know where they are going. The old
Stone House that the Archer Jones are turning into a Poe Memorial
will be opened next week, and a weird collection of Virginia "artists" will be guests of honor, from Mr. Cabell and John [Powell]
to Miss Montague and Mrs. Bosher.[3] I promised to help Mrs. Jones
and I shan't mind because it will all be so absurd. Prince Troubetzkoy comes here quite often now to paint because Amélie hasn't
been well enough to go to New York at all. He is nice—almost like

[3] Kate Langley Bosher (1865–1932), who wrote under the pseudonym Kate
Cairns, was the author of such ephemeral but popular novels as "Bobbie" (1899),
Mary Cary (1910), and Kitty Canary (1918).

a father—I have had so many troubles about The Reviewer and he is always sympathetic—old like a father but more intelligent than most people's fathers. He came one Sunday afternoon when I wasn't well and wasn't seeing anyone, and Alice was away—she only came home yesterday—and he went back in the kitchen and cooked, because he had been painting all day and I don't know how to cook. He is wonderfully efficient. He admires you very much. I've lent Jim[4] In Defense of Women and he is perfectly furious about it. Isn't that queer? I should think if I'm not he needn't be. I met such a strange girl from Greenwich Village last week. It was at a supper after the rehearsal of Mr. Cabell's play—a Miss Williamson—she was so queer looking. There were some men and Emma Gray and other people. Mr. Cabell didn't come. I wish he had, because she kissed some of the men good night, and I would have given anything if she had kissed him. And she asked another to take her to a Country Club dance the next week. It was sad for us because she was entirely surrounded, though they did talk outrageously afterwards. She was quite excited over seeing Mr. Cabell, though she just saw him and that was all, before he disappeared. And she told me that she had heard lots about The Reviewer in New York and was coming to see me, but I shan't let her. She said she knew Mr. Mencken and Mr. Nathan and the Knopfs and Mr. Crowninshield[5] and several others quite well, and she calls Mr. Mencken "Menck" and said he was sweet and adorable, but told me not to tell anyone that she knew him well. She said that when she lived in Washington she used to go to Baltimore sometimes to dinner with him and come back to Washington on the train by herself at night. Did you ever *hear* of such a thing? She must be one of the blondes that you said would wait for him for hours. Mrs. Reynolds told me afterwards that I was a frightful snob and very horrid, but I never mean to be. She said my politeness was unendurable and I really don't know what she means. Mr. Cabell doesn't like Mrs. Peterkin.[6]

4 Jim Allison, a Richmond friend.
5 Frank Crowninshield was editor of *Vanity Fair*.
6 Julia Peterkin, author of *Green Thursday* (1924), *Black April* (1927), and *Scarlet Sister Mary* (1928). Her sketches of Negro life had been appearing regularly in *The Reviewer* since January, 1922.

He said she tired him to death and he hardly ever commits himself so far, so perhaps you'd better not go and see her. She has gone home now. If you will write Mr. Cabell I'll be so glad. I was impertinent to him two weeks ago, and he brought me the Lichfield Lineage. It's just out and he has a few extra copies besides the special five-dollar ones. I think he's going to give you one. Mrs. Cabell has been to Washington and left him for awhile. Mr. Nathan[7] wrote a few days ago and said he was really going to write something before this month was over, but you and Mr. Mencken say he won't. I told him in New York that you and Mr. Mencken said he never did favors, but that we shouldn't regard it as a favor because The Reviewer had practically no gratitude. He said, that being true, he would. Couldn't you write another Tintype when you come South? You give The Reviewer the nicest things it *ever* has from anyone, and the responsibility of filling it is dreadful, because the others do nothing about it except write their own things. Everybody here is so excited and surprised over Mary's last poem. Where are you and when are you coming here? Don't you think it very nice for me to write you this long letter under the circumstances? Does Mr. Hemphill send you the Reviewers and letters? John Powell has written a play about an octoroon—he has just read it to me—you would be interested. Margaret stopped working for The Reviewer several months ago, but we shall always use her name. (She may come back, I don't know.) Hunter has a new doctor and his attacks are becoming more infrequent—but he has never had another with me anyway. I shan't keep telling you things unless you are more responsive. Lady Astor and her husband are coming soon to stay a week here. I think perhaps I'll invite her to write for The Reviewer. She hasn't been here for eight years. Are you sorry and ashamed of having been so perfectly dreadful about writing?

> Very sincerely yours,
> Emily Clark.

Mr. Cabell doesn't know anything about people, does he?

[7] George Jean Nathan.

The Van Vechtens¹ didn't come until late Thursday night and stayed until early Saturday morning. They expected to hear from you and thought you might join them here. What *are* you doing? Mr. Mencken wrote that you'd have to go to a sanitorium for a week or two. Have you gone, and is that what is the matter? I told him that when I heard from you ages and ages ago you had spoken quite beautifully of the scenery and only that, but he said other things had occupied you. He worries over you in every letter. Did he send you a copy of the wonderful thing he wrote about The Reviewer— Violets in the Sahara—in the Sun last week? If he didn't, I will. He put you in it too, as a Southern violet. Guy Holt (Don't tell this) was cross because I said you had done so much for The Reviewer—he acted as if it were all Mr. Cabell. The Van Vechtens are so nice, very fatherly and motherly too, entirely unlike Carl Van Vechten. There were paper-hangers in the hall and so I couldn't ask them here. But I drove them about and showed them some old houses and they met some people and seemed to like it a lot. They say they are coming back and they are thinking of buying a place in Virginia. They had looked at several, but seemed worried about getting servants. Mrs. Sale was in town that day so I couldn't take them to Tuckahoe. We stopped at Reveille, and Mr. Crutchfield must have got in some good whiskey lately, because he had very nice juleps with strawberries and pineapples, and I know Mr. Van Vechten must have liked it because just before we left, he said he was going back with Mr. Crutchfield to look at the secret room in the roof, and when he came back he said they hadn't been in the roof at all, but had had several more drinks. When I had lunch with them at the Jefferson too he had very good cocktails and made them in the dining-room. The garden at Reveille is lovely now and the water-lilies in the pool are in bloom. The Van Vechtens liked it better than any garden they had seen at all. Mr. Cabell was having trouble with his eyes and couldn't see them that day. If they had stayed over a day he could have. He had to spend hours at an oc-

¹ Ralph (Carl's brother) and his wife.

culist's and I think he is frightened. If they could have stayed over I would have taken them to Westover Saturday, because it was open then and will be through this week. Can't you possibly come down by the end of this week? Because you really must see it. I motored there Saturday afternoon and had tea on the beach. It is just thirty miles down the James and a very good road. The garden is perfect now, and it is the most beautiful old house in America except possibly Monticello. Colonel William Byrd, who founded Richmond, and Evelyn lived there, you know, and it is a real manor house, with a beautiful sweep of river at the foot of the lawn. It is two and a half miles wide there. The house is very stately and the old English bricks are a heavenly shade. There are tall wrought iron gates with a crest at the top, and a hall that Elsie DeWolfe[2] has been down twice to look at. It was built in the early part of the eighteenth century, and is quite a different sort of house from Tuckahoe and almost twice as large as Castle Hill. The garden is the largest and loveliest I have seen out of England, and everything is in bloom now, especially roses and honeysuckle. Crowds of people can get lost in the walks and the box hedges are so very tall. Little gateways are cut everywhere, and most of the garden is hidden from every other part. There is a river wall at the foot of the lawn. It isn't very far from Jamestown Island, and I can't think of any place where it is so easy to see satin and powder and perukes. So many old houses are farmhouses and I know there is no other place in America quite like this. It has been closed for several years, and the Cranes, who have bought it recently, are abroad. Evelyn Byrd was the most beautiful woman in Virginia, you know, and the first advanced one. She was taken to England to be presented at court and wouldn't marry the very impressive person selected for her by her father, who was furious. She was brought home and died at twenty-nine unmarried, and was buried in the garden as far from Colonel Byrd as possible, with an enchanting epitaph. She and Colonel Byrd and Lord Peterborough

---

[2] The former actress, under whom Ethel Barrymore had served as understudy in the 1890's, who in later life had become a fashionable interior decorator and partygiver. Still later, after her long spinsterhood, she was to marry Sir Charles Mendl.

still roam the place. None of the family has enough money to own it, and it may be closed next week, and the garden is at its very best now, so you *must* see it. I have to ask you some questions about The Reviewer, but if you are coming soon I'll wait. If there isn't enough money to run it properly as a monthly, don't you think that for a year it could be turned into a quarterly, until it gets on its feet? The Yale and Sewanee Reviews and the Little Review and the Theatre Arts and several other non-commercial magazines do that, and of course we could use less second-rate material in that way. I hate using so many space-fillers. And none of our material is especially current, anyway, except the books. While we were a quarterly, of course, we could only review the most distinguished books and let the others go. I haven't mentioned this to anyone, not even Mr. Cabell or Hunter or the directors, so don't say anything about it. It is only an idea. Burton Rascoe has the leading article in the June issue, and John Bennett,[3] the South Carolinian who wrote Madame Margot, in July, which should satisfy Mr. Mencken. He sends me new and appalling Southerners every week. He wants me to run a series of Southern cities and is going to write me a paper on Baltimore for it. Miss Newman is going to write Atlanta. I haven't decided who had better take Richmond. Wouldn't you like to? Do you think Nellie Tompkins would do it well? But she does nothing now but nurse her family all the time. They *have* sold the house at last, but aren't moving yet. Please hurry and come here and stop ignoring The Reviewer. You are the only person who is so cold to it and your haughty silence hurts my feelings, and its, very much. I'm rather put out with Mr. Rascoe, but don't tell that either. Your telegram was like a ouija board message—you haven't been nearly so bad as this since I've known you and I can't imagine why I bother to write you. But I need to talk to you *very* badly, because I can't explain in a letter how complicated things are. We ought to call

---

[3] John Bennett (1865–1956) was not a South Carolinian but he had made Charleston his home. He wrote about old Charleston legends and folkways in such books as *The Treasure of Peyre Gaillard* (1906) and *Madame Margot* (1921), though perhaps his best-known book is *Master Skylark*, a story laid in Shakespeare's England.

a directors' meeting within the next ten days, and I don't want to do it until I've talked to you. Mr. Cabell is no help at all in this end of it. Of course I know it's dreadful without a secretary. Haven't you got her back yet? I'm enclosing an interview with the Richmond literati from the Leader. Isn't the grouping of them weird, and Mr. Cabell's horrible picture with a crick in his neck? His "ebony cigarette holder" is the ten-cent rubber one. Did you get my letters and Reviewers?

Very sincerely,
Emily Clark.

26

1008 Park Avenue
[June, 1922]

    I realize that I must have been very unreasonable and I'm afraid The Reviewer will become obnoxious to you and others. Alice has been very exasperated at my attitude because the other day Mr. Cabell had to come in and apologize for something he really hadn't done, and she said Miss Margaret Montague was right in the winter when she said my head was turned. I'm ever so sorry, because it really isn't. I never forget for an instant that you and Mr. Cabell are very great men and The Reviewer is very small—never. I don't forget that you have quantities of work and tremendously important things on your mind. I have behaved very badly and given people a great deal of trouble. I compelled Mr. Mencken to write a book review the day he was leaving for New York, and I'm afraid he is quite worn out, but he seems so strong. And I've tormented a number of other people. I shall be more careful, because I don't want them to hate the magazine. And you have been so kind—I'm very humiliated and hope I shall not come to a bad end. The magazine will have to be a quarterly, I think, until next summer. We shall have a directors' meeting in a day or two and we shall publish the July issue—then again in October and at Christmas. Of course it will be much larger, though not four times as large, I think. You are quite right in saying it would be lost as it is now. The real question isn't getting material, though of course that's not always easy. We are, however, acquiring prestige, and have more attention in the papers than any other magazine I know. I think Mr. Rascoe will have a notice in the Tribune next Sunday or the one after. Your friend, Miss Amy Lowell, sent a poem a few days ago, saying that she had seen The Reviewer and admired it very much, and that she was hurt because other people of distinction had been invited to write for it and she hadn't. So you see it is really celebrated! It is all a question of money and the exasperating thing is that it need not have been so. I can't go into the details in this letter, but if one tenth of the thought and energy that have gone into the literary end of the magazine had been put into the business it would now be self-supporting. We have had a fair amount of money put into it and will perhaps have more, but for a whole year—because Margaret resigned last summer—we have had no business manager. We thought we had one in February, but found he couldn't do it, and have only got another on the job within the last two weeks. Nobody has tried to get advertising or circulation and money has naturally been swallowed up. The quarterly seems the surest way to save The Reviewer, and I thought of it because it would give time in July and August to work on the business end of it and collect more money before fall. I think it will be only for a year, and I shall ask all the literary editors to be sure to notice each issue. That will keep it before people. I think the October number will be very good. At Christmas we are thinking of changing the name to a much better one I have in mind, but of course that won't be decided until I've talked to you. I've always thought this an impossible name. The funniest thing has happened. Achmed Abdullah,[1] whom I met accidentally in New York and did not ask to write for The Reviewer, but who is showering things upon it, has written that he will be in Richmond tomorrow night and wants me to have dinner with him at the Jefferson. Of course I wouldn't dream of doing it because he's perfectly impossible, and he's traveling with his agent, Jean [——]. Did you ever hear anything so queer? I had an extremely informal note from her today, saying she liked my things and wanted to see me. I telegraphed them at once that I couldn't do it. But I don't want him to be mad with the magazine, and I think I'd better let them come up here after dinner and see Hunter and me, but Alice is very dubious about even that and I don't know what to do. I've explained to her that if I'm an editor I'm obliged to see people editorially, or get The Reviewer in bad. Abdullah has already been furious once because I took six weeks to acknowledge his contribution, and wrote me "for God's sake not to get in too tight with the highbrows, and to remember that Jack London would be alive when Christopher Morley[2] and Heywood Broun were rotting, forgotten, in their cute little graves." And that all American and English critics were log-rollers except Mencken and Nathan, who though often mistaken had no axe to grind, that Gouverneur Morris[3] was one of the greatest writers of English, that Hearst and Belasco were the biggest men in America, to remember always that Shakespeare and Molière were popular playwrights and that Mr. Cabell was hopelessly précieux, (and Carl Van Vechten too) but had written one good book, The Rivet in Grandfather's Neck, which, he said, was more realistic of Virginia than Main Street is of the Middle West. Because, he said, "*I* know Virginia." How *could* he? I've talked about The Reviewer all the time and I hadn't intended to. I'd much

[1] The novelist and adventurer, who had published such books as *The Blue-Eyed Manchu* (1917), *The Trail of the Beast* (1919), and *Alien Souls* (1921).

[2] Morley had moved in 1920 from the Philadelphia *Evening Public Ledger* to the New York *Evening Post*, where he began his famous column "The Bowling Green." His novel *Where the Blue Begins* appeared in 1922.

[3] Author of such novels as *Tom Beauling* (1901), *Aladdin O'Brien* (1902), *The Pagan's Progress* (1904), and *When My Ship Comes In* (1915).

rather hear about The Magnetic West[4] and I'd like to know when it will begin in the Post. I'm disappointed that you aren't coming here. Mary Tompkins was here a few days ago and said you would certainly come soon, because this was your time of year and you could always rest and sleep here. I felt so reproached because I know it's The Reviewer and I who have made Richmond cease to be restful. I shall try to do better, and I would listen very carefully to you and not interrupt with the magazine. I don't want it to be a terrible pest. I shall go to bed now and have nightmares about Abdullah. He looks like a push-cart person in Pell Street. Mr. Mencken says I must be nice to him, because he is trying to do better. And certainly I've no attachment for Christopher Morley or Heywood Broun whatever. I'm afraid Richmond was more soothing when it meant just the Tompkins and Mr. Cabell. They *are* peaceful. Mary was here for three hours. She said you were very idealistic, and I said that was very wonderful. They are working Nellie to death and I could shake them. I can't imagine why you call her a Nietzschean when she's a mass of unselfishness. I couldn't possibly come to West Chester now. Mary Street is sailing for England the fourteenth, to be gone two months, and when she comes back she will go to Hot Springs to be bathed and baked for her neuritis. So there will be a lot to do for the next month, with the July issue and business arrangements for summer. But I shall be with Rosamund Randall—Beirne—in Ruxton in July, and I'd come to West Chester for a day or two sometime that month or the first of August if it suited you and Mrs. Hergesheimer—and of course you'd tell me if it didn't. I'd like a list of people in Philadelphia who might like to take The Reviewer. Do you know where I'd better get it? Mr. Van Vechten is going to send me the Caxton Club list, because whatever Mr. Mencken may say it isn't primarily the South who will be interested, or who ought to be—it is groups of a certain kind of people everywhere and they are really more plentiful in the North and West

---

[4] A series of articles Hergesheimer had written after an extended tour of the Western states. The series appeared in *The Saturday Evening Post* from September, 1922, to February, 1923.

than here, I think. I don't know whether to ask Mr. Mencken to speak to Hugh Walpole about a paper this summer or wait until he comes in the fall. Did I tell you Mr. Cabell had left his family and had moved into a log cabin across the road and goes home only to eat and sleep? He is so pleased and excited about it, really spontaneous. Mr. Mencken wants a copy of the interview I sent you but I can't find one. I shouldn't have bothered you so, because you must be so dreadfully tired. I'm afraid I'm losing my sense of values. Alice is very cross with me and said you were quite right to speak as you did when I told her. The letter sounded a little like her. But you did better in the West than you thought—you wrote me two letters instead of one. I hope the new secretary is nice. It must be a terrific book to write.[5] I've begun The Bright Shawl and I do like it so very much. You are wonderfully good to us. I am truly sorry and ashamed. I hope you will forgive me.

Emily.

We are going to send sample copies everywhere this summer and will use a number of January, February and May magazines because everyone says they are best. I think Mr. Mencken likes the Scots Grandfather best of the two Tintypes, but for some reasons I like the Absentee Father best—because it's a more unusual situation, and I imagine harder to do.

I've just made the blot—I can't copy it all.

[5] *The Magnetic West.*

27

1008 Park Avenue
[June 19, 1922]

Please don't think I'm a nuisance to tell you this, but I'm *very* worried and very angry, and there's no one else I can ask. I have a curious objection to letting Mr. Cabell know I mind, because he is in a very good humor with Burton Rascoe and apparently sees nothing wrong with the article I'm enclosing. But he is often impervious to fine distinctions. This is from yesterday's Tribune. I hadn't quite known what Mr. Mencken meant when he called Mr. Rascoe a "hick," except that whenever I saw him in New York— he was quite polite to me—he wore queer shirts and he was brought up in Oklahoma. But now I know. Mr. Mencken wrote me the other day that he, B. R., was writing "drivel" and was "fast getting into the Johnny Weaver[1] verein." Well, I think this column I'm enclosing is rotten bad taste and I shan't dare have lunch with Mr. Rascoe again. You seemed not to have said anything the day he mentioned seeing you in New York and you were wise. I'm very angry about The Reviewer notice. It's so outrageously untruthful and inaccurate, and patronizing too, and when more distinguished people take The Reviewer seriously I don't see why Burton Rascoe should patronize it. Frances Newman, as you know, lives in Atlanta and has no more to do with The Reviewer than Mr. Rascoe himself has, which is to contribute an occasional article to it. She is around forty, apparently, even farther from being a "child" than Hunter and me, to whom Mr. Cabell was referring. And I do think it was unpardonable of Mr. Rascoe to ignore Mary, who has helped finance the magazine and sometimes writes for it, and Margaret, who was indispensable to its beginning, and put in Miss Newman. Besides this, I think it very unfair for him to have forgotten that it's my job, without help, to fill the magazine, and that's why I can write nothing for it except those cream puffs at the last minute. With the exception of the wonderful articles you've collected for me, I've had to get everything that goes into The Reviewer without paying a cent,

---

[1] John Van Alstyn Weaver, then book editor of the Brooklyn *Daily Eagle,* had published a book of poetry, *In American* (1921), and a novel, *Margie Wins the Game* (1922).

and write to everyone, and proofread it, and write everything that's unsigned, and interest all the people who have become interested. I couldn't have done it, either, without you, and I remember that always. As long as nothing was said about my writing I think Mr. Rascoe should have spoken of my other work, which is harder. I'm so glad he likes Hunter's and Miss Newman's things, because they are invaluable, but he oughtn't to have given the impression that they help edit the magazine. I think the whole column this time is absurd, including the rehash of the conversation between Mr. Cabell and Mr. Mencken last fall. I think too, as you do, that Mr. Cabell *was* talking seriously and not trying to put something over on Mr. Mencken, as Burton Rascoe, Guy Holt, and the other men who mentioned it to me in New York seemed to think. The story went everywhere until Mr. Mencken was sick of it and I don't wonder. Mr. Cabell, curiously enough, seems to see nothing provincial or foolish about this clipping, not even the part about himself, and that's why I don't mention it to him. He didn't like Mr. Mencken telling that story. Hunter says that if Corra Harris[2] went to Oshkosh the daily paper there would write about it just this way! I'm not speaking of it to anyone but you because no one here knows about such things. I may mention it some time to Mr. Mencken as he is disgusted with Mr. Rascoe already, and he is so beautifully kind himself. He has written everyday lately with suggestions about the quarterly and thinks the magazine may be better this way. I'm so glad you let me know him and I like him better all the time—he and Mr. Van Vechten are the nicest of them, I think. Now I want to ask you this. Don't you think, when the quarterly starts, as it will be bigger I'd better write some book reviews for it? I have put The Reviewer ahead of everything, but as you know I'm not altruistic, and I've no wish to be submerged in The Reviewer. I refuse invitations often on account of it, and I have almost stopped seeing some people I really like, because it interests me now more than any person or thing here. But I don't want to do all this unless it is worth while. Some people think I can write as well or better than Hunter. Mr. Mencken has said several

[2] A popular novelist whose work appeared often in *The Saturday Evening Post*.

times lately he likes my things. Frances Newman says I have an unusually good style, and ought to write something more substantial. She used to quote my reviews sometimes last year in her literary bulletin. Prince Troubetzkoy wrote me the other day about my writing that it had "shimmering wings of which I was unconscious"! And Mr. Cabell and Amélie and Miss Ellen Glasgow[3] like it. This sounds so impossibly conceited and I wouldn't tell anybody but you, but I'm obliged to explain. These little things I'm doing now couldn't be used anywhere else and they get nowhere. And last year you, and some other people, said my reviews were really good. And unless you are writing stories, book articles are more practical than my kind of thing. Of course, I can't write glittering, erudite, complicated things like Miss Newman. Somebody asked me the other day if I'd been brought up on the Bible and Shakespeare because I was so simple and Elizabethan! I'm not as old as she is, with an unlimited background of books, and of course she is a librarian and reads everything that is published. I read only what I want to. And you know I like lots of things besides books. And I can't talk about them technically as Hunter can, who lives with them. But I can, I believe, write better reviews than some of the men, and women, who write them for the Tribune, the Literary Review and other papers. Burton Rascoe has never seen any of mine because he didn't get The Reviewer until last October, when Hunter began writing the book reviews. Do you know of any way I could write for any of the reviews? Because I shall have time now to do things for the Reviewer and other things too. If you told any of the literary editors I could do it, would that be enough, or would I have to wait until they had seen my things in The Reviewer? Because I'd like to do them in the magazine and outside of it. I hope you understand my telling you this. It sounds so frightfully self-satisfied, but I'm thoroughly depressed and disheartened at being lost in The Reviewer, which I have largely made and which Hunter has no responsibility about except to write for. Mr. Cabell strongly opposed last fall having

[3] At this time Ellen Glasgow had most recently published *The Builders* (1919) and *One Man in His Time* (1922). Such better-known books as *Barren Ground* and *Vein of Iron* were not to appear until 1925 and 1935, respectively.

71

more than one person do the book reviews. He said nobody but me could get articles or write conversational things and I must do that. But after all, it's not his magazine. And I want to write for it whatever will be best practice for me. You are more wonderful to The Reviewer than anyone else, and I know you are frightfully busy. I want to talk to you about all this more than I ever have, since the magazine started, but as that seems to be impossible for you now, could you please write me about it? Of course just dictate it if you want to—I suppose you have a secretary now. I truly don't want to be unreasonable but there is no one else I can talk to. I think I ought to be able to use The Reviewer as I please, don't you? Will you think it ill-bred and horrid of me if I remind you again of the Tintype manuscripts you said I might have? I'm afraid Alice would think so. It would cheer me decidedly to have them—I'm more utterly down than I've been for months. I really want you to dictate and answer the easiest way possible. I've already written Mr. Rascoe that I'm very sorry he made a mistake in the name of the editors. Do you think I did wrong? I hope he won't put the letter in his column! Had I better speak of it to Mr. Mencken? I wish I could talk to you.

Very sincerely,
Emily Clark.

The notice gives no idea whatever of the character of The Reviewer and what it is really like, and I especially wanted him to say it didn't pay. It might be *any* literary magazine instead of a very informal one. I'm *furious*.

The Cabinet Photograph, I believe, I like best of the Tintypes, and I'm so very glad to have it for July, because I don't like the June issue much. Mr. Cabell accepted the Beatrice Washburn thing[1] and I think it is so silly and below par. It was wonderful of you to send the Tintype now, because I hadn't expected it before the October number. In July I shall give the reasons for the quarterly and it will appear again October first. John Bennett has a paper on Charleston for July and I hope Mr. Mencken will have Baltimore for October. If not, I'll get Frances Newman to write Atlanta. I really don't think Mr. Cabell knows much about magazines. He didn't think the Southern cities would be any good, and don't you think Beatrice Washburn is silly? Mrs. Cabell took him to New York last week after two years' effort. His Cousin Mary Munford went to see him and told him it was his duty. They will probably be home the end of this week. The Tompkins have taken a house on Park Avenue several blocks below us and will move there in August. I saw Nellie yesterday and she is very homesick and depressed about it. Have you seen Mr. Mencken yet? He wants Henry Harrison[2] to write a paper about him for The Reviewer and to make it "hot stuff." Henry Harrison told me in New York he was going to do it for some magazine and Mr. Mencken thinks it would be fun to get him to do it for this one. He went abroad with Mr. Stewart Bryan last week for two or three months, so I wrote him a steamer letter and told him we invited him to do it and Mr. Mencken didn't care what he said. He has sent a hundred dollars, but that really *isn't* why Mr. Mencken wants him to do it! What do you think of it? Edward Bierstadt has arrived at Castle Hill and he and his wife are separated. Amélie didn't know why, when I heard. She has had to go to bed again, because the Murray Boococks at

---

[1] An essay on childhood entitled "The Unforgotten Country." Beatrice Washburn was on the staff of the New Orleans *Times-Picayune*.

[2] A popular novelist whose first book, *Queed* (1911), had been a best seller. His most recent successes had been *When I Come Back* (1919) and *Saint Teresa* (1922).

Keswick brought their whole house party; including the Duchesse de Richelieu, to Castle Hill, last Sunday, and Amélie hasn't had to talk to twelve people at a time for months. Abdullah and Miss [——] did come that night and I can't make out their relationship. They seem quite settled and he calls her "my dear," but she is middle-aged and unattractive and I thought Orientals adored youth and beauty. Perhaps this is just a bourgeois domestic arrangement and his excitements are elsewhere. But it was very queer. They told terrible things about everybody except Mr. Hearst and Robert Chambers[3] and Gouverneur Morris and Belasco. But he said Mencken and Nathan were honest, though Mencken was a big man and Nathan was just a piffling little aesthete Jew. And they have gone to the Green Tea Pot at Keswick, of all places, to stay several weeks because they saw it advertised in The Reviewer. It's kept by a decayed gentlewoman, you know, and I can't think what she does with them. Lawrence Lee, one of the University students who has just come home, says that Abdullah has amused them a good deal. They motor over and talk to him. It is really too wildly absurd for words— I can't imagine him there. His clothes were better than in New York and he was less oily. I think he had been massaged. He wants to contribute to every issue of The Reviewer but I don't want him to. His paragraphs are coming out later in a book. His name is Achmed Abdullah Nadir Khan, and his grandmother was a Manchu and he says you wrote him a letter about Taou Yuen.[4] Is he lying? Mary has gone to New York and sails for England Thursday with her beloved Rosalie Noland. Margaret is quite good friends with me now, but isn't doing anything about The Reviewer. The thing she can do she won't do and I wish you'd come and reason with her. She thinks you know everything and you convinced her last year. She got hopelessly offended with Mr. Cabell last fall about the dramatic department. She came yesterday and stayed hours and taked very intellectually, so much so that I couldn't say anything at all. Do you know, she

---

[3] Chambers' prolific career as a novelist extended from 1893, when he published *In the Quarter,* through the 1930's. At the time of Emily's reference his most recent novel was *The Little Red Foot* (1921).

[4] A character in Hergesheimer's novel *Java Head.*

74

really knows an amazing amount? I've found out who Mr. Cabell Bruce meant when he said he knew of a probable purchaser of The Reviewer. It's his son, David Bruce, who was in the May magazine and he lives at Ruxton, so I'll probably see him when I go to Rosamund's.[5] Of course, we'd never, never sell it, but if he wanted to be a contributing editor and would pay, would you let him be? I've never met him—he doesn't do anything much now, just dilettante. He was in the war and then he was an attache at the embassy in Rome, because his uncle, Mr. Tom Page, was ambassador then. But now he won't work in Baltimore or anywhere. And I don't think he can really write. He behaves just as Hunter would if he had any money. Hunter has just become twenty-eight and he's still utterly childish. The Van Vechtens sent me a huge box of chocolate creams last week. I was so surprised and cross because nobody but babies likes that kind. And he had such a good lunch at the Jefferson I thought he'd know better. Aren't you surprised? But perhaps he only knows about real food and drinks, and doesn't eat candy himself. You were so nice to write the Tintype now. It is really beautiful, especially the part about not giving her a chance to tell but two things about her youth and her beaux. You were very gentle with her, more so than in your article in the Bookman. I wonder if you remember that last fall you wrote me you were sending me the Tintype manuscripts as they were composed? The first came, and Miss Coombes wrote with the second that you were waiting to send that manuscript when the third was ready to put with it. I'd like tremendously to have them.

Very sincerely,
Emily Clark.

Russell DeVine is our business manager. His great-grandfather was one of the men who helped Poe start the Southern Literary Messenger.[6] I hadn't meant him to use that list of names of people who

---

[5] Rosamund Randall Beirne. Her husband was a writer for the Baltimore *Evening Sun*.

[6] Emily was confused about Poe's connection with *The Southern Literary Messenger*. The sole founder and proprietor of the magazine was Thomas Willis

liked The Reviewer the way he did it. I gave him some press notices to publish, and he asked if many personal things had been said about it in addition to the papers and magazines. So I gave him your name and Mr. Cabell's and all the others I could remember. But I think it looks a little odd and childish. Sometimes I'm afraid The Reviewer *is* childish—especially what I wrote in the June issue. I'm sure the Double Dealer thinks so. What do you think?

White, a Richmond printer, who began publication in 1834. He employed Poe as editor from August, 1835, to January, 1837.

[29]

1008 Park Avenue
[July 15, 1922]

I haven't had an opportunity, to thank you for the manuscripts, because the last ten days have been almost the busiest and most trying of the year. Indeed, it was very kind of you to send them and I hope it didn't give your secretary a great deal of trouble. I like so much having them—even more than the books—and I know you don't usually part with them. It is wonderful for The Reviewer to have the Tintypes—much the best thing that has happened to it. Yes, I did see the May Bookman and thought it quite unspeakably common —the article, I mean—spiteful and in the worst possible taste. It seems incredible that anyone who had stayed with you could have written it. I was surprised and disgusted. I am trying to get thick-skinned because I shan't be fit to edit The Reviewer if I don't, but I'm not having much luck in that way. Nice things happen, of course, but so do the other kind. John Powell took five hours to tell me this week that I was grownup and must act that way. He said something was repeated to him that I said in New York that sounded frivolous and superficial, and I must memember that when I spoke of The

Reviewer or Mr. Cabell I was speaking officially and must be taken seriously—but how unendurable! That is one reason I'm so tired. John and Mr. Cabell are both going to Mountain Lake tomorrow, and neither knows that the other is going. I had lunch with Mrs. Cabell yesterday—they have just finished the oldest daughter's wedding, having dealt with a debutante and a graduation since November. She said, "James won't be bothered." Mrs. Gunn, mother of Harriet Sherwood in West Chester, sent some poetry to The Reviewer and Mr. Cabell refused it but told her to send something else, and I refused that. I hate it when that happens to Richmond people, so I went to see her. But I know she can't understand my sending it back when he asked for it. She said she was going to West Chester. She is rather appalling to look at but quite intelligent. I am leaving town in two weeks and will be gladder than I can say to get away, but there are lots of horrid things to do here still. I shall go to Uncle John for a day or two in Baltimore, because they want me to see Mr. Bruce before I go out to the Green Spring Valley. Ida may be out there as well as Rosamund Beirne, and I'll be in Maryland through August, there and near Annapolis. I might be able to go to West Chester for a day and night in that time if it was quite convenient for you and Mrs. Hergesheimer. I wish you were here now. I never needed advice so badly and there is no one in the world who knows as much about it as you do. Because Mr. Cabell knows nothing about the actual running of The Reviewer and the other men know nothing about the editorial part. I'm more tired, I think, than I have ever been, because I've had to see so many people lately and write business letters, which I hate. There has been no end of questions and complications, and Mary and Margaret are both away. Dr. Tucker and Mr. Anderson are going to have a meeting in October, when some men will probably talk about The Reviewer. It has had none of that sort of publicity in Richmond, and of course I'm glad, but it will be troublesome. Mrs. Cabell told me that Hugh Walpole would visit them here next fall, so I suppose you are expecting him too. He's going to lecture here, I think. Mr. Cabell is writing a story for the Cosmopolitan. And speaking of the Cosmopolitan, what do you think of Abdullah? We have him again in the July Reviewer which should be out today. It was held up because of the statement about the quarterly. One of the Boston papers has been using Abdullah's remarks in The Reviewer! May we have the Presbyterian Child[1] for October? There are a thousand things I must ask you before that issue goes to press in September. I've had letters from the Centaur Bookshop asking for Reviewers with your things, and saying they would have your bibliography[2] soon and one of Mr. Cabell's. Mr. Ralph Van Vechten has been so nice. He is getting us some Chicago subscriptions and he wants me to ask Edna Kenton[3] to write for us. Does she write well? Because if I ask her I must take what she sends. I do think it was splendid of you to remember to talk to him about this in Chicago. I drove with Mary Tompkins today in a little car McCaw Tompkins has given her, and she said that you were very, very kind. And I said Yes, you were. Emma Gray has a daughter— it has just come with quantities of dark hair and its name is Emma Gray. She read Jurgen for the first time the last week before it arrived, which I think was a bad plan, and it gave her such a queer dream. And I bought a lovely dress yesterday. That is all I know, I think. Please forgive me, but I must ask you to tell me two things, soon, before I leave Richmond, as the lists must be made up now. Where can I get a suitable list of people in and around Philadelphia to send sample copies and letters to? We are getting lists wherever we can and we ought to have one there because we send it to two bookshops. Is there a club, or anything, that would do? And please suggest one or two books, novels of course, that are interesting this summer. I want them for something I shall write for October. It is so very important for that number to be good. Mr. Mencken said Sinclair Lewis' book,[4] but I don't want that much, and it may be

---

[1] The last of Hergesheimer's autobiographical sketches, or "Tintypes," as he called them.

[2] The Centaur Bookshop in Philadelphia published a series of bibliographies of modern American writers, the first being that of Hergesheimer (1922). Cabell's appeared in 1924.

[3] Later the author of *The Indians of North America* (edited from Jesuit missionary letters, 1927) and *Simon Kenton: His Life and Period* (1930).

[4] *Babbitt*, of which review copies were available by August.

out too late anyway. I wish I could talk to you right away—you are more help than anyone and The Reviewer couldn't possibly live without you.

Sincerely yours,
Emily Clark.

16 East Lafayette Avenue
Baltimore
[July, 1922]

[30]

I was *so* sorry you didn't come to Richmond the last week-end. Mr. Cabell was away and I would have had a very cheerful party for you. There's nothing but purple ink here and it looks horrid on this paper. I'll be here until Tuesday and then be outside of Annapolis, and I hope I can come to West Chester. Perhaps you could come down there too. I'll write you a long letter when I get there. I'm going out to Rosamund's this afternoon. I had lunch with Mr. Mencken yesterday—he's going back to New York tomorrow to sail Tuesday and came down just for the end of the week. He grows on me tremendously and I like him much better than in Richmond or New York. I can only see him alone here, because he won't go to anybody's house or the Country Club. He says he can't make acquaintances in Baltimore because he lives here and they would bother him. Aunt Rosa disapproves of him so frightfully that I didn't tell her I lunched with him, because I knew she'd argue and I was going anyway. But Frank and Rosamund want to know him and he will meet Frank in the office but won't go near Rosamund. Uncle John has given me a box of embroidered stockings and I'm glad I stopped. I'll write you soon.

Emily.

They sent me Reviewer mail today and I'm exasperated because I told them at the post office to send only personal, and I don't want it. I've been to see Meredith Janvier. He wants you to autograph his books, but doesn't like to ask you.

I've decided to stay here till Thursday morning instead of Tuesday because of a party I have to go to. My address then will be Sherwood Forest, R. F. D. No. 1, Annapolis. Mr. Mencken advised me not to write about books much, and I want very much to talk to you about it, because I don't agree with him. He talked quite wonderfully though—I never heard him do better. We had lunch at a place I never heard of before here, but it is very nice and Hendrik van Loon[1] goes there. Mr. van Loon has married a woman from New York I recognized. She used to keep a tea room down in Fourth Street and everyone in the neighborhood called her Jimmy. He calls her that too, and she is elderly and has bobbed, grayish hair and a stock, and I think he must be insane. But they aren't going to stay married, I heard. Rosamond says you wrote an article for the Junior League Bulletin. Did someone in Philadelphia ask you to? Eleanor Whiting, a debutante of last winter, was here yesterday. She is pretty and perfectly wild, and says she wrote a play and wanted Mencken's opinion and didn't know how to see him, so she took it to him on Hollins Street herself one evening and made him read it, and she is the only Baltimore girl who has ever met him.

[1] Hendrik van Loon was the author of such books as *Ancient Man* (1922), *R. v. R.: The Life and Times of Rembrandt* (1930), *Van Loon's Geography* (1932), and *The Life and Times of Johann Sebastian Bach* (1940).

I saw in the Rascoe column today that you and Mr. Towne[2] had quarreled. He goes to the Troubetzkoys and Amélie says he is very silly. The paper didn't say what about. Mr. Mencken says Mr. Rascoe is a yokel, and he must be. I think the column is terrible. One of the Norfolk papers has had a long editorial about The Reviewer— we are always surprised when Virginia notices us. It is turning hot here and I'll be glad to get away. Are you still reading proof? I want terribly to talk to you. Mr. Mencken says he got The Bright Shawl proof from Knopf and likes it tremendously. He said Cytherea was the best novel about America—better than Mrs. Wharton[3] or anybody, and that you were a great artist. He said more about you than about Mr. Cabell. You never answered my questions.

Emily Clark.

[2] Charles Hanson Towne, a literary man-about-town, was at various times editor of *Smart Set, McClure's Magazine,* and *Harper's Bazaar.*

[3] The novelist Edith Wharton, whose most recent book had been *The Age of Innocence* (1917). In the year of Emily's reference, Katherine Fullerton Gerould's *Edith Wharton: A Critical Study* had appeared.

Sherwood Forest
Annapolis, Maryland
[32]   [August 13, 1922]

You probably don't realize how wild it makes me not to have my questions answered. You should take lessons from Mr. Mencken, who will answer six at a time, all numbered. Then if he forgets one he follows it up with a letter two hours later to explain that he forgot. But perhaps, after all, if you were like him that way, you'd be entirely German too, and insist on everything being done decently and in order, and classified, which I couldn't endure. He is so much nicer than he pretends to be, because he lectured about my not depending on you and Mr. Cabell and people like that—he doesn't count himself because he says he's Southern—but must use nearly all Southern authors. So I didn't dream of asking him to get me anything abroad. But the day before he sailed he wrote me a note and said maybe he would bring me something for The Reviewer from Europe. So it was probably just talk—he did talk for hours without drawing breath and was tremendous—colossal, he would say. McKean Meiere had a little party for me the day before I left Baltimore and Mr. and Mrs. Harry Black came. Mr. Black owns the Sun and says he doesn't go to parties to meet women, except this party. He knew all about The Reviewer from Mr. Mencken, and now he has run an editorial about it in the Morning Sun, besides Mr. Mencken's things in the Evening Sun. Mr. Mencken goes to his house. Aunt Rosa said "No one in Baltimore meets Mencken"—I told her it was because they couldn't and that he was very much run after, really. I told her about Eleanor Whiting going to his house and she had a fit. And I told her the Blacks adored him and the Beirnes couldn't get him to come there and David Bruce wanted to know him and so did lots of others. No amount of attention that anyone gets outside of Baltimore impresses her, you see, because she is a Ridgely and measures everything in terms of Baltimore and is frightfully ignorant except about French books. I explained to her that he wouldn't be bothered by Baltimore people because he lived there and couldn't shake them. She knows a lot more about him than she did before I came—all that I know, practically, except that I saw him while I was staying with her. She is narrow past all belief, especially about Germany, partly because she reads so much French. And because she knows more than most old ladies she is terribly hard to convince, because she thinks she knows everything. And then too, she is a sort of an agnostic, though brought up Episcopalian and that makes her feel terribly advanced and fitted to cope with Mencken. Uncle John is not clever and she controls him and makes him be an agnostic too, which obviously worries him. But you see, he is ashamed not to be one because of her, and because he is in awe of her superior mind. I call it religious persecution. He is a member of the Sons of Colonial Wars and the English-Speaking Union, and would have liked to remain an Episcopalian too. Aunt Rosa is really frightfully intolerant. David Bruce is extremely attractive, not a bit like his father, and the best looking man in the twenties, I think, that I have seen. And I had had to return one of his contributions just before I met him—it was horrid. He buys lots of books and likes San Cristobal best of yours. He collects first editions of Ouida because he says they are records of a dead social system! He thinks you are the most interesting person he knows of because you spent all your money in Venice. He says that is the most perfect thing a man ever did, and if he had done it he would have shot himself when it was over. But I told him you couldn't possibly have done that on account of your books. It is ever so nice of you to want me to come to West Chester, and I think I could come next week, the twenty-first or twenty-second, Tuesday—probably—but that, of course, rests with Mrs. Hergesheimer. I don't know about the connections, and whether you change at Wilmington or Philadelphia. Mr. Mencken said he'd been trying to get there before he left. I'll write down quantities of questions before I see you, so I shan't forget anything necessary. I didn't stay at Ida's—besides her own baby, which isn't so bad—she had two others staying with her. Rosamond has a baby too and you can hear it all the time—she lives in a little stone house. I'm so glad you haven't a baby—it makes the greatest difference, really, in the way I think of you. The woods and water here are lovely, but it's rather too much like camping. The Haskells, who are friends of ours, built this cottage. It is really in the country and they use the nearest post-office, which is closed today so I'm mailing this from Annapolis. But my address is at the top of this letter. Did you ever go to Annapolis?—it's something like Alexandria and Fredericksburg, only with the bay. It is absolutely quiet, and that is good for me, but I'm running short of things to read and that makes me frantic. All I have left now is one Anatole France—Thais—and I've been too busy to read French since I stopped translating for Mr. Liveright, and there's no French dictionary here. So now and then I

83

get stuck. I like letters better than the telegraphic form of communication you've adopted. Have you really forgotten how to write? But I suppose you are still on the book. Anyway, you'll talk to me about The Reviewer, won't you? It's very essential.

Very sincerely yours,
Emily Clark.

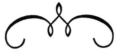

[33]

1008 Park Avenue
[September, 1922]

I've just sent out and bought the Post, and I think The Magnetic West is most beautiful and thrilling. I'll look for it every week until it comes again. There is no one I know, or shall know, as wonderful and as big as you. I liked seeing where you work in West Chester better than anything that I have done, and I felt just as Browning did when he wrote, "Did you once see Shelley plain, and did he stop and speak to you?" I am so terribly sorry I talked so much about The Reviewer and my affairs—it was a waste of time and I wish you had been talking all the time I was there. You are the only writer I know who can put just what is in his books into what he says, and be exactly the same mind that you knew before you met him. But don't you think until Carl[1] came I behaved fairly well? He demoralized me and it was really all his fault that the subject was me most of the time, because he arranged it and then jeered at me. You know that with me it isn't usually so. I'm sorry he amused himself that way because I'd far rather it had been you than me, but he thinks me frightfully ignorant. He is all wrong in thinking I shall be deserted by him and the others and left "old and lonely with Robert Nathan and the Young Intellectuals." Because long before then,

[1] Carl Van Vechten.

84

when Carl and Mr. Cabell and Mr. Mencken begin to grow deaf and senile, *I* shall have to find something younger than them—but never younger than you. I shall always admire you more than anyone, and have a very special feeling about telling you things, partly because you wrote Linda Condon, and mostly because you are yourself. But when I tell you silly things that happen to me, you must not tell them even to your family, or I shan't be able to. Because I don't usually tell anything about myself. And if you get bored with The Reviewer and me I can't possibly bear it. You must always remember too that you are a good deal older than I am, and a thousand times wiser and more brilliant than I shall ever be, and sometimes I'd like to have you explain and tell me things. You said last summer I could always ask you. There are so many things I have to learn for myself with difficulty, and the people I've met in the last year, especially in New York, are different from those I've known before. But of course I shan't ever ask you questions when you are writing a book. You are kinder to me about the thing that matters most to me than anyone else is, and I hoped I had been able to do some little things for you—letters and things—but when Carl said I never gave anything at all you agreed. Perhaps though, you didn't mean it, and I wish there was something very nice I could do for you. Please come in October and stay—you haven't stayed here since The Reviewer started, and we shall grow sensitive about it. I had a wonderful time in West Chester and it was sweet of you to give me the books. I wish we could have talked more about the West and you, and less about viciousness and ankles and eighteenth-century France and me. But that wasn't my fault. I'm truly not so bad as Carl thinks, though not so good as Mencken thinks. Carl says he knows more about me than you do, but he doesn't know as much—no one does, I think. Because I never feel as—well—sort of deferential and entirely trusting—as I do with you. I wish you'd write me now and then because it helps me, but I'll try to write you anyway if it amuses you. Still, I like to be answered now and then. Could we get The Bright Shawl proofsheets in the next week for Hunter to review before September tenth? Christmas is so long to wait. Alice has read Cytherea again this summer, and thinks it next best to Linda, because it does for a middle-aged man what Linda does for a woman. She thinks them the finest of all, and I think I do too. Alice says I'm like Maisie in What Maisie Knew, but I hope not, because I hate her and the book. But oh, what a wonderful title it is! Another thing—don't lose patience with Mr. Cabell, ever. You and Hugh Walpole are the only men he cares a straw about, and he needs you. I know he doesn't amuse you. He doesn't me, either, but he is so tragic. When you get back from Canada I'll send you his newspaper story on marriage, and you'll send it back, won't you? It is about a magician who lived in any ivory tower, as Amélie says he does, and wished his wife "into the middle of next week." I'm sorry Burton Rascoe is in the October Reviewer. It was arranged long ago before he was so unspeakable about you or me, and it couldn't be changed now without an undignified fuss, but next time we'll know better. Thanks so much for being so nice, and don't be cross with me. I hate it when you are. I think Dorothy[2] is perfectly splendid. Tell her everyone I met in West Chester said beautiful things about her before they'd talked to me five minutes.

Emily.

I *wish* you'd send us your Young Intellectuals.[3] It could only amuse, not hurt, because no one would consider *himself* a Young Intellectual!

[2] Mrs. Hergesheimer.
[3] Apparently this article was one which Hergesheimer contemplated but never put on paper.

[34]   [September, 1922]

When you said "kill the sentence about clean hands and a pure heart" did you mean the whole sentence, beginning with "Then it is," or just that phrase? I didn't know, so I sent it to press as it was, but the first proof hasn't come back yet. And do you object to the next sentence after it, because it is very much the same? I thought you were going to correct all the sentences and everything, like last year. I don't think you quite understand that sentence—it isn't meant to be taken literally or sentimentally, but just to express an attitude, like "the cold, black uncompromising North," later on. It is the way Mr. Cabell writes in The Rivet in Grandfather's Neck, although I wasn't thinking of that when I wrote it. I wanted to know what you really thought about the whole paper and if you had any other suggestions, and if anyone else here could have done it better. Do you still think the same about "clean hands and a pure heart" now that I've explained? Would people up there think it was silly? . . . . Mr. and Mrs. Knopf will be here, he wrote, the last of this week, and I'll have them here. Frederick Eddy got a page of advertising for the October Reviewer from Henry Holt, but couldn't get any from Knopf. Tell me, do you think it would be all right for me to speak to him about it here? Or had I better not? I don't know. We give more space to his books than to any others, and he has written that he likes our reviews. Please tell me what I'd better do. And is your Centaur bibliography out yet? I've promised to mention the Centaur in The Reviewer, and when the proof comes I want to say your bibliography is out, if it is. Mr. De Vine is doing splendidly. I need to know these things. I don't mind writing oftener than you do, although you and Amélie are the only people I do that for, and she is old and ill and shut inside of a box wall. When you answer periodically it is all right, but when I'm never answered at all for months, I can't write, and I shall take for granted you don't want to hear. You don't know how difficult it is. Alice said yesterday that she liked your books better than Mr. Cabell's. I hadn't heard her say that before. I'll send you the February Reviewers you wanted this week. When you come to rest in October I'll take you to Westover. Don't you like Virginia any more than Chicago? I'm enclosing Mr. Mencken's article which you said you hadn't seen. There is a lot about you as well as The Reviewer. Also something Mrs. Deland

87

said about you. Isn't she a silly old woman? Mr. Van Loon has cabled the Sun that he has seen no sign of Mencken except floating bottles in the North Sea. They published it.

Sincerely yours,
Emily Clark.

Do you see, Mr. Mencken says the February Reviewer was the best magazine in America? I *want* to know the things I've asked you. *Do* you think it hurts for me to say what I did about the Young Intellectuals? You must specially read Hunter's review of Babbitt and of Prejudices. They are good. The magazine will come out a few days after October first in order to get an extra page of advertising.

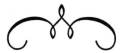

<table>
<tr><td>[35]</td><td style="text-align:right">1008 Park Avenue
[October, 1922]</td></tr>
</table>

I've read The Bright Shawl all over again from the beginning this week—you know I read part of it in The Red Book—and it is so beautiful and unreal. I mean that in a very nice way, like a glorified moving picture flowing across a screen like pictures should be and aren't. It is restful to read, because of that, and more like a painting, I think, than anything you have ever done. Every page of it is gorgeous, especially the Pilar girl from Peru. And you *are* infallible about words. Carl Van Vechten thinks he is, but isn't—just as when he said George Jean Nathan was "pompous" on an occasion when it should have been "supercilious." The people—Heywood Broun is the only one I can think of—who have said there was too much style, are so thick-headed not to realize that all of it is inevitable. And what a shock it must be to everyone after Cytherea—so absolutely cold and austere and proper, the most impeccable young man that I have ever seen or heard of anywhere. I never at all understood why he was alluring to the dancer or to poor little Narcisa, who was so adorable, and whom no one, not even you, took the slightest interest in. But he is a marvelous channel for the lovely, lovely scenes and happenings to filter through. Personally, I should have preferred Andrés. It must be made into a sublimated moving picture, personally directed by you. And it is a splendid story too, but I don't think of it as a story, rather as the shawl itself—all silk and color, and softness and brilliancy. I was very alarmed, and mad too—for fear you'd forgotten to send it, and sent you a message about it. And I'm sorry you've adopted the Mencken custom of signing books on the title page—I used to think they were that way only when they were inscribed for people, and not presents. You know, I told you so when you gave me the little books last summer. And Mr. Cabell says he is inscribed on the flyleaf, just as you used to do, so I don't see why mine couldn't be. But perhaps you will do it later, and I'm tremendously glad it has come. It has a most lovely jacket. Do you think you could get me a jacket for the first edition of Cytherea? You know I told you mine was torn when you were here, and I want it. I'd be very grateful if you could. I don't like this October Reviewer at all. Mr. Mencken likes my Richmond paper very much indeed, and Carl says it is the best thing The Reviewer has published, except of course things like you, and it makes him want to come here. He also said his brother gave a party in New York and that everyone got very drunk, and Mencken went to sleep and snored so loud that the neighbors complained, and you wept. Did you? But that was far, far better than to snore. And Mr. Rascoe wrote about it last Sunday and said that Mr. Mencken slept, and muttered his, Rascoe's, name in his sleep, which I hope with all my heart was untrue. He took no liberties, however, with you. Carl says he has asked Ernest Boyd[1] and Ronald Firbank[2] to write for The Re-

---

[1] Author of *Contemporary Drama of Ireland* (1917), *Appreciations and Depreciations* (1917), *Ireland's Literary Renaissance* (1922).

[2] A belated exemplar of turn-of-the-century British aestheticism, who had writ-

89

viewer and Mr. Boyd will do it if I ask him, so I'm writing. Frederick Eddy, who has been down from New York for the week-end— he wrote the awful thing about Walter de la Mare, but has helped financially—brought me a paper from Arthur Machen,[3] with whom he corresponds. And you promised the fourth Tintype for January, you know. And you told Jim[4] here that it was an oversight that you didn't have one in October—I was so pleased. I'm just over grippe— the fever I had before you came was the beginning of it—and this is my first week out and I'm in the depths of despair. It's so much worse after you are up than while you have it. I keep reminding myself that my thoughts and feelings aren't true, but just the aftermath, and will be over soon, just as the real part was. But that is hard to remember when you aren't sick any more. It is like a bad dream, and I do wish very much that I had never been born, and hope I shan't have to remain indefinitely. But it runs in my head all the time "that no life lives forever, and dead men rise up never." Mr. Cabell says I should have been over Swinburne years ago, and I thought I was. I spoke to Mr. Cabell about The Reviewer, and he promised not to say anything of that kind again. He came here to lunch with Mr. Eddy, and only said what was perfectly nice about it, and has been in an extremely good humor every time I've talked to him since. You said you'd come back here this fall if you didn't go to Salem, and you haven't gone there, so when are you coming back? You know you promised. And you also said you'd certainly write to me when you went home, because I had been very nice. And I told you I couldn't go on writing unless you answered periodically. And I really cannot, even with the best intentions, because utter lack of response disheartens and dries me up. I haven't had a *line* from you since early

ten such novels as *Odette d' Antrevernes* (1905), *Vainglory* (1915), and *Valmouth* (1919). His later novel *Prancing Nigger*, first published in 1924 in New York with an introduction by Carl Van Vechten, was to become his best-known book in the United States.

[3] Author of such books as *The Hill of Dreams* (1907), *The Angel of Mons* (1915), *Things Near and Far* (1923), and *Hieroglyphics: A Note upon Ecstasy in Literature* (1923).

[4] Jim Allison. See Letter 8, n. 1.

July, and that is perfectly terrible, though of course I don't expect you to answer every letter, as other people do. But I shan't believe any longer that you like my letters if you stop me from writing them. I would have been saved from a bad mistake with Mr. Rascoe once if you had answered with just two lines. Please come back here and rest. I don't feel like doing much else, and I'll have Emma Gray all by herself for you, so you can try to make up for not telephoning her when you were here. And I want to talk to you, because there was no chance to before. Things are very critical inside of The Reviewer and I don't know whether it ought to go on or not. So it is very important for you to come, and there will be plenty of people to motor you anywhere you like. Dr. Tucker has appalled the Writers' Club, I hear, by a terrible play about married life, which he wrote and read aloud to them. I don't know if it was his sense of humor or not. Please hurry and write me. I'm sorry if this sounds morbid, but I can't help it. I *am* that way now, but the book is beautiful. And come down here, or I may have a relapse.

Emily.

1008 Park Avenue
[December 1, 1922]

[36]

I've heard from New York that The Bright Shawl is going to be filmed and Dorothy Gish is going to be in it, and I'm sorry, because I don't think she looks the least bit like anybody in the book. I'd hoped that when you gave up, the picture would be given up too. Miss Mary Johnston's To Have and to Hold[1] has just been shown

---

[1] This novel had been published in 1900. Mary Johnston's most recent novels at this time had been *The Silver Cross* (1922) and *1492* (1922).

here and it is scarcely recognizable—the people are so obviously of Hollywood rather than Jamestown. And Ralph Percy, who is one of Miss Mary's usual Sir Galahads, presents the girl with a knife soon after meeting her "to save her from himself!" Which is wildly funny to anyone who has read the book, but may be really the custom on the Pacific Coast. Miss Mary is in retirement at Warm Springs and has not seen it. But it is drawing huge crowds and millions of people must be getting weird ideas of early days in Virginia and the amazing activity of them. I hope you are having a wonderful time in Cuba—your letter sounded tired, and I know you hate not smoking. I'm rather glad you aren't going to lecture at the Woman's Club here because you wouldn't have a free hand. Can't you come when you get back from Cuba and rest? The weather is wonderful, sunny and just cool enough, and some of the Harrisons of Brandon[2] have opened a tea house between Shirley[3] and Westover. They are related to the Byrds and have put some of the original Westover furniture in the tea house. They have beautiful Chinese Chippendale and very good things to eat. You ought to have been here this week though, unless you are dieting, because we've been having Rappahannock oysters and wild ducks cooked with wine. Alice is just back from the Northern Neck and brought supplies. Mr. Mencken has sent me Prejudices III with a German inscription that I can't make out at all. He has signed it on the first page, this time, where I like it, not on the title page where I don't like it, and where you caught the horrid habit. I told him I didn't like it there and he didn't insist on continuing it. He says you won't be better until you "get back to honest

[2] The original grant for this plantation was made to Captain John Martin, who accompanied John Smith on his first voyage to Virginia. Later the home came into the possession of Nathaniel Harrison. In the early nineteenth century an adjoining estate was named Upper Brandon by William Byrd Harrison, whose descendants continued to occupy the home he built.

[3] One of the oldest and finest of the James River homes. The records of the original plantation go back as far as 1611. In 1723 the home came through marriage into the possession of John Carter, and was still the Carter home when Emily knew it.

rye," but I think perhaps you ought to take care of yourself. Of course I'm horribly disappointed about the Tintype for January, because it will be April now before we can have one. But I don't want you to be bothered. Mr. Cabell can't do anything until after Christmas either, but we have Arthur Machen and Ernest Boyd, and a paper from Carl that is *not* Pistaches and Pastiches. I'm so very relieved, because I thought we were having entirely too many of those paragraphs and didn't like to tell him so. But it has evidently dawned upon him. We have Frances Newman for that number too, and it is going to be very much better than the October issue—it will have very few dull things in it. We were so ashamed of the appearance of the last number. Mr. DeVine, who is doing extremely well, but knows nothing of make-up, ordered the leaves cut, which made the magazine an inch shorter and difficult to bind, and because it was bigger it had to be clamped together and looked terrible—like a Baptist Sunday School pamphlet, I thought. But we will go back to uncut leaves for January, and we find we can at last afford a cover and avoid clamps. A quarterly needs a cover. It will have exactly the appearance of the present Reviewer, with the contents on the outside and just a shade or two deeper cream color. We are very excited about having it. We have to go to press before the middle of December, and I have no subject to write about. I've asked the Troubetzkoys and Mr. Cabell to try to think of one, and oh, I wish you were here to think. It's no use asking Mr. Mencken, because he would mean well, but his mind works so differently from mine that it is almost impossible for us to cooperate. And Carl won't even try to think of anything—he urges me to write him flattering things instead of thinking of things for him to do. But he has talked to Ernest Boyd and written Ronald Firbank, though I don't think he always has The Reviewer on his mind. He writes me terrible things, but always one or two very nice ones, and said yesterday that he was thinking of coming here in February. If he does, please, *please* come with him, because I don't want him alone. He still talks about my conceit, and I suppose that does seem specially startling in women. There was a man here from Baltimore not long ago and he talked steadily about himself and how wonderful he was, for two hours. And I listened, truly, without interrupting at all, except just to acquiesce, and was as subdued and admiring as possible. But at the end of that time I *did* think it was time to mention me, so I said, "I think that's all perfectly splendid, but what about me, now—don't you think I'm nice, too?" And he just looked at me, and said, "My God, you are conceited!" And I do think that is unfair, don't you? Are you going to let Prince Troubetzkoy paint you when you get back? When are you going to begin getting things for the Virginia novel? It ought to be laid around 1840, long after the early difficulties were settled, and before the least threat of the War Between the States had come. That was the best time in Virginia. We have lots of books here—Father's Virginiana—and Colonel Byrd's Westover papers. Alice has been reading them—I never have—and he tells scandalous things about everybody in all the Colonies. He seemed to keep in close touch with Philadelphia—his son married a Willing— and he told dreadful things about William Penn and said the Quakers really had a much more amusing time than they pretended. He said Penn had an affair with the Duke of Monmouth's mistress— we never knew that—and they had a daughter who was so charming that she became a duchess. And he tells lots of other things. Frederick Eddy, the man who came down here about The Reviewer and that I had meet Mr. Cabell, is very anxious to meet you, and to have you sign his books. He is crazy about you and asked me to write you a note of introduction, as he is going to Philadelphia soon. I hate to bother you, and you may not be back anyway when he is there, but if you have time I hope you'll let him see you a little while. He has collected all your first editions and your magazine stories, even the old Forums. I wanted the first editions dreadfully when he talked to me, but I showed him my manuscripts and he was thrilled. The other three people he likes best are Mr. Cabell, Arthur Machen and Walter de la Mare. He says he and Carl Van Vechten and Vincent Starrett and Paul Smith[4] know more about Machen than anyone.

---

[4] Paul Jordan Smith had published *The Soul of Woman* (1916). In 1924 he published *On Strange Altars*, and in 1927 (with Floyd Dell) he edited an all-English text of Robert Burton's *The Anatomy of Melancholy*.

Everyone here loves the Bright Shawl. David Bruce wrote me this week that he did too. He wants very much to see you. His father has just been elected Senator from Maryland, and he will be close by in Washington. There hasn't been anyone with a name like Cabell Bruce since the War. Please hurry and come here. I want to hear all about the movies. So does Alice. Ida says—she has just been here— to let her know next time you are in Washington and we will show you the Fairfax County places, Mason and Soe and Fitzhugh. Taylor Burke went to Paris for a month, just as he went to Mexico last fall, and she couldn't go. You see what nice letters I write when you answer now and then. I am much more fond of you when you do. I hope you don't have to drink milk and vichy a long time. I've had to take lots of it ever since grippe and I hate it. Emma Gray said this week she would give you a party. She is fat, but still attractive.

Emily.

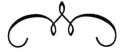

[37]

1008 Park Avenue
[December 20, 1922]

I had a letter from Mr. Hemphill today about your copyrights and I'm so terribly sorry there is any trouble. I'm writing him today and I hope it can be straightened out. The Reviewer would be truly distressed to cause you an inconvenience and I hope so much we haven't done it through ignorance. I will do everything possible to make your articles safe, for they are far the most valuable things we have ever had, and I shall be *heartbroken* if anything has gone wrong. You and Mr. Hemphill must tell me exactly what to do about the next Tintype, which I wish we had for January. Mr. Benét[1] said in

---

[1] William Rose Benét.

95

the Literary Review that it was coming out then, because I had told him it was! I've just read your review of The Cathedral in the new Bookman, and I'll read the book now. I hadn't intended to, because four out of the only five of Mr. Walpole's books I've read bored me. I think it very naive of both you and Carl—judging by what he wrote me—to be so thrilled at learning those things about the Church of England. I could have told you all that Mr. Walpole does and perhaps more. It is quite as interesting and wicked in its way as the mediaeval Roman Church. And I've been brought up hearing bishops and other old gentlemen discuss the windings of it. Bishop Randolph told me once that on a visit to England a British workman wept at the honor of shaking hands with him, because he'd never been so close to an English bishop. Father used to spend months roaming about the cathedrals and he said some of the English clergy were terrible. Virginia used to be a part of the Bishop of London's diocese, and some years ago—before Father's death—King Edward sent a Bible by him (the present Bishop) to old Bruton Parish Church in Williamsburg. The Bishop—Winnington-Ingram—is sweet, but he is different from most of them. We have his picture still in the library here. Father helped look after him. It was before I was grown, but I went to Williamsburg with them. Most of them are very dull and complacent and fearful snobs. When the last Bishop of Virginia—Bishop Gibson—stayed with Lady Astor she dressed him up all the time in an apron and knickerbockers and gaiters because she was afraid they wouldn't treat him with respect if he "looked like a curate." Bishop Randolph—Southern Virginia —was over there at the time and said Bishop Gibson looked very foolish and his legs were very cold. He never let himself be dressed up over there. They are both dead now. The nicest American bishop left is Arthur Lloyd, suffragan of New York, with Bishop Manning. He was Father's best friend and roommate and he is really attractive and very intelligent. I want you to see him, because you think none of them can be at all attractive or have any brains, because lots of them really haven't. He takes The Reviewer and thinks John Partins is worth publishing it for alone, and tried everywhere last winter to get The Alabaster Saint.[2] You must come to New York when I'm there and see him. He used to live in Gramercy Park and last winter he moved to a Park Avenue apartment, and I was there while he was looking for one, so I went up and had lunch with him at the Cathedral with all the clergy and choirboys and deaconesses, and I'd been with Mr. Mencken at the Beaux Arts the evening before. Bishop Lloyd was just as interested as could be in Mr. Mencken and in hearing every word he'd said about everything, and he buys the books that are reviewed in The Reviewer. Alice sent him Mr. Nathan's article in the Smart Set about Bishop Manning. He is a Virginian, although he has lived up there for years. And he is wonderfully attractive, and as you say of Hugh Walpole, utterly without prejudice. You'd like him. He's ten times as tolerant as Mencken, of everything, and hasn't a scrap of reformer anywhere about him. Carl is going into childish ecstasies over every new person he meets, which is different from what I thought—Hugh Walpole is one of them. He (Carl) is coming here in February with David Bruce, and also to Staunton Hill,[3] David's father's plantation in Charlotte County, where your cook, Martha, came from. David's father, Cabell Bruce, has just gone to Washington to be Senator. I wrote Carl about David, so they dined together in New York, and he accepted an article of David's for The Reviewer, that I'd meant to refuse. David is in Paris now, but will be back in January. Carl seems to be expecting you there now, and says you have a contract with Famous Players—Lasky to direct thirty or forty pictures, but that isn't true, is it? Mr. Mencken says he has been offered five thousand dollars a week to star in pictures, but after consultation with his pastor has refused, "because of false notes in the moral tone of the industry." I showed Alice your last letter, and we both thought from what you said that The Bright Shawl was not to be made into a picture. She

[2] See Letter 17, n. 1.
[3] The Staunton Hill plantation in Charlotte County was originally owned by James Bruce. The present Gothic mansion was built in 1848. In Emily's day James Bruce, of New York, transferred ownership of the estate to the Staunton Hill Club, a weekend shooting and social club composed of himself, his brother David K. E. Bruce, and a number of their freinds.

tells me that she wrote you a note from Lancaster saying how much she liked the book, and she is extremely sorry now that she was so frank in her opinions about the movies. Because we have heard since then that the picture was going on—without your direction. I hope they don't spoil it. Is Mr. Walpole still intending to come here in January? Can't you be here with him? And had I better write him about The Reviewer before he comes? I know you wrote him last winter—did you say anything to him this fall? Hunter Stagg is in New York now and I wrote Carl to see him too. We have Machen and Ernest Boyd in January and I have done another Virginia thing called In Velvet. When are you coming here?, and *please* try to be here when Carl is, and I think it will be hateful of you if you go to Chicago soon and don't come here at once. Hunter says Guy Holt is furious about the thing Burton Rascoe had about Mr. and Mrs. Cabell in the Tribune. But Cabell seems to take anything from him. You will have another Tintype after awhile, won't you? And I'll do the very best I can about the copyrights. I think it was perfectly horrid of you to go to Cuba to rest when you said you would come here and do it. And I don't see how it could have been restful in a party. I hope you are better now. Give love to Dorothy.

Emily.

Everyone here loves The Bright Shawl and thinks it perfect. There's a lot about it in the January Reviewer. The Knopfs sent me some cocoa to make me fat after grippe. I hope they send an advertisement. He said they were going to. I think that you ought to write to me as soon as possible now, and I shall be offended if you don't.

The Troubetzkoys aren't going to New York until the late winter, if at all.

Frederick Eddy says the Centaur bibliography is out, and unless you send it to me I'll order it, but I like best to have it from you, because that is the way I'd rather have them. This is not at all indelicate of me, because you said in the fall you were going to send it to me.

I do think it is *horrid* of you not to write me. I want to ask you some things and tell you some things, but I can't when you behave so. I don't even know where you are, and I sent you a letter and a Christmas card. No one—literally *no* one—else acts this way. You said Carl couldn't be counted on to be satisfactory, but only Mr. Mencken and Mr. Cabell could. But you are mistaken—his manners so far have been irreproachable. Hunter wrote me you were very polite to him, and nice, in New York. I don't see why you can't be polite to me. Would you, if I were in New York? I do like you best of them, but I don't know why, because you are often the least nice. And I think it is dreadful to be so inhuman in Christmas week. I can't understand you.

Emily.

Hugh Walpole had to stop with Mr. Cabell this week, because he was so ill with tonsilitis he had to go to New York to be treated. He isn't coming here for his visit for about two months. Mr. Hemphill has been very kind about the copyrights and I hope he and you aren't mad, but if you were that would be some excuse for you. Mr. Mencken has written about The Reviewer again in Baltimore. I have fifteen new pairs of stockings. I cannot tell anything else until I hear. You *are* difficult.

I hate to write you another letter, but I had a talk with Mr. Cabell today, and he got such a strange impression of what you thought of The Reviewer. He said you told him you thought it ought to go on, because it gave us a good time, but that you never read it! And he said you had never told him you thought I could write at all, and that my In Velvet sketch was good style, done after yours, but just your sort of thing, and of course not nearly so good. He said you had never told him you took me seriously in a literary way at all, or thought there was any future for The Reviewer. Was that just Mr. Cabell's perversity, or do you think I can write at all? Mr. Cabell doesn't think that you think the things I write are worth while, and that The Reviewer is just fun for me. Of course it *is* fun sometimes, but it is work and worry too, and I would like to know if you think I have intelligence enough to make it worth while— apart from fun. He said you haven't ever mentioned my Richmond paper to him. I had meant to write some other Virginians like the last one, but I don't want to do it if you think they are just imitation Tintypes—because imitations aren't worth anything. You see, I thought of using some of those people in a book. Do you think it's worth while at all? Another thing—if I have to write regularly, book articles, it will be good for me, just as it has been for Frances Newman. So will you give me a letter for the Herald literary editor in New York, as you said? I believe I can do the work—I still think perhaps I can write. But I was discouraged by what Mr. Cabell said you told him—I know he must have got a wrong impression. Tell me truly, do you feel I've accomplished anything serious or worth while in making and running The Reviewer? Because I have to do it en- tirely alone. If I go to New York about February eighteenth, can you go then? I'm terribly sorry I wrote you all that about Frances Newman. I didn't know then that she was going to West Chester— she told me today. I wouldn't have done it if I'd known—but you probably knew it all anyway. I wish you would let me hear from you—dictate it, of course if you want to. I am very unhappy and confused by the conversations with Mr. Cabell and Frances New-man, both. And for the first time since I've known you I feel that you are sort of strange and inaccessible, and that I don't know how you think or feel about me, or The Reviewer, because of the things they said. Is everything just the same? Are you just the same, and your opinions? And please tell me, do you think In Velvet is any good? Mencken said my Richmond paper was as good as anything Frances has written, but he hasn't mentioned this one. Carl and some of the others have though. Please let me know. And I do want a chance to write more and oftener. Everything seems so queer, and for the first time I have lost confidence in the future. I never have, before. I can't carry the magazine without believing it amounts to something.

Emily.

Is Cytherea[1] finished yet. I'm so excited about it. I wish it would hurry and open. Tell me if you killed Lee Randon. I don't want him killed.

Tomorrow I shall go out and buy a wonderful green hat that I can't afford, to cheer myself up.

I'm sorry I wrote you that letter now. I've just heard something that makes it very important for me to talk to you. Don't you think you can come? I'd be so very glad.

[1] The movie version, not released until 1924.

This is a paper Dr. Tucker asked me to read—he didn't submit it for publication, but I know he'd like to have it published. What do you think of it? I won't use your name, of course. You know you said the night before you left that we must have as many Southern writers on Southern subjects as possible, and this is both. Would it be worth publishing, do you think? I'm sorry I've been such a hell cat, but I was feeling very badly and needed a new hat, and I hadn't heard any very complimentary things, because I'd seen no one for several weeks but Maxwell Wallace and Jim Allison—and Maxwell is utterly matter-of-fact, and Jim doesn't say pretty things, he's only what you call "practical." John Powell is back and I have no respect for his intelligence, but he said lots of nice things—he has just forgiven me for telling at a party in New York last winter that he called me up at midnight and said he couldn't live more than a year. You know, you told me I oughtn't to have done it. But he *did* promise to die within the year, and he hasn't done it, and it was so absurd. I asked him about Freud, because I'd just been talking to Frances Newman, but he said I was the healthiest person he knew—sunshine and flowers and poetry and all that—and must never think of Freud. So I felt renovated. That's why I told you all those wonderful things about myself, because I felt the need of hearing them—but if I hear a great many now I shan't do it again for a long time, and will be very modest. I wrote you the letters with all those queer things because I was very upset and excited at hearing them—no one had ever talked to me like that before except one girl in New York. But you oughtn't to mind, because it was all very interesting. Delia's[1] party was the best I've been to in Richmond for a long time, you should have been there—it is a beautiful house, also beautiful food and beautiful clothes. I like Mme. Sylva[2] lots, and I'm going to hear

[1] Delia Tompkins.

[2] Marguerita Sylva had been a member of the Manhattan Opera Company under Oscar Hammerstein. She later made many vaudeville and motion-picture appearances.

her tonight. She is on her way to Florida and Cuba. The man talked about Mr. Cabell and said terrible things. Usually it makes me mad, but I was too cross with him from the day before to care, or to defend him. They wondered if his child was imbecile, but I explained that he wasn't—he's really worse than that, something queer. He remembers things better than most children do, and whenever I see him he kisses my hand in a dreadful sticky way and catches the hem of my skirt and holds it. I think he is a stray figment of Mr. Cabell's brain—a nature myth, really, one of those things that grew on bushes in Anaitis' garden.[3] Lots of people have read the Bookman piece[4] and are twittering about it. I saw in F. P. A.'s[5] column that Edna Millay was back, and at some party. You know, I told you she was coming. Please hurry and tell me you think I can write, because Mr. Cabell said you considered The Reviewer a plaything. He *always* says that. And you *don't* hate Richmond, do you? You said just before you left that it had been so horrid and it bothered me. Can you be in New York the week of the nineteenth? Let me know. I may be with Patterson (Rose) Dial instead of Martha Roberts. I shan't have Mrs. Reynolds anyway. Mary Tompkins has just come and I had to say I was out. She comes all the time this winter, I don't know why.

Emily.

[3] Born in 1915, Ballard Hartley Cabell was Cabell's only child of his own, his wife's sixth. Cabell explains in *As I Remember It* (p. 83):
> [He] developed into that which the advertisements of "special schools" call tactfully "the exceptional child." His body had grown quite normally, I mean, although it remained dwarfish; but his mind must stay forever—so said the omniscient grave doctors who had made a speciality, along with some opulence, of such mishaps—the mind of a child. Yet I found as the years passed that his mind was astute and nimble and remarkably well balanced through its entire extent. The trouble was, so nearly as anybody can phrase the matter, that a part of his mind was missing. Of mathematics, here to cite his main lack, Ballard had not ever any notion. And in consequence, of any affair into which mathematics entered, such as money values, he had no notion.

[4] Cabell was featured in "The Literary Spotlight" in *The Bookman* for February, 1923.

[5] Franklin Pierce Adams' column, "The Conning Tower," appeared in the New York *World* after moving from the *Tribune* in 1921.

I bought the Herald yesterday and I can write much better book reviews than any of those extra ones in there, I *know*.

Mr. and Mrs. Archer Jones are going to New Orleans this week and stay in the Vieux Carré and buy old things, and she is going to collect lots of erudition about New Orleans just as she already has about Virginia. She really knows a good deal. Mr. Jones was pleased with you for snorting the way you did out at the cabin.

N.B. This is a nice letter, not a horrid one. *Don't be afraid to read it.*

I can't understand Mr. Cabell about The Reviewer, or what he really wants. He has something he is thinking of developing into an article for the April issue. Besides that, he seemed so amused when he said you didn't read The Reviewer and didn't mention my writing. He laughed and laughed more than I have ever known him to. It was only a few minutes, but he is coming here alone toward the end of the week, and I suppose he'll talk about it further then. He, I believe, thinks nothing is any good but a book, and says what Frances Newman is doing will come to nothing unless she can write a book. But he said I had some years advantage of her in age, although I ought to begin soon. Yet he seems to take Burton Rascoe quite seriously, and he isn't writing a book. I shall start in and read French as much as I have a chance to, and try to translate for Mr. Liveright—that will be good practice. With The Reviewer to carry —Hunter has been away and Mary ill and hasn't touched it for months—there has been so little time, together with some newspaper work I've been doing here which hasn't helped at all. But I must just work all the time and give up parties entirely, just as Frances has always done. She says she never goes to Country Clubs or anywhere, except with literary people. Do you think that would be best for me? I'm sure I could do books for a New York paper, because Mr. Clover used to like those I did for him, and Mr. Knopf often quoted them in his advertisements. Frances has done it too in her library bulletins. I don't ever write dull ones, anyway. Do you think the Virginia sketches are worth going on with? You see, I was going to use them as the basis of a book. I shall try hard to change and improve. I've been far, far too childish and immature, but I feel a thousand years older now. I wish you'd let me help you too with your French translation and papers. I can do it rather well, and I'd love to help you sometimes, because you've helped me so much. I've never been any use to you at all, but I truly am not a fool. Love to Dorothy.

Emily.

Please write me something before I see Mr. Cabell, which will be about Friday. I don't believe for a minute that you talked entirely differently to him from what you did to me. But he did torment me horribly, anyway. I'll write an entirely amusing letter next time, but I can't think of such things now.

[42]   [February, 1923]

I couldn't go away when I had intended, because I caught a bad cold Thursday and had to stay in for several days, but I'm better today. And I didn't telegraph because I didn't know what I was going to do. I was so relieved at hearing from you—never as much so—I think I must have taken cold on account of feeling you were displeased, because I hardly ever do it. This is the first day I could write. Hallie—our maid—has almost as much curiosity as you—she has just eaten one of the oranges off the little bush on the dining-room table to see if it was good, but it didn't hurt her—nothing does, not even asphyxiation. You know she'd just been asphyxiated the first time you ever came to the house. I shall write a paper about peacocks for the April Reviewer. It should be in Mr. Cabell's manner instead of yours, to mollify him—he has never been so ruffled with me as he was about In Velvet, and I think that is why he tormented me so about it and I wrote you that silly letter!—but I don't believe my peacock paper will be in his manner, after all. Carl says In Velvet was kolossaal. I've just had a note from him about his Alabama trip—he seems to expect to stop here on his way North— and he says Frances Newman told him last week that The Reviewer was going to stop. He seemed much perturbed. Either he misunderstood her utterly—because when I discussed it with her I told her it would certainly go on unless I found something I'd much rather do, which I don't expect—or Carl was merely romancing, as he does sometimes. I never know, in a letter, whether or not he is serious. Do you? I tell you this only in order that you may flatly contradict such a report in case you should hear it. Of course you already know it is going on—I adore The Reviewer and think it the most interesting literary thing in the world, next to you. There is something very silly in the new Bookman by Mrs. John Lightfoot, whom you don't like, about Mr. Cabell and the terrible Writers' Club[1] here. I'll send it to you if you don't see the Bookman. John Farrar announces that she is "in close touch with things literary in Virginia," and that is a lie, because she isn't in touch with Mr. Cabell or The Reviewer, and they are the only things literary here. I do think the Bookman is hopeless, and I hope you'll never write for it again, not even to please Hugh Walpole, whom everyone, apparently, wishes to please. Mrs. Archer Jones writes from New Orleans that she has discovered how the Double Dealer is financed. I didn't know there was any possible mystery about it, because it is run by Jews and it is a well

[1] "Are Writers Human?" by Nan Maury Lightfoot, *The Bookman*, March, 1923.

known fact that Jews are all rich. Did Cytherea [the movie script] have to be changed, and is it quite finished? Carl says Marie Doro[2] likes it. I wish I could read it. You will be swamped with invitations when you come again to Richmond. Delia and Emma Gray want to give you parties, and Mrs. Gill, too, is very excited about you, and I don't think she will invite any of us to her party for you. I've never seen anyone make such a stir in just two or three meetings. And Billy and Dick think you are marvellous for a novelist, and seem to consider you a hundred per center—but their wives know better. Delia and Emma Gray are copying their dresses from a Godey's Ladies' Book for the thing they are going to have here April sixth— you must see them. I had a letter from Frances Newman before she sailed. Do you think she has anything that could be used for the April Reviewer? About my plans—they partly depend on yours, so please telegraph me when you get this. I'll go to New York this week-end, if you'll be there then, and are going off to Florida or somewhere, as you once said, later. But if you'll be in New York for some time I'll go a little later. Of course I'd adore to see Cytherea, but I imagine that is quite indefinite. Next to that, I'd rather see the Moscow Players. It is quite necessary for someone, besides Hunter, to go to New York within the next four or five weeks, and I must go within that time. I can't stay but a week, because I must stop in Baltimore and Alexandria. But as I said before, I'm not going unless you are to be there, if only for a day or two. So I can come this week-end or later, whichever you'd rather. Please telegraph me if you can, when you get this, so I can telegraph the girl I'm staying with. I've told her two or three different things already, poor thing! I do want ever so much to see you—Dorothy too, I hope she is going. But if you are too busy this week-end I'll come later. I'm developing a large Southern correspondence, which bores me horribly, in order to have a good report for Mr. Mencken. I think you are wonderful and it will be so comforting to look at you, and I am really nice now. I'm

[2] Marie Kathryn Stewart, who under the stage name Marie Doro had begun her career in 1903 in such plays as *The Billionaire, The Girl from Kay's, Little Mary,* and, most notably, in Richard Harding Davis's comedy *The Dictator* (1904), in which William Collier and John Barrymore appeared.

reading lots of Henry James. Were you bored with all the letters! I sent you a message by Mr. Hemphill about Dodges and Fiats before your telegram came. There is no one so sensible as you. I broke two engagements last Saturday, with Carl and someone else. I'll come now whenever you say, so let me know. I have an appointment with Mr. Liveright too, about the French books. I'm sorry to ask you to telegraph again, but I can't help it.

Emily.

You must see Hickory Hill,[3] near here, before you begin the Virginia novel.

---

[3] Located twenty miles north of Richmond, Hickory Hill was originally Anne Carter's share of her father's estate. The first house was built in 1820 by her husband, William Fanning Wickham. In 1875, after this building burned, the present house was built by Williams Carter Wickham.

1008 Park Avenue

[43]   [February, 1923]

I'm sorry about the Fiat, because I liked its looks so much. But I realize that Fiats and other things must be got rid of, if they prove intractable. And that a Dodge that will respond when the time comes is preferable even to a Rolls-Royce that will not. Thank you for your letter. I have profited by it, not being a fool, however much I may have acted like one. The letter was written by a great author, and as Burton Rascoe remarked in the Tribune of Albert Jay Nock,[1] "he need not fear, although I am younger and less familiar with the classics, that I shall fail to understand him." If I hadn't been so

---

[1] One of the editors of *The Freeman*. He had recently published the book *The Myth of a Guilty Nation* (1922).

badly frightened, I would have laughed . . . but I did not laugh. I hope with all my heart that the letter was a warning, and not a summary removal of all Fiats to the junk heap. And that you will accept my sincere and permanent apologies. I'm so sorry Cytherea goes badly. I've thought about it a great deal—though Heaven knows I've given you no reason to suppose that I think of anything except myself and my petty affairs—and so far I can't see it as a play at all. Because of that I'd like enormously to see it when it really is a play. I know that the best critics, including Frances Newman, for whose opinion I have a real respect when in my right mind, likes the Black Pennys best, but I love Linda and Cytherea, who belong always together in my mind, with everything, on one hand, and nothing, on the other. I believe Mr. Cabell does too. A few days ago a man in the movie censorship office—they censor them here, you know!—called me up in a hurry, and said that Java Head had come in unexpectedly for a private showing, and invited me to see it. I was quite excited and rushed down there, but it had already begun. The Salem pictures and long shots are, as you said, unusually lovely, and the detail so good—pillow cases, worn stair carpet and all that. But Leatrice Joy is by no means Taou Yuen. After all, though, how could she be? She is more Madame Butterfly than Manchu, I think. Alice is so pleased with the first edition Bliss, especially now that Katherine Mansfield is dead, which I consider a calamity. It was ever so nice of you to think of getting it from Meredith Janvier, and I hope you saw his shop. I spent a long time there the last time I was in Baltimore, and he badly wanted some of your manuscripts. We are very distressed because some wonderful Rappahannock River oysters came to us after you left, and they are one of the things you could have eaten. Alice, having grown up on the bay, won't buy Richmond oysters. But, I, having grown up here, have an ignominious time with these other oysters, which are abnormally large, and either choke and leave the table, or cut them in two, which last makes Alice's blood run cold at the sacrilege of it. But they aren't as nice now that we can't have beer with them anymore. I'm going to New York, I think, next Saturday or Sunday, the seventeenth or eighteenth, and I'm writing you because you very kindly told me, the night before you left, that you could be there almost anytime except the week-end after the fifteenth, when Mr. Walpole was coming to you. I'll probably get there the middle of that week-end, and be there only for another week, as I've promised to stop in Baltimore a day or two before I go home. David Bruce is having a party, and there is stacks to do here with Hunter and Mary gone. But I don't want to go unless you can be there even for a day, so if you aren't going to be there anytime in that week I'd wait and go another week. I don't mean by that, that I'd expect to see you for more than an hour or two, because I know how busy you are, truly. But an hour or two would be more important than seeing all the other people put together, so I hope you'll let me know if you are going to be there any part of that week. Telegraph, of course, I mean, don't dream of bothering with a letter. Mr. Mencken is giving me an audience there in regard to Southern Letters, and I am, under his orders, pursuing a Gerald Johnson[2] down in North Carolina, who I think, takes life and the poor South very hard, and writes like H. L. M. He (H. L. M.) is very kind, far more so than he has any cause to be, and I do like him truly—not that it is of the slightest importance whether I do or not. It would be nice to see you together again—the only time I ever did, both Emma Gray and I thought it was wonderful. I don't forget that The Reviewer and I are lucky in the people who are good to us—one in particular has been so good that I have grown more skeptical than ever about "Southern gentlemen." Mr. Mencken wrote a scream of a letter, the funniest yet. He also said he saw you in Baltimore, but you didn't appear in New York, and he feared your "old war wounds" were troubling you. I hope you found some things of Frances's that would do for The Reviewer. She said she'd ask you, and some of them might do. I think I must have been possessed of more than seven devils, not to mention a severe case of loathsome feminity, to drag in all that silly personal stuff with a person whose brain is so good that the rest is unim-

[2] At this time Gerald Johnson was on the staff of the Greensboro, North Carolina, *Daily News*. He later became associated with the Baltimore *Sun* and published such books as *Andrew Jackson* (1927), *America's Silver Age* (1939), *American Heroes and Hero Worship* (1943), and many others.

portant. If you haven't already done it, I wish you'd destroy those horrid pages—oh dear, but that sounds Victorian, "Burn this letter"! Doesn't it?—Mary Tompkins seems to be downstairs again—she told me the other day that you had come to her rescue on three important occasions, which sounds very dramatic and interesting. I'm reading the new Germinie Lacerteux,[3] and it is a beautiful translation, rather literal, as I like it. Mr. Liveright likes it free, but I think French prose too perfect to be free with. I shall be, in New York, in a house with Patterson Dial,[4] *not* Mrs. Reynolds, at 35 West Seventy-fifth Street, your "Rose," you know. She is lovely, with incredible hair. She is in Fury [the movie] now with Barthelmess. I'm not sure that you'll be willing to see me at all, but I'll be more relieved than I can say if you telegraph that you are! If it is as clear as your letter there will be no doubt of my understanding. By the way, I saw Mrs. Sale today and ordered one of the Historic Gardens of Virginia for you. It will be ready early in March, and it was so lucky that I saw her, for nearly all of the first thousand numbered copies are ordered in advance, and the others won't be out until fall. It made me more cheerful than I've been this week to be able to get you a book you might want, "with my compliments." It has Castle Hill, Westover, Shirley, Tuckahoe, and many others that you haven't seen yet, including our own old one in Halifax, which is gone now. I hope it is a nice book, but it may be a mess, because some of the women in charge of it are so silly. Prince Troubetzkoy is making the frontispiece. They are in New York now, and I'll see them when I go. I don't know whether or not your Miss Landon is with them. Ernest Boyd has written a most amiable letter, admitting that "rage and despair had torn his soul," because everyone had Reviewers but him, but he is now restored to calm. A frantic letter from Hunter says that I must on no account open my mouth in the Algonquin except to put food in it, because everything that is said is instantly repeated, and usually repeated wrong. Poor child, he seems to have had some rough experiences.

[3] The novel by Edmond and Jules Goncourt, translated into English in 1922, with an introduction by Ernest Boyd.
[4] An actress who belonged to a prominent Richmond family.

He also said that, with late hours and dubious gin, he was losing his looks, which entertained me tremendously. I hope I shan't miss Carl in New York—he was expecting to go to Alabama sometime in February "to see the birthplace of Tallulah Bankhead," and to stop here on the way back. But I'd rather miss him than you. I don't think he and David Bruce will have their Staunton Hill party until spring, when it would be nice if you joined them, and used the place in your Virginia book.[5] David would be thrilled, more because you spent all your money in Venice once than because you write beautiful books. He has nice things to drink. Emma Gray is still insisting that you get in touch with her New Orleans friend, of the pink pearls and daily quart of champagne. I saw her mother, Mrs. White, today, who is beautiful, more so than Emma Gray since she got fat, and she said she wondered if we realized how good you are to The Reviewer, and I said yes, I realized better than she did. You enchanted all of them by saying such nice things about Bessie Watkins. They think so too, and feel that more people should know it. I've had a talk with Mr. Cabell and he says he only meant— and said the same thing to Frances Newman—that he was afraid I'd get more interested in editing The Reviewer than in doing work of my own, and he wanted to prod me. I explained to him, as you did to me, that for the present The Reviewer was work of my own, and would make it easier for me to get other work noticed. I also explained to him that I had done as much as lots of people my age have. He worries too because Hunter doesn't write a novel at once, and I think it would be fatal if he did—for a year or two. . . . I don't believe Hunter ever gets mad with him. It's queer. And I've stopped getting mad with people too—it bores them and will make me get thin, I know. However—and Alice will bear witness to this —I never say bad things about you, only *to* you—but never again, I wouldn't dare. It seems rather strange to write you such a long letter when I've just deluged you with letters, but I remember that, until two weeks ago when I ceased writing real letters and descended to fits of hysteria, you used to find them wildly diverting, and this

---

[5] *Balisand,* Hegesheimer's novel, which appeared in 1924.

one is, don't you think, a return to my "earlier manner," as they say of people like you and Mr. Cabell and Henry James? I'm going to a party Tuesday given by Mrs. Gill, who sat in front of you that terrible night at Reveille, and that you thought so pretty and chic. She was so pleased that you noticed what she was like when she took off her hat, and wants to see you when you come again. You *will* come again, I hope? She said you were attractive even when you snorted and squirmed. Don't imagine that because I'm babbling like this, I don't feel very serious and really frightened, and realize what I've done and what your letter meant. I do. I realize that it might be unforgivable, but you are always generous and I'm hoping that, as I've never done it before, you will believe that I shall never do it again. I admire you more than anyone, and always shall, and value your friendship—quite apart from The Reviewer—more than any that I have ever had. If you let me keep it I can safely promise that I shall never handle it roughly or stupidly again, but treat it just as I do your manuscripts, which are the best things I have—much better than my lace, which I never wear, or my grandmother's emerald, which I cheerfully lost. There is no reason why I should save all of my intelligence for my work, and use only impulses with people. I wonder if the peppermints were all broken in the mail. Another unfortunate impulse. The new Dial has an even queerer installment of the Sherwood Anderson story[6]—he is, beyond doubt, insane, and the Dial too, a little. Mary Street has just sent a special delivery from Hot Springs for me to write some people there what the policy of The Reviewer is, and I don't know. Give my love to Dorothy. I think she is wonderful.

Always sincerely yours,
Emily Tapscott Clark.

[6] *Many Marriages,* published in book form in 1923.

Richmond, Virginia   1008 Park Avenue

[44]   [February, 1923]

I wrote you a letter this morning, but forgot to put in one thing, and this will probably reach you first because it is being mailed from the station. I feel as if I ought to be struck by lightning when I think of having said "fibs" to you, when you are absolutely the most honest person I've ever known, even more so than Mencken. I was *unspeakable,* and—how it hurts to say it—common, too. I can never forgive myself, but please you try to forgive me. The week has been bad enough to amount to a real Katharsis—isn't that the way you spell it? I even went to church this morning to please Alice, which shows that my spirit is utterly crushed and broken. It was really fun though, because there was a diatribe about Dr. Grant, which made me decide to run in and embrace him if I am in his neighborhood. Keep this letter till the one written this morning about Fiats and Dodges comes. Patterson Dial says she is devoted to Dorothy Gish and Richard Barthelmess. I've been so abjectly penitent and so horribly worried that two days ago I showed Alice your remark about the Fiat and told her I'd been abominable beyond words and asked her if she thought you'd ever forgive me. She was amused about the automobile—I was not, and am not now, but am utterly tragic—and said you might forgive me if you were really fond of me, but that I couldn't expect everybody to put up with what she did, especially a genius. I explained to her that no one else had to. Then she said that whatever I had done was the result of being selfish and spoilt for so long—she sounded just like the place in Figures of Earth, where half of the people said "that simply showed you; and the rest of them assented that indeed you might well say that, and they had often thought of it, and had wished that young people would take profit by considering such things more seriously." But she never said I deserved to be forgiven. She seemed to think you might do it like God. And she was amazed to hear I'd *ever* taken liberties with you, because she knows how I feel about you. And I'm amazed too, and aghast. And when I think of everything about you and your books and your Tintypes, and yourself, I cannot understand myself. She always thinks it's my fault when dreadful things happen, though she's very fond of me, and advised Mr. Cabell last winter to drop me when I behaved so badly to him. He didn't do it, but if he did I wouldn't care at all in comparison with you, and I'm so frightened about the Fiat. As I told you, I even went to church. And if you will come back to Richmond, instead of saying I'll give you parties and take you for drives, as I used to say, I'll promise to let you beautifully alone, and never telephone you or write you notes, or urge you to do things, whether you are working or not. I can offer no more than that.

Very sincerely yours,
Emily Clark.

Wait for this morning's letter.

[45]   [February, 1923]

Have you ever noticed how Ernest Boyd says "everyone in town," and C. V. V.[1] says "all New York," when they mean about fifteen people who are doing the same thing? And Mrs. Gordon Battle's[2] friends say it when they mean everybody on a certain part of Park Avenue, who lunches at Pierre's. It seems to be a Manhattan peculiarity. I'm not staying in Central Park West, as I said I would, because Martha Roberts has someone else there now, and Waverly Place is too far down. Lots of people have spoken of your interview in the Dispatch here. I do hope you'll let me look at you again,

[1] Carl Van Vechten.
[2] The former Martha Bagby, of Richmond, now married to George Gordon Battle, a lawyer. At this time the Battles lived in New York.

but I'm not at all sure, since the Fiat has gone. If you won't, now, I'd rather put off my visit until you will! You'd find me as calm as Alice—I can say no more than that.

I hope you won't be bored to irritation when you finish this. I don't see how I could have expected you, or anyone, to give every second and every thought to me!

I must have been insane to get vapours, and rather vulgar vapours too, with you, who of all people are most sensible. If your letter had been a cold shower it couldn't have worked quicker. Mrs. Caperton[3] wants to give you a party with all six curly blonde daughters in evidence and their best clothes. I think it sounds rather nice. They are all so *perfectly* pretty, without being beautiful, and they all have brains. Carl must see them too, as "the fast set!"

If you still like silly letters, that don't ask you to do things, even when you are very tired and busy, I can always write them. I won't decide positively about New York until I know about you. I *hate* myself for having asked you impertinent questions—when all the time I feel just as Hugh Walpole said he felt about Conrad when he was younger—only more so, because you are just as big as your books. Did you know Conrad may come to Richmond in April?

It wasn't nice of me to call the child a nature myth, but doesn't he look like one?

Such is very natural perversity that I've been telling everyone here—they don't appreciate it—that F. Newman's work is wonderful. I've written Hunter what you said of it too, because he has never understood it. I don't, quite, but I shall try right away. Not naturally mean, really, you know that. Trying hard to make amends.

[3] Mrs. Helena Lefroy Caperton had been a schoolmate of Nancy Langhorne Astor. She published a number of stories in national magazines and had six strikingly blonde daughters who were among the main social attractions of Richmond.

16 East Lafayette Avenue
Baltimore
[46]   [February, 1923]

They use purple ink here, I can't help it. I've had such a good
time that I want to write you a nice letter, all in good humor. I
stayed in New York two days longer than I intended, because the
Dana Gibsons[1] gave the Troubetzkoys a Chauve-Souris party, and
I missed seeing it last year. But I was disappointed in it. And I
never saw the Moscow Theatre, because seats had to be got so far
ahead. I told Carl I stayed over to see him, so when you see him,
don't tell him anything different. He said I was very unflattering
and annoying to come when he was away, and to come to see you
instead of him, and that he was going to be wonderful to me, and
give me a party if he'd been there, so I wish I could have stayed for
it. As it was, I only lunched with him, and Fania Marinoff and the
Ernest Boyds and Helen Westley and Philip Moeller.[2] Carl was
sweet, and said he adored me and The Reviewer, and that if I ever
stopped it he would continue it himself. And Ernest Boyd said he'd
do another paper for the July issue, and that The Reviewer was
better known than it had ever been, and was by far the best of the
non-commercial magazines. I thought that was extremely nice, from
him, because he is so critical, and not interested in me personally.
I'd had lunch two days before with him and Mrs. Boyd alone. She
had to go to a matinée, so Mr. Boyd and I went to a bookshop together, and looked at lots of books. He was lovely—I like him tremendously, although Hunter couldn't bear him—he is so easy to
talk to, and understands everything I mean. And he said he was
glad to see that I kept my head very well. If that were always true!

---

[1] The Charles Dana Gibsons. Gibson was the creator of the Gibson Girl—also
the Gibson Man, modeled on his dashing friend Richard Harding Davis—in the
famous drawings he did for *Life* and other magazines and books around the turn
of the century.
[2] Among this group of writers and theatrical people, Helen Westley was particularly in the news at the moment for her performance in *Peer Gynt*. As already
noted, Fania Marinoff is Mrs. Carl Van Vechten, and Philip Moeller was a popular playwright.

But I don't much care for Mrs. Boyd. She chatters so all the time and pays no attention to me, and just looks blank and says "Comment?" whenever I speak to her. And interrupts her husband when he is talking to me. She is frightfully bourgeoise and unattractive, and treats me as if I were a jeune fille or an imbecile. I've never seen her alone, but I don't think I like her. The only nice thing she said to me was that I wrote irresistible letters. But I think Mr. Boyd one of the nicest people I ever met. I was a little disillusioned with Carl, although I'm very fond of him. He has gotten fatter since last summer, which he shouldn't have done, and is so gossipy. They talk about each other *all* the time, and crane their necks to see who everyone in the Algonquin is with. Fania Marinoff is attractive enough for the stage . . . I don't think she especially takes to me either, although she was much politer than Mrs. Boyd. And I watched her cook, in their apartment, and it takes breeding to look well while cooking—she looked a trifle shrewish and East Side. All this is *very* confidential, for no one but you. I said only lovely things about everyone while in New York, because I learned a lesson last year through Guy Holt. I had dinner with him this time, before I left, to please Mr. Cabell, and we both behaved very nicely, but I shan't ever really like him. I'm not crazy about Philip Moeller— he roars at everything Helen Westley says, whether it is funny or not, and she is so repulsive. Amélie and Pierre say she is positively obscene and loathsome in Peer Gynt, and calculated to make every man leave the theatre more strictly moral than he had ever been. She said in her terrible voice that she wanted something "dainty and French" for lunch, and at once began to devour hash and apple pie in huge, sickening quantities. She didn't notice me much either. I think wives and mistresses of literary men are rather impossible, all but Dorothy. I don't think Mr. Huebsch[3] at all attractive, although he is intellectual. He is too personal and obvious, and rather impertinent, considering that he is a Jew. He took me to the Lafayette and asked me if I liked to fall in love with people. I told him I hated it, because it upset me horribly. Then he asked if I liked

[3] The well-known publisher B. W. Huebsch, who published *The Freeman* from 1920 until 1924. In 1925 he merged his firm with the Viking Press.

to have people fall in love with me. Then he called me a moth, and said they were very lovely, but were sometimes more interesting after their wings were singed, and that mine would be if I came to New York often. Frances asked me to write her what I thought of him, but I haven't done it yet. He also called me a "young girl," which made me furious. He was tremendously nice about The Reviewer, and said its possibilities weren't half explored, and that my "In Velvet" was beautifully done. I went to the Brevoort with Abdullah, and made Miss Wick go too. We went to his apartment first for cocktails, because I wanted to see it, and he played some Scriabin, and did it extremely well, and said Carl knew nothing of music and thought he knew everything. He has a terrific anti-Van Vechten complex—I think he is the least bit gone on Fania Marinoff, and says she told him she was horribly afraid of Carl, but he was probably lying. He adores Fanny Hurst and Gouverneur Morris and Hearst and Belasco. His apartment is *wonderful,* by far the best I've seen. Burton Rascoe and John Farrar had both told me about it, but he won't often admit the Young Intellectuals. He has gorgeous prayer rugs on the floor, walls and divans, inherited from his family, and copper bowls which he says—and no one is in a position to dispute!—have been handed down since the year 850, when his Moorish ancestors occupied Spain. And beautiful dragons and Buddhas, all studded with turquoises. He has some delightful pictures and books, and a beautiful thing that he burns incense in all the time. He is an orthodox Mohammedan, and he has an inherited volume of Hafiz, the Persian poet, handwritten and hand-illustrated. I don't think I've ever seen so many interesting things in such a small space. He says he can't stand Burton Rascoe's parties, because none of the people there have any background. Mr. Rascoe gave me Pender Among the Residents[4] to take home and review. He'd intended having Ernest Boyd do it. Did you see his Reviewer notice in the Sunday Tribune? If you didn't, I'll send it to you. I wasn't crazy about it, but this time I thanked him very nicely. It was quite inaccurate, because I didn't mention The Reviewer to him

[4] The new novel by Forrest Reid, author also of such novels as *Pirates of Spring* and *The Spring Song.*

119

when I was with you, but several days later. He told me Sinclair Lewis had had to leave Hartford, because he kissed the wife of the president of the Rotary Club, and had gone off to the West Indies quite drunk, by himself, and didn't know where he'd live now. He also said that Mencken had given him (Lewis) the theme of his next novel, and was discussing it with him. It will be a college professor. Mr. Mencken telephoned me the day you left, and said his laryngitis was worse, so he was leaving a day sooner, and asked me to have lunch with him Saturday in Baltimore, but I wasn't here Saturday, and when I did arrive his voice was quite gone and he was laid up. I talked to his sister—did you ever meet her? So I missed him here. I didn't telegraph you about coming to David Bruce's party, because it proved to be not especially amusing. His brother and sister-in-law, whose large house he was living in alone, had to return unexpectedly from Porto [sic] Rico because his sister-in-law was taken ill. So David is at Ruxton with his parents, in senatorial solemnity, and parties there aren't very much fun. He and Carl are still corresponding, and he wants us both to come to Staunton Hill in the summer. I've promised to get David invited to Castle Hill too. He has a romantic affection for Amélie, whom he has never seen. I'm not a bit excited about him anymore, and have quite ended my wild experiment with him. He is coming to Richmond soon. You shouldn't have mentioned the experiment before Patterson Dial, because I don't tell them to anyone but you—certainly not to women. David wants you to be his guest for the next Green Spring Valley races, which are very nice, and he will put you up at the Baltimore Club. He says The Reviewer is the most chic and charming and airy magazine in America, and his favorite of them all, after La Vie Parisienne, but that I need a course of solid reading, beginning with the Iliad and the Odyssey, and including no living authors. Do you think so? He was at Princeton with Scott Fitzgerald and John Peale Bishop and Edmund Wilson, Jr., although they are older. And he says Mrs. Fitzgerald can drink more than any woman he has ever seen, and is a trifle ordinary and Alabamian, but has brains. He was rather in sympathy with them there, but afterwards they went in hard for writing, and he went in for diplomacy and society. He is really beautiful and thoroughbred to look at, but not as attractive as I at first thought. I love Baltimore, and don't want to go home tomorrow, but I must, because The Reviewer must go to press. People here are perfect to me, both men and women, and I have parties every minute. They treat me as if I were rather important, but they are a little like Richmond people and don't like things to get too literary and serious, and they say that being an editor hasn't changed me at all. I believe though that I'd rather live in Richmond, and have The Reviewer, than in New York, although I'd like to spend more time in New York. Because even the people there who are comfortably off, like Carl, live in what I call discomfort. And they are just as trivial in their way as Southern people, and gossip all the time. The people at home are often horribly boring, but they are much better bred. It is hard to know which is preferable. I went to a nice party Saturday night in a perfectly lovely old house out in Beekman Place by the river. Margalo Gillmore[5] was there, and she is a darling. And a moving-picture director, Levino, just from the Coast, who told about you and Rupert Hughes at a party in Hollywood last spring! I gave your note to Mr. Maurice[6] and he said he'd certainly have me if I lived in New York, but that Mr. Munsey[7] wouldn't let the books go out of town. I heard that from someone else too, and I'm so sorry. But it was sweet of you to write the letter. I'll do some for Burton Rascoe, and perhaps for the International Book Review. I stole the Post with Gold Petals[8] from Pat Dial's apartment, and it is lovely. Won't you send the bibliography soon? Also my cigarette holder. I'm so sorry I was careless and left it with you. Amélie has given me a box of her cigarettes which are just the right size for it, the first I've had, so I want it. Pierre has a place in the Forties, where you can get both cocktails and wine and wonderful food. Amélie said I had great talent and great

---

[5] A popular actress, who had recently appeared in *Alias Jimmy Valentine* and *He Who Gets Slapped*.

[6] The New York critic Arthur Bartless Maurice.

[7] Frank Andrew Munsey, the magazine publisher (*Munsey's Weekly*, e.g.), who now owned the New York *Mail, Sun and Globe*, and *Evening Telegram*.

[8] The title of one of the installments of Hergesheimer's series *The Magnetic West*, then appearing in *The Saturday Evening Post*.

charm, but that my head was being turned and I did things that weren't me at all. Unlike what Ernest Boyd said! She said she was the same at my age, but that I must get straight. My head *is* straight now—I've thought so very hard and been so frightened. Please come to Richmond soon and let the longing ladies give you some of the parties, if only for the week-end, that they've planned. I shan't be asked to all of them. Alice sent you messages when she wrote. I hope Dorothy's ear is well now. Give her my love. This house has some lovely old furniture, and I think it will be left to me. But it's not the kind you like best. Please telegraph me some time, if you haven't time to write. I wish I could read Cytherea.

Emily.

I spent the last part of the time in Washington Square with some Virginians who have an apartment there. Such nice doors and windows. Pat Dial still has no engagement.

[47] 1008 Park Avenue
[March, 1923]

The most wonderful thing has happened, and I'm so excited. I wrote a sketch called Stuffed Peacocks for the April Reviewer— Mr. Cabell wanted to see it and I showed it to him. He said it was "excellent," and that the style was mine and not yours! He still says In Velvet was yours, and though he thinks yours is beautiful, he has a *fit* if I seem to be imitating you, because he says I must write like myself as I already have a definite manner. Perhaps though, if I ever wrote like him he'd feel differently—I don't know. Anyway, I decided to show this paper to Mencken, because I've never sent him one of my manuscripts to read, only other people's. He wrote back that very day and said he liked it lots, and asked to have it for the Smart Set if I didn't need it for The Reviewer, and if I'd make a different ending, and if Mr. Nathan liked it too. Of course I think The Reviewer is more distinguished than the Smart Set, but I want to publish things in other places, so I wrote a different ending that same day and sent it back to him. He wanted it more dramatic, like a story. The next day I wrote something called White Angora, in two or three hours, for The Reviewer. Then Mr. Nathan wrote and said Stuffed Peacocks was extremely good and he was delighted to have it. I'm so glad, because I've never sent anything to any magazine but The Reviewer. I've put it off because people told me one had to be refused ever so often before they were accepted, and it makes me so perfectly wild to be refused things that I haven't had the courage to go through with the beginnings of writing. But Mencken gave me a good start by asking me, instead of my asking him, and I shan't be so afraid after this. I really wasn't thinking of the Smart Set at all, only The Reviewer, because I didn't think it was Mencken's and Nathan's sort of thing. But this is the wonderful part—a few days ago Mencken wrote again and said if I would write twenty or thirty more sketches of that sort—old Virginia types but done differently from the way other people here have done them—Knopf would be very glad to get them, and he—Mencken—would see that they were brought out in a book. He said if they were as good as Stuffed Peacocks it would be an excellent book, and I must begin it at once. And that he'd like to see some of them. So he has White Angora now, and hasn't told me yet what he thinks of it. It is different from the others, because instead of being just another old lady, it's an old man and woman and a sort of situation. I don't feel, now, like writing about anyone my own age, but Mencken said that was all right. I'm alarmed about the book though, because I'm afraid some of the people will be recognized. The first two papers—In Velvet and the Peacocks—are cousins of mine who are dead, but I haven't enough dead ones to make a book, and I think Mencken wants most of them rather disagreeable, like the first two. Peacocks is hateful, openly so, not subtly so, like the Velvet one. And people will be furious with me, but I'll have to risk it. Mencken likes the Peacock paper best of all my things, and Richmond next best. Now, I must hurry with the book, because I've always wanted to publish one by the time I was thirty, and there's not much time. After thirty, I've never felt things would seem quite as important and interesting as before. Don't you think it's perfectly splendid? I'm growing almost to love Mencken, he is giving me such an unexpected chance. I didn't realize that things so light and slight could make a book. He is having a terrible time—you know he was sick when I was in Baltimore, and then his mother was desperately ill, hardly expected to live, and now his sister has fallen down the back stairs, and he hasn't been able to get a nurse for her because they are all busy with influenza. And I think it is sweet of him to have my things on his mind, and I'm sorry I said he was heavy and German, and I shan't let Carl be disrespectful about him again, and tell me things about Miss Bloom (Blum?), or whatever the lady's name is. I'm sending you Stuffed Peacocks because I'd like tremendously to know what you think of it, if you don't mind, but it is in Alice's room now, and she is asleep. So I'll mail it later. I wanted to tell you all about it at once, but I'd written you so many letters I decided it would be heartless to write another for a long time. But I can't keep from telling you any longer, because I'm so thrilled about writing a book—more excited than I've ever been in my life. And I wanted you to know, and I hope you think it is very nice. Do you? And do you think I could get it out in time for next Christmas? My first review—Pender Among the Residents—is in the Tribune today. It is nearly a column, but I'm cross as usual with Burton Rascoe, because he killed the three sentences toward the end that were the point of the whole thing, and that leaves the review almost meaningless. I know he did it because Ernest Boyd had expressed a quite opposite opinion, and he is outrageously influenced by both Mr. Boyd and Mencken. It makes me very mad. Alice has been very ill indeed since I came home and I've been badly frightened, but she is better now and is going out again. It always makes me feel horribly queer when she is sick. Carl says Mr. Walpole writes him very often, but that you never do. But you don't write me either. Carl writes almost as much Italian as French now in his letters, and I can't understand him. He was a little cross with me, I think—he wrote me from Alabama saying he'd like to stop in Richmond on his way North. I didn't answer, because I was in New York, and the letter was forwarded me just after you left there. So he didn't stop here, and reached New York just before I left there. But I'd rather he'd come in the spring anyway, when he can motor, and see some of the river places, and I very specially don't want him without you. Alice particularly wants you with him too. He says you've been telling him for years that you would bring him here. He thought I shouldn't have gone to New York when he was going South, and miss him both there and here. Franklin Spier told Hunter that The Blind Bow-Boy[1] was homosexual, and I'm *sorry*. I hope most people won't see it, anyway. But if that is true, what an absolutely *wonderful* title! One of the best I've ever heard. I thought it was silly until I knew what it meant. But I wish it didn't mean that, all the same. I heard so much of that sort of thing in New York that my head swam. Virginia McFadyen—Mr. Björk-man's wife, who has the ingénue part in The God of Vengeance—said it was no use trying to explain to me because I was "so fearfully normal." That whole company—Provincetown—has been arrested lately, but they are out on bail, playing to packed houses. . . . But I didn't repeat anything that I was told to anyone up there. You are wise not to live there, because even the most reckless of them never, never talk about you. Mencken feels as I do about Mrs. Boyd—he says if it weren't for her husband he wouldn't care if he never saw her again. Louis Untermeyer sent his paper in time for the April Reviewer, but there is nothing in it anywhere near your Tintype, and I'm so proud of that. There is no one else at all like you. Most other writers just seem like the pack of cards in Alice, and when you say I'm indiscreet about them it's largely because I entirely forget they are human and think of them only as creatures that write. I never feel like saying things of that sort about people here, or in Baltimore or Washington, or West Chester or anywhere else I've stayed; but they behave so strangely, and say such devastating things to, and about, each other, that it's hard to take them seriously outside of their books. However, I am learning, and I was much older and wiser this

[1] A novel published by Van Vechten in 1923.

time than last time—because no matter *what* they told me about each other I just said "Really?" Mr. Cabell told me to do that before I left here. I've just been over The Reviewer subscription list with Mr. De Vine, and it has grown so much more under him than I realized. I hadn't seen it since before Christmas. It is *very* fashionable, more so than literary, and is very amusing! Lady Astor takes it, and the Edward Stettiniuses and Gibsons[2] and others in New York, and the same sort of people in Washington and Baltimore and Charleston. The Richmond people are the same kind—none of the writing people here except Mr. Cabell and Mrs. Bosher and Miss Glasgow take it. Dr. Eckenrode and the Writers' Club hate it. Isn't it funny? Carl got me a paper for the April issue that I don't like, and he has asked Ronald Firbank for one for July, and I'm afraid to think of it here in Richmond, because I'm reading his books now. But Carl has helped more about getting papers than anyone except you, and says he has it on his mind always, and I hate to discourage him, because he is so kind. Mr. Cabell's little boy is very ill with pneumonia. I talked to him over the telephone today and he said he was critically ill, and seemed very depressed. Of course it will be much better if the child dies before Mr. Cabell discovers that he is really abnormal, but all the same it will break Mr. Cabell's heart because Ballard is the only thing he really cares about except his books. Mrs. Richard Crane has finished furnishing Westover. We are going to ask her here next week. She and Mr. Crane are living at the Jefferson and spending weekends there now. She is very pretty, and someone will take you down there if you like, when you come again. Mr. Crane was minister to Czecho-Slovakia for awhile, and his father to China, and they have some very nice things. She is going to have David Bruce there this spring or summer, and I've promised to get Amélie to ask him to Castle Hill just for the night. Mrs. Archer Jones wants to drive you around. Mr. Jones is crazy about you. They are just back from New Orleans and Charleston and she has a lot of clothes and is giving some parties—one for Mrs. Oliver Iselin tomorrow night. Mrs. Iselin is the one who lives at Aiken and Southampton, but she has bought a country place in Virginia where

[2] The Charles Dana Gibsons.

she comes quite often, and has horses, and Mrs. Jones' athletic daughter adores her. Mr. Jones is suddenly taking a great interest in The Reviewer—I think you must have put it into his head—and has some business ideas for it. Louise Burleigh's time is up with the Little Theatre League, and Mrs. Jones put on a rather ordinary play Thursday evening in which Emma Gray was incredibly good—better than anything amateur I've ever seen, and better than some on Broadway. The Little Theatre here bores me horribly, and I hate amateur plays and am very prejudiced about them, but Emma Gray really excited me. I haven't had a real illusion from any acting in years except Charles Gilpin's[3] in The Emperor Jones—I missed the Moscow Theatre—but this was rather extraordinary. You remember, you were impressed by her in the dreadful Passionate Pilgrim. Well, she was even better this time. I didn't dream she had so much temperament and I could murder Billy Trigg when I see his complacency and think of what she might have had—with her beauty, her breeding, her temperament, and her gorgeous voice. But I think this play was quite good for her, and the things that people told her afterward. She has decided to get thin again now, and she told me she would do it as soon as possible. I don't think she will ever have anymore children either and this last won't be a baby much longer. She has made me frantic during these last months, because she can be one of the loveliest and most magnetic people—universally so, I mean—that I've ever seen, and it is wicked for her to let go. Before she married Billy men adored her, and I've always believed she had talent too—but too much money and a conservative family. Apart from liking her—as I do—it infuriates me from an artistic standpoint. She and Delia Carrington have an act in Godey's Lady's Book dresses in the Chauve-Souris thing that they are having here the sixth of April and you told them you would come and see them—I wish you would! I'll have a party and so will they. You need never go to West Avenue again, you know—I haven't, since you left, and never did until you came. I think it was a very erratic thing for you to do.

[3] Charles Sidney Gilpin, the Richmond-born actor who had recently starred in John Drinkwater's *Abraham Lincoln* (1919) and was currently starring in O'-Neill's *The Emperor Jones*.

Mrs. Gill, that you liked, has just bought a house near the Country Club, and is moving there in June. Mary Tompkins says she called my thing in the January Reviewer a Tintype because she thought that was the literary name for it, and not *your* name for them, and that you were overcome with mirth. I don't wonder. Have you changed your mind about sending me your bibliography? It is very indelicate of me to speak of it again. Abdullah has just sent me an autographed book, and says he is sending another, but they look very queer with the other books. I had an invitation yesterday to go to New York this spring and stay in a house in Beekman Place and I'd adore it, but I don't think I possibly can. Beekman Place is the only part of New York I'd want to live in, and this is a mid-Victorian house with high marble mantels. I can't stand most of the apartments. The Virginia Garden Book won't be ready until late April, because Prince Troubetzkoy was late with the frontispiece—the Castle Hill box drive, and it should be lovely. Does Cytherea have to be changed any more? I'd give anything to read it, because I hardly know anything at all about it. We want you to come very much this spring—"with the robins," didn't you say? Alice too—she is very fond of you. The weather is getting to be perfect and you must see Hickory Hill, the Wickham place in Hanover. It is one of the best gardens in Virginia. The same people have always lived there, like Shirley. They take The Reviewer too. And you must see the Byrd furniture at the Blue Teapot because you might want it. It was the *Green* one you went to in Albemarle. And if you go to England you should come here first. Don't you think it is nice about the Smart Set and my book? I'd like to get it out in time for Christmas. Please help me think of some subjects when you have time. Margaret Fawcett,[4] who lives in Beekman Place, is very fond of Thomas Beer,[5] and wants to have him there with me. He was abroad this time. She says he never goes to the Algonquin, and very seldom to literary parties. Do you like him? Patterson Dial's mother, that you met at Reveille, died suddenly of pneumonia a few days after I left New

---

[4] The daughter of movie actor George Fawcett.
[5] Beer had most recently published the novel *The Fair Rewards* (1922) and the biography *Stephen Crane* (1923).

128

York. Pat has been at Reveille and now has gone to Florida. She will come back here and not go to New York for some time. She seems all in. I didn't care for Mrs. Dial at all, but I'm very sorry for Pat. I still make up my eyes a little and do different things with my hair, just as I did the last time I saw you, and sometimes I am picked up on the street, but I think I shall keep on. I think, in some ways, Baltimore is the best place to live, because it combines this and New York. You do think it would be nice for me to have a book, don't you, and you'll read my Peacock paper? Please come soon.

Emily Clark.

1008 Park Avenue
[48]   [March, 1923]

These are notices of Java Head, in the Richmond journalistic manner. I've just got them from Mrs. Channing Ward, a Chicago woman who came here several years ago and signs herself Helen De Motte in the Leader. She doesn't write for the other two papers. She says she wrote you last year about Tol'able David, and has wanted to meet you everytime you've come, but hasn't known how to do it. She adores The Magnetic West. Emma Gray and John Powell say she has a good deal of musical ability. A lovely set, Java Head, but your story all ruined. I had dinner at the Triggs' last night and told Emma Gray—they had just been—that I was sending you these. She sends you a message—not in Billy's presence:—She says if she runs away and leaves her family, children too, will you get her a job?—In the movies or on the stage, perferably the stage, so as not to waste her voice. Somebody should stir Billy up. Emma Gray will have lots and lots of money when her mother dies, and I think then she ought to endow her two children and leave them. She has had a girl here from Philadelphia who knows Harriet Sherwood, who is here for a few days, and I asked them here together. I'd never talked to Harriet before and I think she is rather nice. She told Emma Gray and Delia that you were the most attractive person she'd ever met. I'm bursting with excitement, and I can't tell Mr. Cabell because the little boy still may be dying, and I'm obliged to tell you at once. I don't know if I told you that I met old Dr. Clifford Smyth in New York, who has the International Book Review. He told me he might send me a book, because I told him I could do it, and because of what you wrote Mr. Maurice I asked him if he'd like you or Mr. Cabell or Mr. Mencken to tell him so. He said no, that The Reviewer spoke for itself and me. He was perfectly sweet, though very vague, and I didn't take it seriously. But I think he liked my review in the Tribune—although it was rotten because I hadn't written any since The Reviewer first started and Burton Rascoe killed the best part— I had such a nice letter from him today saying he liked my things and he was sending me two novels to review in that mail. He didn't say what they were. And was going to send others. I think criticism is futile and boring, but I'm so glad he wants me to do it, and I like having things in several different places. Besides, I think this is far more distinguished than the Tribune, because you did Hugh Wiley[1] for it in February, and Carl had Machen. I'll be thrilled to the core at being in what you were in, but of course I won't have much space. *Don't* you think it is nice, this and the Tribune and the Smart Set serial and the book prospect all happening in two weeks? And think how I plagued you this winter and last summer about wanting to write for other things right away. And you said it would happen in time—I'm so ashamed of myself. I had a wonderful letter about The Reviewer today from Baltimore. I love Baltimore and wish I could import about six of the men there for my personal use here. I like them better than Richmond or New York ones. McKean Meiere wrote from there this week that Léon Bakst[2] was staying with Mrs. John Garrett, a very rich woman there, to paint her, and he'd just

[1] Author of Negro stories, such as *The Wildcat* (1920) and *Lily* (1923).
[2] Lev Samoilovich Bakst, the famous stage designer for Russian ballet productions.

had dinner with him and thought he'd write for The Reviewer. But I don't think he would be much good for us. Amélie met him in New York this winter at a party for her and Clare Sheridan,[3] and liked him. Billy Trigg said last night he'd buy fifty copies of my book to give for Christmas if it were out then, and so would lots of others. But sometimes I wonder if anybody would really like it. Mencken seems to think so, but I don't know. I've suddenly begun to get fat. I began drinking milk several months ago, hoping it would happen, and it has just begun to take effect. I'm so pleased, because I can stop it when I want to. Perhaps it is the Smart Set and not the milk. Ida Burke is going to spend two weeks here in April. She said last time she was here that she wanted to show you Fairfax, and that if you wrote about Virginia you ought to see it. It is the most historic of the counties, with beautiful houses, very old ones, and she has a very nice car. It is quite near Washington. I've done nothing but work this week, and have seen almost no one. I don't know how long it will last. But I feel very uncertain about the book. I think you are more wonderful than I've ever thought. Mr. Conrad may come to Richmond this spring to see John Powell. Do you think he'll write for The Reviewer? I have such a nice hat now. Everyone thinks it is the best I've ever had. Is Cytherea finished? I hope you think everything I've told you is exciting.

Emily Clark.

It was Mr. Meiere who gave me the party that Harry Black came to, and Mr. Black has given The Reviewer another notice.

[3] Mrs. Clare Consuelo Sheridan, author of several books about her travels.

If you are buying Virginia books—I think you said you were, get Mr. William Cabell Bruce's Life of John Randolph of Roanoke —(Putnam). It is very fine, one of the best things of the kind that has been done, and includes a great deal of Southern Virginia besides Randolph himself. He used some of our letters. Mencken says Philip Alexander Bruce's History of Virginia is the best history written in America, but we have that here if you ever want to read it. We haven't the Randolph one. Mencken, I hear, is going to tea with Mrs. Arthur Kinsolving in St. Paul's Rectory in Baltimore, to meet a Harvard professor. It is the most extraordinary thing I ever heard, but I understand it is true. He will probably join the Maryland Club soon, and go to the Country Club Saturday evenings. I am worried about Horrible Henry, as Harry Black calls him. Edward Bierstadt, I know, although no one has told me, wrote the Bookman paper about Mr. Cabell.[1] It came to me like a flash, and Mr. Cabell believes it too. So does Hunter Stagg. I don't know why I didn't think of it long ago. The part about Mr. Cabell's ignorance of history, sociology and economics gives Mr. Bierstadt away absolutely, and no one but him would be irritated by Mr. Cabell's dislike of Woodrow Wilson. He has been hard up, you know, and has done all sorts of things— even sold all his first editions and his correspondence with Mr. Cabell and Lord Dunsany. You must read the Randolph book. John Randolph was the most brilliant and interesting, and in some ways the most aristocratic, man who ever lived in Virginia, though not the most famous. His letters especially are quite wonderful.

[1] "The Literary Spotlight," *The Bookman*, February, 1923.

Richmond, Virginia　　1008 Park Avenue

[50]　　　　　　　　　　　　　　　　　[April, 1923]

I've found the carbon copy of Stuffed Peacocks and am sending it now. And an hour ago came a letter from Mencken, enclosing the carbon of White Angora in the April Reviewer. His letter this time was the best yet—he said Angora was enormously good and would do perfectly for my book; and that I must go straight on writing the book, but not to hurry, because Mr. Knopf would print it instantly. He also said it would have a very good chance of success. He gave me an outline for it, and said I must call it just "Virginia." I hadn't even thought of a name yet. He said I must just go on putting into the book anything that came into my head, and that all of it that wasn't needed for The Reviewer I must send him with a view to the Smart Set, because he likes my things a lot. He says I've found just the subjects for me—that those first little things, in The Reviewer last year, were good practice for style, but that now I must go on with this, because nothing like it has been done here. He said too, that my paper on Richmond, which I hadn't thought could be used again, would make a good preface. He wants me to do some colored people next, and then some people who have recently come to the top socially in Virginia. But I dread going into that—I can do the remnants of the old régime so much better, see them so much more clearly, than the new people, or the people of my age. But I'll try. Do *you* think "Virginia" is a good title?—I don't know. Frances Newman wrote today that she wanted to write a disagreeable paper about France for the July Reviewer, a paper that no one would print but me. It's all very well for her to be disagreeable about France, but I hate to think of what may happen to me when I get through being disagreeable about Virginia. I'll probably have to go and publish The Reviewer in Beekman Place, where I hope you will visit me. They have colored servants from Virginia there, and long mirrors like ours, and dining-rooms with candles and flowers, that aren't used for anything *but* dining-rooms. It is the only part of literary or artistic New York that I can endure. Do you think, when I've done about a dozen hateful chapters, I might insert Amélie and Castle Hill, done romantically, in the grand manner? I'm so excited, and shall write another paper this week, for the Smart Set this time; and then one for the July Reviewer. I'm writing another review for Mr. Rascoe soon, but—I'm hopeless contrary—though I've wanted to do some reviews because I thought Hunter and Frances were getting good practice with them, now that I'm doing them I'm bored to death, and can't get my mind on anything but Virginia and the aborigines. Please tell me what you think about this. I want to know what you think more than what anyone else does. And suggest something if you can, because *you* know Virginia too, and I need suggestions. Those I could get from people here would be no good whatever. Mencken seems very interested. It is only in the last few months that he has seemed excited about my things. His family is getting well now. I do want to get something done while I'm still young and it is fun. Please write me—I *wish* I could talk to you about it. There is no one here who is any good, and even Mr. Cabell is shut up with his little boy. Tell me about Cytherea. I wish you'd come down here. I hope you don't mind being asked to read these.

Emily.

Of course there are things in both these papers that are fiction, but the larger part is true.

[51]   [April, 1923]

Do you like The Reviewer this month? Mr. Cabell thinks The
King Had Seven Wives is a masterpiece. It is certainly a masterpiece
of imitation—the author is seventeen, and she sent Mr. Cabell the
paper and he gave it to me, just as Carl did Henrie Waste's.[1] Mr.
Cabell is delighted and very flattered, and says Elizabeth Nelson[2] is
brilliant. His little boy is getting better now, and I think it is a great
pity, but he is almost bubbling, for him. The High Place[3] will be
out in August, he says. Henrie Waste is really a Stettheimer, sister
of Florine, and Carl calls her a young author, but Hunter says she
looks over thirty-five. I'm so glad the Tintype is in this issue, because
it makes it entirely different. I like every issue with a Tintype better
than the others. Don't you think Hunter's review of Many Marriages[4] is good? But I don't like the book. He sat next [to] Sherwood Anderson at John Farrar's Bookman lunch, and he wanted to
know about the South and slavery and our attitude toward the
negroes, and I was so annoyed, because Hunter knows nothing at
all about it. I'm quite sure that neither of his grandparents ever
owned a slave, and Hunter has no right to any attitude toward the
negroes. But he is working hard and I am pleased with him. He said
Dr. Canby[5] and everybody at the Bookman party treated The Reviewer with great respect. I've just been to a party for Stephen Lea-
cock at the Country Club, and he is very tiresome. I was the only
person there who wasn't middle-aged. He told jokes all the time
and quoted things Irvin Cobb said to him. He knows Hugh Walpole. Mrs. Caperton and Mrs. Archer Jones locked horns though,
and that was very amusing. Mrs. Jones' son, Osborne, is rushing

[1] Henrie Waste (pseudonym for Ettie Stettheimer) had recently had a first
novel, Love Days, accepted by Knopf, and it had already created a stir among
several critics who had seen it in manuscript or in proof.

[2] Elizabeth Nelson had contributed the story "The King Had Seven Wives" to
The Reviewer.

[3] Cabell's new novel.

[4] The novel by Sherwood Anderson, published in 1923.

[5] Editor of The Literary Review of the New York Evening Post from 1920 to
1924, when with several associates he founded The Saturday Review of Literature.

Helena, and it worries her. Helena, by the way, is going to be presented at court in London this summer—you know they have very impressive relatives in England, baronets and bishops and a distant earl. And she will be one of the prettiest things that has ever been seen there, but she hasn't any money, and Mrs. Caperton says they need it over there desperately now. That is why they sent the celebrated Lady Ursula and Wanda to visit her here. Well, some man at the Club told Mrs. Caperton how pretty her daughters were, and she repeated what you said to Sara at Mrs. Jones' party about pretty, attractive girls not needing to know anything. And Mrs. Caperton said they did know something, and that in spite of looking like wonderful desserts—that isn't what she said but something like that—they were really very efficient. She said, "Emily, *you* know they are efficient," and I said they certainly were. And Mrs. Jones drawled out, "They dress efficiently, beyond a doubt—remarkably picturesque little creatures." But Mrs. Caperton wasn't a bit dashed. Helena sat in Osborne's lap at a Sunday night supper there not long ago, and ate her salad, and I don't think Mrs. Jones liked it. I shall have a Caperton—their number is unlimited, you know—to see you next time you are here. I went to a very young party by accident not long ago, and talked to a boy younger than any I've seen for years, and didn't entirely realize before how utterly they'd changed since I was the age of that party. The masculine methods are especially startling. They don't stop for amenities of any kind. One remark especially. I'll tell you about it when I see you, for a story for the Post. But I think I shall be a recluse for awhile now, like Miss Willa Cather, because I don't know anything at all and I don't see how I can write a book. I am depressed about it—do you think I need to have read a great deal before I can write a book about Virginia? Did you think the papers I sent you were rotten? I've been afraid you did, because I haven't heard. I was ever so glad to get your letter, and when you have time I'd like to know if you think they are any good. Because Mr. Mencken is really very easily pleased. He even thinks Scott Fitzgerald writes well. Mr. Cabell said he saw in the Times last Sunday that you were in California, but he didn't know whether it referred to last year, or now. I didn't think it could be true, because you didn't think you were going when you wrote me. *Are* you in California with Mr. Walpole? Mr. Cabell says he is coming here in June. I wish you'd come too, because I want to see him without Mr. Cabell. Please tell him to come and see me. I'll invite him here anyway, but I'd like him to come without a party. I think his books are rather dull, but he must be very nice, and he is so excited about American writers that I want him to say something nice about my book when I write it. Mr. Cabell says he will, too. He says all I need now is to get the book written, because all of the conditions are unprecedentedly favorable. Amélie and Prince Troubetzkoy are very thrilled about it. Amélie is so pleased because Bakst especially complimented the Maharajah costume she designed for Pierre to wear to a ball for Bakst. Amélie says I must come to New York for part of next winter with them. She has inspired a Mrs. Wright, who is only about twenty-five or six and has a lot of money, to start what Amélie calls a salon, and she is beginning with Bakst and John Barrymore and Clare Sheridan! Amélie doesn't like New York parties, because she says people who are doing the same artistic things herd together and get more and more narrow, and purely society people herd together and get more and more vapid. She says when she used to go to dinners in London there would be a writer and a bishop and a politician and an explorer and a debutante and a duchess and an army officer all at one dinner, and that is the way she likes it. I think that would be best too. She says New York is just a cluster of villages, with very little communication between them. I think Amélie is wonderful, even if her books are trash. She is one of the few women I've ever seen that I'd want to be like. Sometimes I think it is almost better to be a personality than to write remarkable books, because even if the books do live you aren't here to care about it. Of course, if you can be both, like you, *that* is best. But most people can't do that. You know you said in the Bookman that you were affected by Hugh Walpole personally, and didn't criticize his books, and I think that must be what puts his books across, because I'm convinced they don't amount to much. Besides, a real talent wouldn't waste itself lecturing either. Sometimes I think it is more desirable to be Amélie than Willa Cather, though Mencken says Miss Cather

137

is the most wonderful woman in America. And Amélie is so thoroughly polite that nothing can break it, just like Alice. I can be quite hypocritically nice to everyone until I lose my temper, and then everything goes. And they make me, and nearly all women, seem quite naked and indecent by comparison. They admire each other very much too. But I have an idea that Amélie can be rather terrible, alone with Landon or Pierre. I've never seen her off guard, any more than I've seen her without her makeup. Mr. Cabell would simply pass out on the spot, if I said to him what I've just said to you, which of course I wouldn't dream of doing, because he is truly a great economist. He would have a thin time too, if everyone thought, as I have spells of thinking, that personality is more important than immortality. Aren't you *thrilled* about having both? I told John Farrar in New York that I'd like to write reviews, and he looked skeptical and so I left some early Reviewers, when I used to do some books, with him. He sent them back this week with a very nice letter, saying to write at once for the books I'd like best to review for them. I sent Dr. Smyth two reviews this week. Don't you think I am a very literary person? But I hate to write about books, and in the next few days I'm going to write about Henry Anderson and send it to Mencken for the Smart Set. Everyone would see it and recognize it in The Reviewer, which is, as Carl says, a "family paper." But it will be safe in the Smart Set, and can be changed for the book. He is one of the new Virginians, and a triumphantly successful one. I shall write up the affair with Queen Marie of Romania, and Mr. Mencken will think it is fiction, but most of it won't be. But I can't call my book "Virginia," as Mencken wants, because that would be too pretentious, and prejudice people in the beginning, don't you think so? It would sound as if I really thought I'd covered the ground. I hope when you come you'll have Carl for a day or two here, because I find that in February he had some of the Cabell books for Mr. Cabell to sign. No wonder he was irritable when he'd made all his plans to stop here. I'd never seen him anything but very gay, and he looked positively sulky in New York and told me I had the most annoying ways of anyone in the world, and my behavior was unflattering in the extreme, although he was fond of me, and I didn't realize then quite what was the matter. So I sent him some beaten biscuit a short time ago, because he'd never seen them, and said he wanted to eat them here, and he was very pleased and said he ate the first ten without stopping. And wanted to know if I made them. Did you ever hear anything so wildly funny? Mr. Huebsch writes that it would be "greatly to the advantage of the social life of New York" if I came there to live. But I don't think I shall. Not unless you find me a New York man with lots of money, who would endow The Reviewer and let me live in Virginia part of the year and publish it, and do just as I pleased. Then I would marry him if he asked me to. Can't you arrange it? Mary Tompkins says you often do that for people, and offered to, for her. And I can be very nice when I try, and I wouldn't let him know, until things had already gone too far, that I was the least bit literary. Because I was rigidly trained in my youth here not to appear so, and nobody can look more vapid, more deferential to vapid people, than me. I need an endowment for The Reviewer, and the only person I know now who could supply it would never let me spend much time on it, or on anything like that. I've just realized I've asked you for three things in this letter: to send me the book, and send Mr. Walpole here, and find me the man I've described. But that isn't unreasonable, is it? And I know you can do everything. I've scratched out the bibliography part, and you must consider it unasked. I've just told Alice I asked you, and she said it was indecent, and I must not. She likes The Presbyterian Child best of all your Tintypes, and she wants to ask you some questions about Mr. Mencken when you come. The Troubetzkoys are very fond of you. Are you going to have him paint you? Ida is coming tomorrow with Taylor, for two weeks. I've been telling David Bruce about Linda Condon—he'd read all the others —and I told him it was the most wonderful because it told *all* there was about women. He can't quite understand it and likes the Black Pennys and Cytherea, which he says is an ultra-moral book, best. He says I'm obsessed by Linda, and I suppose I am.—I can hardly wait for you to see my makeup and my hair. I wash it every six days now, and am almost as dizzy a blonde as the Capertons. Prince Troubetzkoy thinks it is a great improvement. Please hurry and come, if just for a week-end. We both want to see you. I've never done anything about your copyrights because I've never been told what to do, and I'm waiting to be notified. A former Yale boy, Montgomery Evans, has just been down. He met you at Dr. Phelps'[6] there, and visits the Brintons in West Chester. He wants to see you again. He is interesting, and loves The Reviewer and is collecting a file. He is going to England to visit Lord Dunsany this summer and bring me something from him. He loves Linda too, best. Tell me, when you can, about my papers, and if you think it would be worth while for me to write more like items, because I ought to begin. When will you go back to Dower House? Alice wants you to come and tell her the "amusing, significant things," and I want to show you Hickory Hill.

Emily.

Alice thinks I ought to make people leave at twelve o'clock now, if there is just one, and not a party. Someone stayed until one last night and she thought I shouldn't have allowed it. She always blames me, never the man. I wish you would talk to her about it and tell her how unreasonable and embarrassing it is. Your last letter was so nice. I like especially for you to talk about the weather.

⁶ William Lyon Phelps, who became widely known for his book department, "As I Like It," in *Scribner's Magazine.*

[52]   [May, 1923]

I want to know if you like Lustre Ware—please hurry and tell me, and write something on it to go with Mr. Cabell's. I want it back. Everyone, even Mr. Nathan, has written me about it, and I do think you might. I'll send you a list of the Virginia books here in a little while, but I shan't write you anything much until you've written me, although I know a great deal. Ida said before she left that you were coming there for a week-end in July, and that you were bringing Carl or Mr. Mencken, but I hope now it will be Mencken, because he would be of much more use just then than Carl. He could read all my things and tell me about them. Carl is better, though, just for pleasure. Ida said she'd take you both down the Potomac in a boat one evening, and that would be lovely. Several of the houses face the river. It would be a very nice party, I think. The Cabells have asked John Powell and me to tea on Sunday afternoon, and I was so surprised. But I don't know if John will be back —he has been seeing Mr. Conrad in New York. I'm wild to write about Mrs. Archer Jones, and how she uses Poe for the honor and glory of Mr. Jones, and how he'd resent it. For the Smart Set, I mean. Mencken wants some climbers. But I don't dare. I'd explain how she uses that old house and her money to get some things which she can't get just through her personality. But I don't think I'd better do it. I wish you'd send me Proust and the Flower Beneath the Foot.[1] It is terrible to remind you, but you told me to. I do want to be literary, but I can't get books like that here, and you were going to bring me the Firbank one, and forgot. Alice would think this dreadful, but I'm not really embarrassed. Please tell me about my paper soon, and I'll write you a nice letter, without asking for anything. I hope you'll come back soon. It is very generous of me to write you. I hope you won't be cross.

Emily.

Hurry and write me. I think it is terrible that you don't.

[1] By Ronald Firbank (American edition published in 1924).

I do want Lustre Ware back, unless it is lost, because Mr. Cabell wrote something very nice on it, and I keep the manuscripts that
he has written on. Mr. Cabell said wonderful things to me about
my writing two days ago—he likes Lustre Ware better than anything I've done—and told me it had a quality that was unique. I
said I'd write you a nice letter after you sent me the manuscript and
Proust. If the manuscript is lost that can't be helped, but you told me
four times, and again just before you left Richmond, to keep on reminding you about Proust. And you said first I must read him. I
need to, because everyone in New York has read him. No one here
has him except Hunter and Mr. Cabell—the one you gave him—and
theirs are in English, and I want to read him in French. Mr. Hemphill told me that to get things from you, one must insist, so I'm insisting, and you told me to, too. You wrote about sending Alice
things, and not a word about me. Alice hadn't complained either,
so why worry about people until they do complain? I am complaining, you see. When you have sent me Proust, or notified me that it
is on the way, I shall write you a wonderful letter, and another with
what I think of him after I've read him. Emma Gray and Billy are
in Philadelphia for a day or two, at Chestnut Hill, I think, visiting
someone named Ferguson, who is going to marry someone in West
Chester named Brinton. I'm glad you'll see Fairfax soon. Ida talked
lots about your going there, and is tremendously pleased with you. I
too shall be pleased with you when you send me Proust, and I shall
show it very beautifully. And remember, you first offered him to me,
and then told me many times to remind you. I sent you a June Smart
Set today, with the first of my papers for Mencken in it. His own
things are unusually good this month.

Very sincerely yours,
Emily Clark.

The books have been coming, and the letter your secretary sent, too, from the Centaur.[1] I think you were prefectly *splendid* to send them to me, and I am so pleased with you. It was sweet of you to do it, and I hope you weren't cross with me for insisting. I think I'm going to like them lots—I'll tell you all about it when I've finished. They aren't as easy as Anatole France. I'm reading some in Du Côté de Chez Swann now, because I've heard so much about that, but I'm going to read the homosexual part soon, because I'm so ignorant about that, and I want to understand. Ida says if I live with nineteen men—which she doesn't advocate,—I will not be sophisticated at the end. And that I will ask the nineteenth man just as amazing questions as I did the first, and they will never feel they have got anything stale or shopworn. She thinks I will not grow dull. But I shan't put myself to so severe a test as she mentioned. And I do want to learn as much as possible. Mr. Cabell is *crazy* about my writing now. I've just shown him Caste in Copper, and I showed it to Mencken too. I wanted to send it to you, but thought you might be too busy. Because you just tell me my things are "well done," and I already know that, before either you or Mencken tells me so. I want you to say which are best and where they are wrong, and what I'd better change, and make suggestions for me. The others always do that—but then, they haven't given me Proust, but just their own books. And I suppose everyone can't do everything. I still love you best, and always shall, but don't tell me again that my things are "well done"—say something new and surprising, and suggestive. But I think you are wonderful, and I wish you'd hurry and send the six women[2] to Alice, because I want to read them. This is a good time to do it, because she is in bed for a few days. I'll list our Virginiana as soon as this Reviewer goes to press, and send you a bibliography. It will take several days, I think. And I'm sending you the Virginia Gardens book when it is out in two weeks—the publication was delayed because of

---

[1] The Centaur Bookshop in Philadelphia.

[2] A series of six portraits of dream women, for which *McCall's Magazine* had contracted to pay Hergesheimer $15,000.

Prince Troubetzkoy. They got back to Castle Hill this week for the summer. They have just written me about Stuffed Peacocks and think it is my best paper. The Bruces have just sent me Mr. Bruce's Life of John Randolph of Roanoke, that I told you to buy, and you ordered John Marshall instead. It is a ten-dollar book, published by Putnam, but you must buy it. It's just the period you want, and it is a *bird*. Old Mr. Bruce raked up all the scandal in three counties, and told dreadful things about nearly everyone, except my grandfather and great-grandfather Clark, who lived nearby in Halifax. He said lovely things about them, and I think it was very nice of him. John Randolph isn't as celebrated as John Marshall, but he was an aristocrat, and Marshall was a backwoodsman. And he was the most intellectual man of his time, and wrote wonderful letters to lots of important men and women—almost as nice as mine—and he lived in the early nineteenth century. Roanoke was the name of his place in Charlotte County, near the Bruce's place and ours. I'm enclosing David Bruce's remarks about The Bright Shawl[3]—he is very fond of the story—in a letter from him last week. It hasn't been here yet. Why *did* they make Dorothy Gish a star? No one that I know thinks she has either beauty, charm or talent. Pat Dial says she is extremely good and kind, and has all the bourgeois virtues, even to sleeping in the same room with her husband with her hair in curlers and white vaseline on her lashes. But those are scarcely qualifications for the stage. I went to see Fury not long ago because Pat was in it, and she was infinitely better than Miss Gish, who has such absurd small-town mannerisms, and even more absurd legs. I liked Mr. Barthelmess enormously in Tol'able David, but I don't especially care for him any more, because he is always just that in everything. I do think the movies are hopeless. I'm also enclosing an editorial from yesterday's Baltimore (Morning) Sun which will amuse you, and probably irritated Mencken. You know his paper, the Evening Sun, is very advanced, but the Morning Sun is conservative. This is the first time I've ever cut up a letter (David's letter) this way, and I wouldn't do it now, if it were at all important. I make this expla-

---

[3] The movie version, in which parts were taken by Richard Barthelmess, Dorothy Gish, William Powell, and Edward G. Robinson.

nation in case you again say that I'm indiscreet. I really am not, you know, about anything that matters. Frances Newman . . . tells me that she hears in Paris that Lytton Strachey is addicted to strange pleasures. Oh dear, the world is hardly fit to live in—do you suppose it's all talk, or are they really like that? But I've never heard, even in the green heart of Greenwich Village, that you were queer. Emma Gray said the other day—apropos of Machen—that you said Frances Newman was really wicked, and Mr. Cabell disagreed flatly. He said you were wrong—that truly evil people were never openly malicious, because that armed you in advance, and for that reason wasn't dangerous. He said he had known wicked women, and that they were sweet and charming to everyone, but meant nothing by it. And that no one ever suspected them of a thing, and often felt extremely drawn to them. And he said *they* were the people who worked havoc and were really evil. It was interesting, because he so seldom expresses an opinion. And he quoted what the darkies say about it's being more deadly to use molasses than vinegar when you are trying to catch flies and break their wings. I tried to find out who some of these deadly females are, but, as usual, he wouldn't tell. So now I shall be suspicious of all amiable women I know, and comparatively at ease with Frances. Mr. Cabell is *so* aggravating. But I still don't know whether he or you has the correct idea about wickedness. There is so much I don't know—I get depressed. But while I'm talking about him I must tell you something *very* nice that he said to me. I said I was worried at not having read more, because I wanted to write. Of course I've read more than most people my age here, but nothing *at all* compared with Hunter, and Frances Newman and Edmund Wilson and Ben Ray Redman and all the Young Intellectuals in New York. And I told Mr. Cabell that sometimes I thought I ought to shut myself up for six months and read all the time, and not go anywhere, before I wrote another line. And he said I mustn't consider such a thing, and must just read what I wanted to read, and put all of them out of my mind, because I had something unique that they didn't have, naiveté, he said. He said I'd never get anything that I had to say out of books, but just out of my personality, and I must go on reading just for pleasure. Wasn't that nice?

He is nicer to me since I started these Virginia papers than he has ever been before. And Mencken wrote yesterday and said Mr. Nathan liked the papers just as much as he did, and please to hurry and send them some more. And Ernest Boyd wrote today, and said Mr. Mencken had told him about it, and he was sending congratulations. I was very impressed with that. And Carl wrote and said they were good enough to cause riots here, and that I had been very cruel to him because I hadn't written. He said Fania Marinoff was opening in Captain Applejack in Washington and that he might go down there in a week or two, and if he did he'd come here. Won't you come too, because I don't want him alone. I'll telegraph you when I know. Mr. Cabell says Hugh Walpole is coming here this month for just two days, and that I shall certainly see him. Would you write Mr. Walpole first, and tell him about me and The Reviewer? It would be *such* a help to me. Mr. Mencken says you and he found good beer in Bethlehem at ten cents a glass, but that you both kept perfectly sober, and got to bed every night by eleven-thirty. . . . White Angora made some trouble, so I've told Mencken to sign my Lustre Ware, in the July Smart Set, "Priscilla Hale," because that sounds New England and misleading. I hate to give up my name, even for just once, because I need it in the beginning, and if I'd disguised Lustre Ware better I wouldn't do it now. But it might make trouble for The Reviewer, as Henry Anderson is a director. I'll manage the next one better, so I can sign my name. Isn't it wonderful that Mr. Mencken writes and asks for them? I've taken one of Emma Gray's poems, A Pretty Woman, for The Reviewer. I've just got a lovely dress. Aren't the six women finished? I went to Mr. Beard's yesterday with Mrs. Archer Jones and he said he wished you'd buy the Mary Washington highboy. When are you coming back? I want *dreadfully* to see you. You promised to talk to me about my book when you were here, and you never did. The woman who sold me my dress is a German Jewess—very attractive, and she knew Arthur Schnitzler,[4] and said he begged her to go off for a week-end with

[4] Schnitzler's most recent books at the time were *Casanova's Homecoming* (1922), *Dr. Graesler* (1923), and *The Road to the Open* (1923).

him at a dance in Berlin, and said lots of the things to her that he uses in The Road to the Open. She has a post-card from him, but didn't keep his letters because she didn't know he was going to be so important. You'd better come here in June, because it's cool and lovely and green here now, and no one goes away before July. And you *ought* to be collecting more material for your book. John Powell is back and is pleased with me again, but says I've pushed him aside when he was the first person who knew I had "butterfly wings" and that he loves me always. I'm enclosing a paper he wrote on Conrad. He saw him in New York. It may entertain you, as an aftermath of Margaret's party. Hunter's Russian mistress from Greenwich Village came down to see him this week and stayed at the Jefferson. He wouldn't let me see her, although I told him he could bring her here to call. *Can't* you come back soon? We want to see you. Give my love to Dorothy. When are you going to begin the Virginia book? Isn't this a nice letter? Please write me *soon,* and more interestingly. I think you are wonderful—more than any of them.

Emily.

[55]   [June, 1923]

This is John's[1] article, reprinted in the Leader—I told Mencken what he said about Roger Casement being Kurtz, and he didn't see how it was possible. But John told me that years ago. He is always saying that Conrad is misunderstood, and thinks he is the only person who understands him! Was it nice at the Bach Festival. Don't

[1] John Powell.

tell anyone about Hunter's Russian—no one here knows it but me. She was art editor of Broom[2] before it expired, and went abroad with Alfred Kreymborg[3] and Djuna Barnes[4] to start it. She doesn't go with the Algonquin crowd, but with the very extreme ones—Miss Barnes and the Kreymborgs and Edna Millay and Ezra Pound and Floyd Dell. She gives Hunter presents, and came here just to see him, and does the things you'd think he would have to do for her. I can't see what she gets from the relationship. He came here last night after he'd taken her to the train, and seemed absolutely *flat*. I think she must have started it because I don't believe he would have known how. Mr. Cabell doesn't know about it.

Emily.

I think you ought to write me soon. You had better come down before it gets hot.

[2] The magazine edited by Harold A. Loeb and Alfred Kreymborg, published sporadically from 1921 to 1924.

[3] Playwright, poet, and critic, Kreymborg at the time of this reference was known for such books as *Mushrooms* (1916), *Blood of Things* (1920), and *Less Lonely* (1923).

[4] Later known particularly for her *avant-garde* novel *Nightwood* (1936), Djuna Barnes had at this time published such books as *The Book of Repulsive Women* (1915) and *A Book* (1923).

THE REVIEWER
Richmond, Virginia   1008 Park Avenue
[56]   [June, 1923]

I'm sending you more of your Virginia publicity. Don't you think I'm a good clipping bureau? I see by the papers again that you are in California. *Are* you? Please tell me. Mr. Walpole is coming for two or three days this week to see Mr. Cabell and Miss Glasgow. Can't you possibly come too? Have you told him all about The Reviewer? Please hurry and do it, because Mr. Cabell says I'll meet him, and I'd rather it would be explained in advance. Please come. It turned *quite* cool yesterday, and I've had to wear a sweater all day. I'd rather meet writers under your auspices than Mr. Cabell's. I have another review in this month's International Book Review—Scissors —but old Dr. Smyth is so horrid, he won't sign my name. Everyone else does. Carl has just sent me the blurb which will be on the Bow-Boy jacket and it is very nice. Will Mr. Knopf give me one just as nice? And the new jacket to Peter Whiffle, eighth edition. Do you suppose Carl is by way of becoming a celebrity now? A celebrity outside of New York, I mean. I wanted some information for the contributors' column of The Reviewer, and sent him a special delivery telling him to send it at once. He did it at once, but I believe it woke him in the night, because though he said nice things he sounded the least bit brisk. Carl is lovely always, but I believe telegrams and special deliveries go harder with him than they do with Mencken. I've never sent them telegrams though, only special deliveries. Ida wrote yesterday that she was busy soothing Alexandrians because of my White Angora. She said she would be disappointed in me if I let them upset me. Ida admires you tremendously and I'm so very glad she met you. *Where* are the six women for McCall's? Alice would think it terrible to remind you, so I shan't mention her, but *I* want to see them terribly. I've just read Casanova's Homecoming,[1] and also your review of it in the Nation, which I saved from last year. It is far the best review by you that I've read, but of course it is hard to review a book when you have to avoid all mention of the book, and only say the author is nice, like with Mr. Walpole and Mr. Wiley. We've read your Walnut[2] and like it lots. Mrs. Jones has sent it to Mr. Beard. I like Proust a lot, and haven't found anything very wicked yet. It is most beautifully written. Please send the six women. I have bought a new hat with money from Mencken, the Smart Set, I mean. I feel very proud of it. They have beautiful

[1] The novel by Arthur Schnitzler, published in the United States in 1922.
[2] A new story by Hergesheimer in *The Saturday Evening Post,* June 2, 1923.

149

cheques, with red Cupids and little devils stamped on them. I wish I could see you. Let me know if you are in California, and send the six women. And come with Mr. Walpole. I'm invited to a party Tuesday to meet Mme. Jonnesco, representing Queen Marie of Romania, and sister-in-law of the prime minister. And we would take you. She is coming down from Washington. I've been reading your bibliography, and I want to see Blue Ice and Read 'Em and Weep.[3] Is there any way I can get them? Mr. Cabell has given me a paper about himself for the July Reviewer, by Aleister Crowley,[4] an Englishman. Carl has Firbank for October. I don't believe Mencken likes David's writing. Hunter's Russian girl was good for him. He is going abroad this month for two months.

Emily

Hunter is going with Montgomery Evans, the boy who spoke to you in West Chester. I *do* think you ought to write to me.

[3] Two magazine pieces by Hergesheimer, which appeared, respectively, in *The Saturday Eevning Post* (December 13, 1919) and *The Century* (January, 1920).

[4] One of the curiosities of modern British literature, Crowley was the voluminous author of assorted esoterics in verse and prose: e.g., *Aceldama* (1898), *Ahab* (1903), *Konx om Pax: Essays in Light* (1907), *Ambergris* (1910). Most recently he had written *The Diary of a Drug Fiend* (1922).

[57]   [June, 1923]

I'm *very* excited—Mr. Mencken has just written me that he has seen the Knopfs and they will publish my book as soon as I send it, "if Guy Holt doesn't steal it." Of course I wouldn't let him have it for anything. Mr. Mencken talked as if they would all be shrieking for it. He said he was "very eager to see the next chapter." *Are* you in California? Why *don't* you say something? Mr. Cabell says he has seen it in the paper seven or eight times. Where are the six women? Alice will be hurt if you don't send them, although she didn't tell me to say so. Mr. Walpole was expected tonight, but was taken sick in New Jersey and has to come a little later. Miss Glasgow is having a supper party for him tomorrow night if he is here then. I'm the only person at all young who is asked, and I think it is sweet of her. The others are middle-aged Bryans and Branches and Williamses. She likes my Stuffed Peacocks lots. I am giving Mr. Walpole a party too. I asked you to come to it and I think it is *horrid* of you not to. If Mr. Walpole is coming down from New Jersey why don't you come with him? Please hurry and write me. I want to see you. Everything is going wonderfully.

Emily.

I'll write you a long letter when I've heard where you are.

I'd meant to stop with the card, but I have just heard that the Garden book will be out in a day or two, unless another delay occurs. I went to the party for Mme. Jonnesco, the Romanian lady, yesterday, and she was lovely. She said she'd send me a signed photograph of the Queen when she got home. Queen Marie is coming to Richmond next winter, without the King, and stay at the Jefferson. On account of Henry Anderson, I suppose. The Romanian attaché, who was at the party too, was so nice. His name is de Pilis, and he talked to me a lot of the time and said he'd have me see the Queen when she came. I *do* like Continental men when they are well-bred —they know such a lot, and say just what you want them to say. This one talked about European politics, and I talked about them too—quite intelligently—you would have been surprised—at least I think I must have been intelligent, because he looked as if it were quite all right, and continued to talk. He said he found Southern women very understanding, more so than Northern ones. He is part Austrian, and speaks seven languages. I didn't tell him I was writing a book or mention The Reviewer, or anything, but just conversed politically. Carl says I won't want The Reviewer now, because I will soon appear in the Saturday Evening Post and the Atlantic, but I *adore* The Reviewer and feel that I couldn't live without it.

Carl says he couldn't either, and would continue it himself if I stopped it; that he no longer sets a two-year limit to a magazine, and this is an exception. Not even Emma Gray is asked to Miss Glasgow's, though she's always asked everywhere. No one under thirty-five but me, Miss Glasgow said. I feel very important. And I met Richard Crane, who has Westover now, yesterday. He used to be minister at Prague, and he takes The Reviewer, and as soon as I met him he said he'd read all my things in it. We will take you there next time you come, so you can see how it looks, furnished. He has brought tapestries from Europe. Please come with Mr. Walpole and write me soon. Are you beginning the book yet? Did you get John Randolph?

Emily.

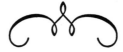

1008 Park Avenue

[58]   [June, 1923]

These are all of the books which, I think, might possibly be used for reference. Most of them can't be bought now, but Dr. Henry McIlwaine, at the Virginia State Library here, could arrange for you to have any books you wanted. Mr. Edward Valentine knows a lot, and you can see him any time. Although he put his head on my shoulder last Sunday and said he didn't think he'd be here very long—he is old. Mr. James H. Whitty, 1700 Brook Road, the Poe authority and president of the "Shrine," is a terrible crank, but knows a lot about Virginia. You'd better hurry to communicate with these last two, else Mr. Valentine will die and Mr. Whitty will go crazy. I wish Father were here—he could really help, and he'd be *thrilled* at your writing this book. He was on the boards of lots of Virginia historical and genealogical societies, and edited things for them, like Arnand in Linda. I'm very excited about your writing it. It is shrieking aloud to be done, and no one down here can do it. It isn't Mr. Cabell's sort of thing, and none of the women can do it at all. I never can, even if I write better than I think I shall. Mr. Cabell can't write about early Virginia. He is always writing about modern Virginia, but the things he wants to say about it are so dreadful they terrify him, and so he calls it Poictesme. But no one seems to know that but me. You talk about early America in those Saturday Post stories, and in some of your books too, as if you really felt it. So do I, sometimes, and of course Virginia is so much the most important part of America. Everything else is commonplace, besides this as it used to be. Just going through those books made me so glad to be Virginian, although it isn't much good now, and put me for the moment out of the mood for my malicious sketches. And think what you did, in Java Head, with a drab, impossible, middle-class place like New England. And what you *could* do here. You *must* write a Virginia book. And of course, as you said, it must be political, because everything serious here was centred then in service to the State and Church. Of course now, it's just money, like everywhere else. Mr. Walpole, as you probably know, was ill in New Jersey and couldn't come here, so I didn't have my party. But Miss Glasgow went on with hers, and I'm sorry you weren't here, though Mr. Walpole wasn't, because it was one of the loveliest parties I've ever been at, anywhere. The house is so nice anyway, and she wore such a perfect dress, and there were only about thirty people and *banks* of flowers, and an apparently unlimited supply of really good things to drink—for women too, tell Dorothy. Gordon gin and punch and Scotch and soda through the whole evening. And a negro Glee Club—they sing better than any other negroes here— sang in the garden afterwards, when it was too dark to see them. Everybody sat on the back porch then, which is quite large, and it was covered with vines and flowers and was very nice. You know her garden is nice too, because it has a high wall around it, and has jessamine and magnolia trees. Miss Sally wants those darkies to sing for you—they are her protegés. The party was just as I expected, mostly rich and middle-aged bankers and things, and their wives, with nothing interesting about them except their clothes, and it made me feel very young, for the first time in years, because there was no one *at all* anywhere near my age. Miss Glasgow made me stay with her through supper, but Mr. Cabell was with me on the porch afterward—he was the only writer there—and you know he says in Jurgen that everyone is most truly themselves in the dark, but he was just as he is by daylight, except a little more expansive, so he must be truly himself all the time, with no complexes. Miss Glasgow asked me quantities of questions and was ever so nice to me—she didn't notice me much in the past, but she was as sweet to me that evening as Amélie is, and asked me to come to see her whenever I could and tell her what I was doing. She said she specially wanted Mr. Walpole to know me, because she thought we'd like each other, and said I was the author of an important Virginia book of the future! Wasn't that wonderful? And she said if Mr. Walpole should come the next day, just for a short time—which he didn't—she was going to have me meet him, though she couldn't have another real party for him. She liked my Peacocks and semed to know about what I was doing. And she told me some *screaming* things about Gertrude Atherton,[1] who rushed her in New York, which I'll tell you another time. She said she hoped I'd stay myself in spite of contacts with the New York crowd! She said she liked you very much indeed, and that you were a real artist, and she hadn't known when you were here last time. And she asked me *lots* about Carl, because Mr. Walpole had told her he was wonderful, and a great friend of his. And that if you brought him down here she hoped you'd let her know. She'd never heard of Carl until Mr. Walpole told her, so I'm having her read Peter Whiffle now. Mr. Cabell and I said bad things about you on the porch. He said you never wrote to him, and I said you never, *never* wrote to me. He also said he'd sent you a picture of himself, which, he thought, would *compel* you to write and acknowledge it. He's given me one, too, signed. I wish I had yours. Not the one in the bibliography though. Mrs. Knopf wrote me yesterday, without my saying anything to her, and said

[1] The novelist Gertrude Atherton, whose most recent books at this time were *The Sisters-in-Law* (1921), *Sleeping Fires* (1922), and *Black Oxen* (1923).

Mencken had told her about my book, and she and Mr. Knopf were eager to see it, and please send them some manuscript as soon as I can. Isn't it splendid to have her ask me for it? But it was you first, and not Mencken, who told them about me. I am worried sometimes because you won't correct my manuscript and write me letters and do some of the things the others do. But you told most of them about what I was doing, and brought Mencken here, and I never forget that. I think you are much more wonderful than anyone, but I do wish you'd write me some time. I've had only one letter from you since you were here in April, and sometimes I'm so afraid you are dead. Are you? You talk sometimes about feeling badly, and if you died I could not bear it. I'd stop The Reviewer at once. I'm more fond of Mr. Cabell now than I would have thought possible once, but he's not like you, and whenever I see him at a party I wish that you lived here. Mrs. Jones has a plan for The Reviewer. She wants us to have our office at the Poe house, and get all the visitors there to subscribe to it, as the successor to the Southern Literary Messenger. And Mr. De Vine, you know, is the great-grandson of one of the founders. When I was going through the old books yesterday I found some bound volumes of the Messenger—I'd never seen any before—and it is rotten, if Poe did edit it. The Reviewer has it all over it in every way. But I wish I were sure that I could ever really write, and that it is worth while to try hard. Emma Gray said you told her you wouldn't advise her to now, as much as you would have a few years ago, because it was twisting things into unintended channels, and that you told her something about settling down. Do you think I'd better settle down too? I'm not sure that I can. You ought to come here now, before it is hot. I've gone about a good deal lately, and I never stir when it's hot. But I hate people, and run away from the telephone and the doorbell more and more. Hunter told me yesterday I had a perfectly dreadful disposition, with no affection in it, and that it was horrible of me to think people were so repulsive and to be so nice to them and pretend I like them. And that it would make me a terrible person. And David Bruce told me last time he was here that I was selfish and cold-blooded; and that I could be one of the most remarkable women of my time if I were nicer and warmer. If I thought that, I would try to feel warm to everyone right away. But nearly everyone is so horrid or so tiresome, and I don't like either kind, do you? I told Mr. Cabell I was never happy, either here or in New York, because here I thought people were stupid and complacent and dull, and there I feel superior all the time, and not at all disposed to be intimate with anyone because they are so underbred and malicious, and utterly lacking in manners and really like insects or animals, more than people. And I feel so hateful inside, that things I think are really going better with me than I deserve. Mr. Mencken told me to let Knopf have my book instead of Guy Holt. He needn't worry. I wouldn't let Guy Holt have it for anything—I can't bear him, and I wouldn't want to be issued from Greenwich Village. And I wouldn't consider Mr. Huebsch either, or Mr. Liveright, because though they have some literary discrimination they are impossible in other ways. I had liked Mr. Liveright, because his face and manner are good, but the last time I was in New York he informed me that he had "made a lot of money in the last year." *That,* to a person who could have no possible interest in, or concern for, his income! But it may be the custom in Jewish circles. It about finished him with me though. I'd rather have Mr. Knopf than anyone—I liked him lots. He is so simple, really like a gentleman. If he wouldn't do it, I'd rather have Doubleday, Page than anyone, wouldn't you? I've met Mr. Nelson Doubleday here, and he is really good form. But Mr. Knopf would be more of a compliment than anyone, because he publishes the best books. And I'd be all swelled up with pride to have the same person you have for your books. I'm going to Ida's for early July, because that is the only time the house won't be full of her rather dull relatives. But I'll be back here before I go anywhere else. Please try to come here soon. Hunter, and Margaret Freeman, are both sailing for Europe this week, and I'm sunk in melancholia because I'm not going too. Please come down here when you can. The next Reviewer will be good—all Southern too except for Ernest Boyd and Edwin Björkman, which will please Mencken. But he wrote me to urge you to write for us as often as possible, because, he said, any magazine, North or South, ought to have you if they could get you. I wish you'd write about old furniture for us. Gerald Johnson, a North Carolina newspaper man, a discovery of Mencken's, has written the most amusing article we've ever had—not the best, but the most amusing. Be sure to read it. I have an extremely good paper on Paul Morand from Frances Newman. I like to have all of her things, on any subject, but I was disappointed she didn't do The Fair Sand of France, as she at first suggested, instead of a literary paper. Because The Reviewer is a shade too literary anyway—it alarms me a little every time it comes off the press. A Western paper said not long ago, that "The Reviewer, edited by Emily Clark, had a distinctively Southern literary touch." It said it was one of the most literary magazines in America, which is very odd, when it has one of the most un-literary editors. You are the least literary contributor we have—Ernest Boyd and Carl Van Vechten fairly *ooze* information. But I like everything of Frances Newman's, and I shall ask her to write about France for October—it will do just as well then. She sent me this just before [she] left for Berlin, where she is now, and it is very timely, and will be good for us, I think. I have lots more to tell you, but I can't now. I'll tell the rest when you've answered this, or when you come. The part about Mrs. Atherton is very funny. Alice was very *displeased* with me when I told her I'd asked you for the six women—more so than anyone has been since you and she were so outraged by my telling Carl that Hunter bored me. She said I acted like an infant, and a bad one at that, to you. The Russian, by the way, seems really in love with Hunter. She telegraphed him today that she did not expect, or want, technical faithfulness, but that he must be sure to come back to her. It is bringing Hunter out tremendously. I imagine she has had to manage most of the affair. He doesn't tell anyone but me, and you must never tell this, or anything. Because I write you anything that comes into my head about anybody at all, that I wouldn't tell other people. Miss Glasgow called you and Carl and Mr. Cabell "the younger men." I'm so glad you aren't really that, because if you didn't have some extra years and Dorothy I could never write you such nice letters. My letters to what *I* call "the younger men" are much duller. I suppose that's why I'm considered cold-blooded. Miss Glasgow said

Alice was one of the most beautiful women she'd ever seen. I wonder if she is—it's hard for me to tell, I'm so used to her. I'm terribly sorry I spoke of the six women, to you or her, so please consider it unsaid. *Please* write me. That would be next best to coming. Are you cross with me for insisting on having Proust? I'm still reading it and I love it, and I've learned a good deal from Swann. And I'm reading Masefield a lot. If you haven't time to write me, then dictate, because I want to know whether you are in California, or living at all. What *are* you doing, and when are you beginning the book? I was going to persuade Mr. Walpole to write for The Reviewer, so I'm sorry he didn't come. Mr. Cabell says we have got on. Everyone seems to like him except Ernest Boyd. He told me in New York that he didn't like him at all, and told me why. I hope this will be of some use.

Emily Clark.

Hunter is crazy about you. He said you were so nice to him last time. I told him I'd tell you about the girl. No one here knows.

Don't ever tell anything I tell you. Miss Glasgow said she would not have had anyone else my age to the party. Do you think I'm as important as that? I think it will be unpardonable if you don't write me right away, and I can't write you another letter like this if you don't. Don't ever tell anyone I hate people because nearly everyone thinks I like them, and I never tell them I don't.

THE REVIEWER
809½ Floyd Avenue
Richmond, Virginia   [June, 1923]

This is The Reviewer's new paper. Mr. De Vine did it, without consulting us. We'll have to change again if we go into the Poe house, and Mr. Cabell says then we must be called, "The Reviewer, Formerly the Southern Literary Messenger"—The Messenger having been suspended only about seventy years! The Double Dealer has just become a quarterly too, but I think we have more chance of being permanent than they have. I'm sending you a very slushy review in today's paper by Stewart Bryan, of Mr. Rosewell Page's life of his brother, Mr. Tom Page. It is not exactly the period you want, but relates closely to it, and might be a good book for you to have. Of course the book is hopelessly sentimental and Old Virginia, and all that, but Mr. Cabell says it is fairly vivid, of its kind, and Arthur Bartlett Maurice gave it an enormous amount of space in the Herald. Robert Cortes Holliday said a lot about it in the Bookman too, and said it was a very authentic picture of an old Virginia gentleman. I'm not at all sure, though, that Mr. Holliday is a connoisseur of Virginia gentlemen. Of course I never knew Mr. Page until he was old, and he was a fearful windbag then, but so are most old gentlemen down here. He was, at the same time, a perfect and intact survival of the Virginian country squire and gentleman politician of the early nineteenth century, which is what you want, and I think you might get some atmosphere from the book. I haven't read it. My occasional conversations with the author have robbed me of the heart to try it. Mr. John Patterson says Paul Morand wrote "The Steamship Tenacity."[1] He didn't, did he? What Frances says doesn't sound at all as if he did. She doesn't mention any plays of his at all. It is an extremely good paper, and I am so glad to have it. I hope though, that she will write about France for us too. She did write me personally something about the author of "The Steam-

---

[1] *La Paquebot Tenacity* (1920), a comedy by the French dramatist Charles Vildrac.

ship Tenacity," because I liked it in New York. But I'm sure his name isn't Morand, is it? I don't think she likes France much. But all the same I'd like to spend several months there and dislike it for awhile. She is going to England soon. Margaret Freeman is going to study *interior architecture* in Paris this summer. Isn't that queer? And another friend of mine is going in September to take the same course that Frances took at the Sorbonne. I don't believe I'd study anything—Mr. Cabell said it wouldn't do me a particle of good. That's very discouraging, I think. I'm even more thrilled about your book than I am about my own. That is the Perfect Tribute. It simply *must* be done. I'll send you notices of anything I see that might help you. You could always use the books here whenever you were in Richmond. I hope you aren't cross with me about Proust, but I'm beginning to be frightened. Are you cross about anything? I apologize, whatever it is, and will never do it again. Please hurry and write me.

Emily.

Montgomery Evans is going to see Lord Dunsany, whom he knows. I don't know whether he'll take Hunter or no. He told Hunter you were nice to him in West Chester, and nice about The Reviewer. He has been to see the Brintons again, I think. Emma Gray has just had her tonsils out, and I believe it will make her thinner. She told John Powell she was very fond of you, and it made him cross. He is *very* cross when I tell him so too. Are you perfectly pleased with me? I don't mind when John is mad, but I do, when you are.

I'm very low today—I've just had a letter from the wife of an old friend of Father's into whose hands the April Reviewer has lately fallen, and she is heartbroken over my White Angora. She says she doesn't see how I could "cold-bloodedly have made two such dear saints appear so ridiculous." That the world is full of trouble anyway, and it is "wicked to use a gift from God to hurt people's feelings and make more trouble." That her husband says my things are brilliant, but she says I'd better not have any brains at all than use them that way. That I ought to write things to help people, instead of hurt them, and that if I don't, I will hurt myself as well as many other people. And that she feels impelled to tell me all this, because she still thinks of me as "little Emily Clark," that her son played with, and she can't bear to see me started in this present path. And more, oh pages more, to the same effect. It is really unreasonable of her, because I collected traits from several people and lumped them together, and if she chooses to attach all the unpleasant attributes there are to her two friends, then I don't believe she can consider them as saintly as she pretends to. Someone else, too, thinks the sketch is about a man and woman that I never even heard of! What do you think I'd better do? Fortunately, my paper for the July Reviewer, that I sent Mr. Mencken this week to read, is about an old servant of ours. And that could agitate no one, because no one, at least will identify their dear friends with a colored woman! In identifying hers with my White Angora, the lady who wrote me the letter said something far worse about them than I would have dreamed of saying! Emma Gray was disappointed at not seeing you in Philadelphia. She likes you lots. *What* do you think I'd better do? I'm low too, because the proofs of my picture—the first I've had taken since I was six—have just come. And I'm annoyed at the way I really look. Cameras are so frightfully cool and unbiased. David Bruce wrote in the same mail that he'd just read my Peacocks and loved it, and I must get rid of my "social complex," and go on. But oh dear, I don't know. But I'm lowest of all about my Virginia book. What *had* I better do?

Emily Clark.

And yet it would be very hard for me to let writing alone.

[61]   [July, 1923]

We went to see The Bright Shawl yesterday—these are the clippings. I've never seen lovelier pictures, but Dorothy Gish was too painfully absurd for words. *How* could she have permitted herself to be placed in such a humiliating position, before an unlimited audience? She must be a person of no perceptions at all. I've never understood how she managed to get by even in her usual parts, with no equipment except facial contortions and uncouth feet and legs, but this was worse. And she was so *common*, and so American, and so utterly un-seductive when she first rolled her eyes at the young man from the balcony. It was enough to fix his mind permanently and unreservedly on Cuba. I think Richard Barthelmess is always rather attractive—he has a nice smile—but he can't wear a stock well. He looks short and hump-shouldered. But he is appealing in a way. The other people in the cast are more satisfactory, I think, perhaps because they don't matter so much. After all though, all moving-picture people look more or less what they are, and that is a fearful thing to say about them. I have never seen even one who was not second-rate, and who didn't resort to tricks. And of course the *beautiful* story was mangled past recognition—and the horrible McKinley stuff. But, as pictures go, it was a good picture, far better than To Have and to Hold, and lots of novels that have been filmed.

But I have no faith at all in the future of pictures—I don't think anything can be done about them, and no one can make me believe that the people who act in them are of normal intelligence. Are you really so very fond of Richard Barthelmess? You seemed to be, in New York, but I don't believe you could really be very good friends with a movie actor. Rudolph Valentino had an engagement to dance here a few weeks ago—he had to break it—and I knew some girls who were going to see him. It seemed so queer to me—I wouldn't have walked to the front window to look at him. Of course I think Mr. Barthelmess though is immeasurably superior to him. I feel very unreasonably cross today though, because I hated to see a story I love so garbled—and the dreadful domestic scene in the ship's cabin at the end. But then, this will only be for a little while, and the story is for always. And the Havana scenes were very lovely indeed. What a pity Mr. Barthelmess can't have a few extra inches, since he lives to be looked at. And *I* could have writhed and contorted, with no training at all, more effectively than Dorothy Gish did. She is obviously proper to her very core. He doesn't look uncompromising though—all the come-hither was with him, which is exactly the opposite of the story. What tortures you must have gone through in New York, when it was all being done. But I won't quarrel about it anymore just now. Did you have a nice time in Canada? I shan't get away before August. Ida's father died, and there were a great many Reviewer complications. We changed printers again, and I had to read a great many proofs because I didn't want to take chances, and the first time they left out *all* the French accents. I certainly hope the magazine will be out this week, since it has "July" on the outside cover! You must be sure to read the leading article, by Gerald Johnson, Mr. Mencken's especial admiration. Mary is at Hot Springs and Hunter is abroad, and in their absence Mr. and Mrs. Archer Jones have proposed an appalling plan. It had to be hung up until The Reviewer was out, but will, I suppose be settled next week. That is another reason why I couldn't leave in July. They have a plan to amalgamate The Reviewer with the Poe Memorial, which would mean, I suppose, financial security. But they

163

want to drop Mary entirely, and not call Hunter an editor either, but have him write book reviews—and just keep Mr. De Vine and me as the staff. They say that Mary is negligible, and that Hunter has nothing to do with carrying or making the magazine—that he only writes for it, like any other contributor. That is true, but it would be unthinkable to drop them, and that the Jones' scheme will have to be abandoned unless they will accept my terms. I'm afraid it is going to be a very difficult situation. If there were any other pos- sible way of getting money I wouldn't consider them for a moment, because I'm very much afraid they may try to interfere with The Reviewer and I want so much for it to stay independent. But no other scheme has been suggested, and the magazine is obliged to get a limited amount of money somehow. What do you think? Of course I can never let Mary and Hunter know that such a suggestion was ever made, and I can't mention it here at all. I'm not even writ- ing Mr. Cabell about it. Which makes it especially lonesome and difficult for me. There is no one to help me argue with them. Of course I'd love to go to West Chester and it is sweet of you to ask me. Would sometime around the twelfth of August suit you and Dorothy? I've promised now to go to Ida's sometime in August, and to go to Maryland for one or two visits while I'm away. July is hectic, with these horrible things to settle, and I'll be glad to get away. It is almost impossible to write, when all of The Reviewer is on my mind, but I wrote something Sunday that I'm sending Mr. Mencken this week. I don't know whether it is good or not, but it is nearer a story than my other things. It is called The Ravelled Sleeve, and is so gloomy that I scarcely recognize it as my own. It almost might have come from the Middle West, except that it is very Southern. It's a "po' white trash" tobacco field story, and I can't imagine why I wrote it. I'll show it to you. I want dreadfully to talk to you about my things—I have attacks of fright about them. I'm really an unusually light-hearted person who doesn't really dislike anyone unless they interfere with me, and the things I write are either so malicious or so mournful that they look like changelings to me. But it is the way they come, and I can't help it. I hope they will get gayer as I grow older and more experienced. I sent you an

August Smart Set[1] today, with my Lustre Ware, signed Priscilla Hale like New England. I hate to give up my name even once, because I need it now, but this subject wasn't sufficiently disguised. Before it appears in a book I'll change a number of details. It was wonderful of you to remember The Reviewer in Wisconsin, and I do like the paper very much indeed, and rather agree with it. I was afraid she was going to praise Many Marriages, but she didn't. I consider it a failure, because he made marriages of all kinds, legal and illegal, so unattractive. I'd like ever so much to see Miss Latimer's things.[2] The Reviewer could not live without you. I'm very flattered because Mr. Mencken is urging me in every letter to come to Baltimore or New York as soon as possible! He has not shown this degree of eagerness to converse with me before. John Powell has left for Mountain Lake, which seems to have become a Home of the Arts. I'm quite sure he is annoying Mr. Cabell. He went down to Oyster Bay twice to spend the day with Mr. Conrad at the Doubledays'. I asked John why The Arrow of Gold was different from his other books, and he said it was autobiographical and the others weren't. That Conrad had *known* Dona Rita. Poor Mrs. Conrad! How dreadful to be married to a man who had known a woman like that. She must get only warmed-over remnants. But her pictures look too phlegmatic to care. I'll be so glad to see you. You are so good to me—more so than any of them.

Love—

Emily.

Alice and I loved the six women. I'll write you about them in another letter soon. What do you think of the Jones' plan? I wish I could talk to you. Give my love to Dorothy. No one knows about the Jones' but you.

[1] The story appeared in the August issue, not in the July issue as Emily had thought it would appear. See Letter 54.

[2] See Letter 77.

Mr. Mencken loves The Ravelled Sleeve and it will be in the
Smart Set. He says it is a story, not a sketch. Don't you like Gerald
Johnson's article in this Reviewer? I had such a nice letter from
Hugh Walpole today, written, not dictated, from Edinburgh. I left
a note at Miss Glasgow's for him the day before her party, asking
him to write for The Reviewer, and explaining that it was the same
magazine you had told him about. Miss Glasgow forwarded it to
him, and he wrote and said he'd love to write for The Reviewer;
that he was finishing a small book now, but would write something
in October for the January Reviewer; and that he adored America
and was coming back. I thought it was very nice of him. I'm *really*
writing to tell you about Lustre Ware. Although your lovely story
about Richmond[1] appeared in the Post the same week that Lustre
Ware appeared in the Smart Set, I'm obliged to tell you that Priscilla Hale absorbed most of the spotlight. Everybody is talking about
her, and this issue of the Smart Set is completely sold out, although
it is unpopular here. I thought, for that reason, that it (the article)
was safe from any attention, but some man ran across it in the
Westmoreland Club, and told all the others. Then there was a rush
for the newsstands. Some people are even subscribing, to see whom
Priscilla will write about next, but I have already killed her. Here-
after I shall appear under my own name always. One or two people
think I did it, but I am lying about it steadily, and there is so much
talk that I'm really alarmed. You see, it isn't as if I'd only made fun
of the hero of the sketch—but I made fun of the whole city, and
of the English lecturer, too, which was very reckless. One or two
people think Mr. Cabell wrote it, but he is safely out of town. Many
people think Ellen Glasgow wrote it, and Mrs. Sallie Nelson
Robins, a Richmond literary lady, says "it is the most brilliant thing
Ellen ever wrote, but very unkind"! I saw Mr. Stewart Bryan today,
and *he* thinks I wrote it, although I denied it. He said it was brilliant, and he wanted to congratulate me. Some people like it violently, and others dislike it violently, but practically *everyone* has

[1] "Oak," *The Saturday Evening Post,* July 21, 1923.

read it and is talking about it. People who scarcely knew before that I was writing at all! Isn't it a scream? Mr. Anderson is out of town, and I hope he'll never see it. It was fearfully reckless and impudent of me, and I do feel nervous, because I'm not of an age yet to take such liberties. Mencken and Nathan, of course, are charmed, and they sent a notice to the News Leader saying that Lustre Ware, by a Richmond person, was about to appear. But a friend of mine on the Leader told me when the letter came, and I kept it out of the paper. I do want so much to see you and ask your advice about my book. I never really talked to you about it when you were here. Do you like Lustre Ware? Mr. Cabell thinks it the best thing of mine that he has seen yet. Caste in Copper is certainly harmless enough. So is The Ravelled Sleeve. Please write me *soon,* and tell me if you think it was dreadful of me to do this. Your story is *beautiful,* and I like it so much. I'm not sure, though, that you could get black-eyed peas when crabs are still very small. It has exactly the right atmosphere. You were very gentle with the Westmoreland Club. When will you have another story anywhere? I always get everything you have, right away. I think you are perfectly wonderful, always.

Love from
Emily.

[63]   [July, 1923]

This is The Ravelled Sleeve—a carbon copy and quite filthy and blurred. It is the only one I have, so I have to ask you to send it back—and I hope you can read it. I hadn't intended sending it until you said you'd like to see it, because I thought the manuscripts might be a trouble. I'm never quite sure if you like my things, be-

167

cause you have never said anything specific about them—only sort of indefinite things about their being "well done," or something of the sort. I've always wished you would really read them carefully and critically and say what you thought; where they were good and where bad. That would be a help. You didn't say whether or not you liked Lustre Ware or Caste in Copper, and if you liked the last Reviewer. Mr. Cabell likes it and thinks it one of the best, but Carl says my paper and Gerald Johnson's are the only good things in it, and that some of the things are *awful*. Do you like Gerald Johnson's? Carl says it is a good idea, badly written. He said I'd make a great mistake ever to let The Reviewer stop. He says so in nearly every letter, although last summer he said no magazine ought to live very long. He says he would continue The Reviewer himself if I didn't. David Bruce saw Carl in New York week before last, when he went up to be best man at a wedding near New York. They seem quite crazy about each other, and Carl has written to rebuke me for having turned down David's last paper—on Walking-Sticks. But I shan't take it. David always wants to write on wines and walking-sticks and things like that. Carl talks to David and Hunter about me, and tells them how corrupt I am, and I wish he would not, because then, the next time they see me, they want to proceed along those lines, and it only makes extra trouble. Carl thinks I could give lessons in wickedness to everyone for years, and says that I said something to him about Guy Holt and Ben Ray Redman in a letter that will prevent him from ever being able to look at them again without being overcome with mirth. Mr. Cabell gave me that paper about himself by Aleister Crowley. Mr. Cabell wrote me today, and says he doesn't agree with Mencken about The Ravelled Sleeve being a story, that he thinks it a sketch. But he said, "to my finding it is excellent." He said too that what I had done so far was "much more than competently done." He said "I now incline to remove you from the class of persons who are going to write by and by, and consider a book inevitable." Wasn't that nice? But Lustre Ware is still making a frightful amount of talk, and more and more people are saying I did it. Miss Glasgow is one of the people accused of it, and I have an engagement with her soon. I shan't let her know I did it. Some people still don't think it's me, because they think it was written maliciously, by a man who is a political enemy of Mr. Anderson, or by an older woman here that he didn't propose to. And they all know that I feel no malice toward him at all. I've never met him except at parties. I rather like him, and would really hate to hurt him in any way. They can't understand that such a thing could be written quite without malice, as a purely literary exercise, just like running scales on a piano. They don't realize either that I made just as much fun of Richmond, and the English lecturer— of everyone, in fact—as I did of Mr. Anderson. I don't know if he has seen it—he is out of town. They all say it is brilliant, and some of them say that if they had known how to do it, they would certainly have done it. But I shall never try anything so reckless again, for I'm feeling like Lucrezia Borgia and Margot Asquith and Clare Sheridan rolled into one, and hate to leave the house for fear I'll hear something further about it. It is such a frightfully small-town attitude. Mr. and Mrs. Archer Jones will be back from Atlantic City in a few days and then the question of The Reviewer and the Poe Memorial will have to be settled as soon as possible. What do you think of their plan? I have two ideas in my head that I want to write about, but it is so hard to write when I'm constantly involved in what is not literary. And Mary Street is never involved in anything, and yet she writes scarcely at all. It seems so queer. I'm most horribly tired and want to get away. I'm glad you'll be in Dower House so soon. I hadn't thought you'd get there before fall. It is lovely of you to ask me, but I shall not be able to go to West Chester toward the end of September. I'm more sorry than I can possibly say, because I'd love it. You see, I have to be here the last part of September because the proofs of the October Reviewer will be coming in then, and there is no one to read them but me. I'm afraid I'll have to be back here from Maryland fairly early in September, although I don't know yet what day. No one else can get out The Reviewer. I'd adore seeing you because I want to talk to you more than I ever have—specially about my book—because I don't trust all that

Mencken advises about that. Mr. Cabell isn't much help about that either. And I want very much to see your New Dower House and your furniture too. Hunter has spent several evenings with Arthur Machen in London lately. He had a letter to him, and is quite entranced with him. He took Montgomery Evans, the boy you talked to in West Chester, with him, and they seem to have all got very drunk together. Mr. Machen takes them to his pet Pub, and then they wander through Soho, and he tells them how it used to look. I don't think Hunter is being faithful to the Russian. He writes me dreadful things. Hunter is lacking in almost everything that belongs to a man. I've never seen anything else at all like him. Mr. Mencken roasted Machen in the last Smart Set, and Mr. Rosewell Page's life of Mr. Tom Page, too. They don't usually see the Smart Set here, but everybody saw this issue, because of Lustre Ware, and some of them are furious with Mr. Mencken for his remarks about Mr. Tom Page. Some are not, but the Bryans are mad. They are talking of answering it in the Leader, and the Times-Dispatch ran a violent editorial against Mencken recently. Of course it is all very absurd, and they ought not to act so, but I do wish Mencken could have let old Mr. Page alone, since he is dead, and nothing that anyone says can affect the situation now. Alice sends her love, and is very much pleased with your message. She will write you later. Historic Gardens of Virginia is at last ready—it was promised in December!—and the books are being distributed now. Some people already have it. I haven't, but I know I can send it to you within the next few days, and I hope it looks as well as it ought to look, considering the time and trouble they have taken. The Reviewer delays are nothing to this one! I'm sending you another Reviewer. I had a review of Ethel Sidgwick's last book in the Tribune Sunday. Have you seen any of my reviews? Mr. Cabell says I musn't write any more for the International Book Review unless Dr. Smyth signs my things. Mencken says Dr. Smyth is an ass. I write for three things now besides The Reviewer. *Please* tell me if you do, or don't like The Ravelled Sleeve. J. B. C. says it is "Sleave" in Shakespeare.

I love you.
Emily.

Isn't Dr. Smith's[1] paper a scream? I had to put that in for Virginia. We so seldom placate them.

[1] C. Alfonso Smith, whose paper in the July issue of *The Reviewer* was entitled "Americanism: A Challenge."

[64]   [July, 1923]

I sent you Historic Gardens of Virginia today. It has a few smutty places on the cover, and inside, but I did *not* put them there —the printer must have, because I mailed it about two hours after it was sent me. The writing about the gardens is mostly fearful drivel, but the pictures are good. Prince Troubetzkoy painted the Castle Hill frontispiece. The whole book was made here in Richmond. Barrister Lodge is my great-uncle's house, and was not built until about 1830. My grandfather's house, a few miles away, was built before the Revolution, but that garden is all gone, and the porch has fallen in, so it couldn't go into the book. Mrs. Hertle, who writes about Gunston Hall,[1] the Mason place, is a very rich Chicago woman, the present owner. Staunton Hill is David Bruce's father's place, and Berry Hill[2] is where Mrs. Crane, who owns Westover now, came from. Most of the Halifax and Charlotte and Pittsylvania places are relatives of mine. I think it is a great pity that all the accounts of the gardens are so silly.

[1] The home, overlooking the Potomac River, built in 1758 by George Mason, author of the Virginia Bill of Rights and the first Constitution of Virginia, and one of the authors of the Constitution of the United States. The owner Emily refers to was Mrs. Louis Hertle, whose husband had undertaken a comprehensive restoration of the building and the grounds.

[2] The home of Malcolm Graeme Bruce in Emily's day. Located in Halifax County, it was one of the few old homes in Viriginia that had never been owned by anyone except descendants of the original owner.

I spent two hours with Miss Ellen Glasgow yesterday and told her that I wrote Lustre Ware. She was lovely about it—you know she is Henry Anderson's best friend here. She said she didn't think he'd seen it, because he'd been out of town, but if he did see it she would let me know, and give me a chance to explain to him just why and how I did it. She seemed to understand that I wasn't malicious about it, but just used him as I would a lump of clay, and became entranced with my own idea. She was ever so nice. People are still talking about it, and I'm horribly afraid it will get into Town Topics. It is the sort of thing that does get in, and I should be ill if it did. She said she liked you lots, and better last October than ever before, and she hoped she'd see you next time you came. She said she thought Hugh Walpole was responsible for some sort of misunderstanding between you and her, in telling you something—I don't know what. She may not have wanted me to tell you this. Carl wrote yesterday that he was sending me The Blind Bow-Boy at the end of this week. He said the first two editions were already sold. He enclosed an editorial from the Sunday Times about Ernest Boyd's article in The Reviewer. I'm always more pleased when there is an editorial about us than with a notice in the book section, because that is wonderful publicity. The Times has had four editorials about The Reviewer. I wrote a letter to the Lynchburg (Virginia) News a few days ago, asking them to mention The Reviewer in their book notices, as the New York papers did, and they published the whole letter as a news story in their Sunday issue. It took a column, and then they added half a column of their own about the magazine, and about what an interesting letter it was! I hadn't intended it to be published. Another Virginia paper gave us a long notice too. Mr. Mencken says this is an extremely good number, but I don't see how he can really think that, because he hasn't said any special things in it were good, except my paper and Gerald Johnson's. He said Rosamond Beirne's was "slush," and Dr. Smith's was "drivel"—which it *is*—and that "Miss Newman's article is, as usual, too ornate and vague. Her style grows worse, not better." All that is word for word, so I don't see how he *can* admire this issue very much. Frances Newman wrote me that she liked "Paul Morand" better than anything she had done, but I don't, do you? I like her "Atlanta" best, and the "Allegory of the Young Intellectuals" next best. Her sister told me she tried it first on the Freeman and the Tribune, and so I told Mrs. Patterson she ought to give me first choice because I had given her her start. Besides, my other contributors write their things especially for The Reviewer. Mrs. Patterson told me I musn't feel that way, because Frances had her living to make, now that she has given up the library, and The Reviewer didn't pay. But I explained to her that I was writing for more paid periodicals than Frances is, and carrying the entire magazine, and doing some newspaper writing here, and writing articles specially for The Reviewer, and going to some parties too. I said it quite delicately, of course, not a bit like that. But you can't reason with Mrs. Patterson—she is, as you said, just utterly stupid. I shall tell Frances though. It will be easier to talk to her, when I see her. I think I'd better make *my* style a little *more* "ornate and vague," and begin to write about Virginia "in the manner of Sir Thomas Browne." Mencken says *my* meaning is always fatally clear, and it is. I heard someone say the other day that an enfant terrible was living in their midst. They meant me. Oh dear, the last ten days have been a *nightmare,* and I am a wreck. I don't think I can write anything more for a week or two. I don't see why the Times had an editorial about Mr. Boyd's article, but I'm glad they did. Mr. Boyd has surprised me so—he looks a little forbidding, though I liked him. But he writes the most wonderful Irish sort of letters, very queer, coming from him—just like somebody down here would write. He said the other day that I was so charming it would be dangerous for him to live in the same place with me. All this is very confidential. Carl says he is cutting him out. I am *very* unhappy—Mrs. Archer Jones has made her Reviewer proposition quite clear—she will finance The Reviewer for three years, down at the Poe House, to give it time to establish itself, and will pay Mr. DeVine a salary, but she will own more of the magazine than the editors do—unless I can drive a harder bargain with her. She says she will keep her hands off, because I have proven that I can carry it, but I don't trust her entirely. It does seem too bad, that when I made it and have got for it all the prestige it has now, that she should own more of it just because she has some filthy money and I haven't. And *with* her money, she couldn't have done for The Reviewer, to save her life, what I have done. I know that sounds conceited, but it's true. I stayed at the Country Club with her all this afternoon and talked about it. She was extremely complimentary to me, but I don't trust her with so much share in The Reviewer. I could have an equal part with her, if I would drop Mary and Hunter, as she wants me to—she doesn't like them—but I simply *won't* do that, for anyone. I came home and cried—something I don't do once in five years—it was very babyish of me to tell you that. But I am so tired, of that, and Lustre Ware, and everything. I'll be better tomorrow though, and will wish I hadn't written such a letter. Fundamentally, I don't believe that I can be really modern or pessimistic. I'm incurably convinced, except in acute spells of depression like this, that nothing really terrible can happen to me! I wish you were here, and I could talk to you. I want *dreadfully* to see you. I can't talk about this to anyone else, and I'm not really as gloomy and unattractive as I sound. I *never* dissolve in tears where anyone can see me, and abnormally seldom even when alone. And I have some wonderful new shoes and stockings. Miss Glasgow and Carl didn't like the Crowley article on Mr. Cabell. I explained to them that Mr. Cabell gave it to me to publish. I told Miss Glasgow that you were the only person, of all those who have helped The Reviewer, who had *never* been helped *by* The Reviewer. She said that was wonderful, and I told her that *you* were wonderful. Write me soon. I *wish* I could see you. I don't expect to leave here now before the middle of August, and don't know yet how long I'll stay. With all my woes I continue to grow fat. Isn't it queer? I only need about five pounds more. I'm painting my mouth violently. All men like it except John Powell, who says I must represent "a mellow Virginia culture," and not an "Algonquin Cutie." It smells sweet too, and he says that is vulgar. If you don't like the garden book, it is considered a very good investment.

Miss Glasgow likes your Richmond story best of those about furniture. Write me. You are more wonderful than anyone. That is why I tell you about things, even when I have to write them. I hope they don't bore you. I'm so tired and cross tonight. Next time I'll write a really delightful letter.

Love—
Emily.

Tell Mr. Hemphill I wish he would negotiate with Mrs. Jones for me. It would be a help, and he could represent me. He did with Miss Hoopes, you know. I wish he lived here. I'm devoted to you.

Do you think The Ravelled Sleeve is any good?

Mrs. Patterson said she appreciated what The Reviewer had done and we weren't a bit disagreeable. I think she is thoroughly well-meaning. She was very pretty, I hear, when she was young.

(I love you, just as I said last time, and I don't love them)

(I didn't say it that way of course).

I've told you nothing but horrid things about everyone. I didn't mean to. I wouldn't have felt cross with Mrs. Patterson except for Lustre Ware and Mrs. Jones.

Give my love to Dorothy. I am mad with Mrs. Cabell. Alice is displeased with me too, because I've been so *hateful* for three days.

[65]   [July, 1923]

It was outrageous of me to write you all those Reviewer complications last night, and say that I wanted to talk to you about them. Because nobody in the world can possibly settle such questions but me, and no doubt they will be settled soon. I ought to have been very glad that Mrs. Jones wanted to help. I'd much rather talk to you about something nice and interesting than horrid business matters, so don't bother to answer all those questions, and just dismiss it. I feel much better today! And I'm horribly ashamed of myself for unloading my affairs on you, and worrying you when you are busy. And, as I said, no one but me can possibly decide, anyway.

Miss Glasgow said she thought it was perfectly *terrible* of Mr. Cabell to marry Mrs. Cabell, and she didn't believe he could stand her at all. She said Mrs. Cabell was at once the most middle-class and the most dominant woman she had ever known, and that she couldn't talk to Mr. Cabell when his wife was present.[1] She said Mr. Walpole wasn't as attractive this last visit as he was the other time—that he had lost his boyishness. She seemed to think he was coming back next year and just visit—not lecture. Is that true? I saw in the paper that you said you were coming to Miller and Rhoads'[2] book fair in the fall, and that he might too. Miss Glasgow will have a book of short stories out in the fall. She asked questions about Carl, on account of Mr. Walpole. I think Carl is very excited over his increased success. He sent me a French review from Le Figaro. It may please you to hear that Delia Tompkins has had ptomaine poisoning. She is not going to die though. McCaw Tompkins has given them a big car, but Mary still thinks she is ill, and won't drive it. Emma Gray has gone to Massachusetts—Magnolia—until

[1] When in 1913 Cabell married Mrs. Emmett A. Shepherd, the widow of a lumber merchant, Richmonders of social pretensions viewed the event with certain snobbish reservations. Cabell was aware of such feelings and, indeed, seems himself to have shared them in some wry Cabellian fashion. Moreover, as he later wrote, "my wife and I did not ever have anything in common except only a certain fondness for each other," and he had the impression she had never read a single one of his books. Such aspects of the marriage were plain for all to see, but what truly mattered about it was less visible. In Cabell's words again, "this brown-haired, soft-voiced but emphatic woman entered into virtually everything I wrote; she contributed to never so many of the feminine characters in my never so many books; and she provided me with glad reams of phrases very far beyond my own inventiveness. Then by-and-by she made more facile the writing of every line that I got down on paper throughout some thirty-five years, those so remote seeming years during which her protectiveness enabled me to revise all the short stories and novels I had published before I knew her." In describing her death (1949), he added the deeply felt words, "But she meant more to me than all the books in the world" (*As I Remember It,* pp. 11 and 111).

[2] A leading department store in Richmond.

sometime in September. Did you ever hear of a Gertrude Carver,[3] of Merion, Pennsylvania, who writes verse? Harriet Sherwood's sister, Mrs. Leas, sent me some to look at, and says she is often in the magazines. We are having a hot water furnace put in and the house is a perfect mess. I don't like the radiators either, but it will be warm anyway. You always said you were frozen last winter, if there had been ice cream. Mr. Cabell isn't writing at all this summer. He says he feels completely feeble-minded, and doesn't even read. Are you writing? Will you have any more stories soon? I have just discovered that Henry Anderson has not seen or heard of Lustre Ware, and I feel *so* much better. Alice says I'm like a house catching fire and having always to be put out. But you musn't let my communications worry you. I shan't bother you again. You must come down here when our house is straight. I'm *so* ashamed of telling you I cried. Don't tell anyone.

Emily.

3 Author of poems which began to be collected in volumes in 1924. *Jupiter's Moons* was the first.

[66]   [July, 1923]

Carl has just sent me a paper from Ronald Firbank for the October Reviewer, called A Broken Orchid, and all done up in lavender. Carl is very proud of having got it and says he is wonderful to me, and that he had to ask for the paper hundreds of times before he got it. But I am very embarrassed, because it is homosexual. I think, and no one here would like it if they could understand it—but they won't understand it and then they will be bored. So it won't help anyway. Carl says he sent me The Blind Bow-Boy the first of the week, but it hasn't come yet. I don't think Katherine Mansfield and Middleton Murry could have had a ray of humour between them, do you? I'd never be sentimental enough to keep that sort of journal. I don't keep any, but if I did I'd haunt anybody who published it. Sometimes I've thought of keeping a record about you and Mr. Cabell and one or two other people, but I would never tell anything *I* thought in it. And I think it was ill-bred of him to publish that part about her wanting him to kiss her in the middle of the night, don't you? That sort of thing sounds so unattractive to people who are not involved. It is a *great* mistake to tell about it outside of fiction. It will all come out later in the Yale Review too, and make them both seem absurd. I am interested in reading her journal though, and the Adelphi. I think she was very remarkable, but I don't think she sounds like an attractive woman, and perhaps it is just as well she died young, before she became unendurable. Alice is *quite* crazy about her. I think The Reviewer is better than the Adelphi, more well-bred and not so intense. I don't really like any literary women except Edna Millay, and she doesn't sound literary, any more than you do. I specially like: "My candle burns at both ends; it will not last the night. But ah my foes, and oh my friends, it gives a lovely light." And I like the one about Hell that ends, "It is not so dreadful here." Carl Van Doren had a nice paper about her in the June Century, called Youth and Wings. Of course, her being still young, helps, because literary middle-aged women are even worse. Or any sort of middle-aged women—I hope I die young. I shan't ever be old or fat anyway, because no one in my family ever has lived to be either. I wish you'd get Edna Millay to write for The Reviewer, and you promised I could meet her some time. I love her. Carl writes me "Firbank's views on the West Indies are quite different from Joe's." I should hope they are. I wouldn't speak to you if your views about anything were the same as his. I hate him. I asked Mrs. John Skelton Williams yesterday why they had such awful drivel attached to the pictures in the Garden Book. She said they got the people who had the letters and records to write the accounts. But they show few signs of letters and records, I think. Ravensworth and Woodlawn in Fairfax, and several others too,

178

should have been in it. There will be a second edition, increased to two thousand copies, because so many people want it, but this edition is the best to have. I was so pleased a few days ago because an old lady told me that I was more like *old* Virginia, and "atmospheric," she said, in manner, than anyone she knew of my generation. Mentally, you see, I'm *much* more modern than any of them, but she doesn't know that. I told Alice, and she said it was because for four months every year until I was grown I lived on a plantation inside a box wall, with nobody to speak to for miles around but negroes and tenants, and very old books. Most of them here of my age have never been on plantations at all, but here in the winter, and resorts in the summer. I told Mary Tompkins this week she was a cockney; because she hates the country and doesn't know Virginia outside of Richmond. She has never seen the place they came from, and thought I was queer to have thrills whenever I go down the River Road. We are having the rooms papered, as well as a furnace put in, and you must come and see us as soon as it is straight. Delia Tompkins is getting quite well. She is not going to die. I have a bright yellow dress. I never had one before. I shall use lots of make-up with it.

Emily.

Hurry and write me. I've written you *ever* so many letters.

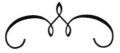

[67]   [August, 1923]

I shan't tell you any more about Mrs. Jones and Lustre Ware. It is ever so nice of you to still want me to come to West Chester, but I shan't do it if it interferes with any of your plans. I'm not leaving here next week, as I intended, because The Reviewer's affairs progress so slowly and complicatedly, and I'm not willing to leave until they are settled. I could go to West Chester around the last of August or first of September, or about the fifteenth, probably, of September. I don't know yet just how long I'll be away. But if you are moving, or at the seashore, or anything, at those times, that will be quite all right. I'm not leaving here until week after next, certainly. Of *course* I'd love seeing you, but you musn't change anything you are doing, or bother about it. I shall probably ask you a great many questions when I see you, although I thought your letter was a trifle brisk about it. Did the Garden Book ever reach you? I mailed it a week ago Wednesday, and if it hasn't come I must see about it. I shan't "pitch Mary and Hunter overboard." I am *very* kind to them, although I feel very malignant toward them for going off and leaving me in this situation. It might be a lesson to them if they got a severe shock. I am very bored and disgusted with them. Mary does practically nothing at all for The Reviewer now, and it requires all the attention anyone can give it. But she feels entirely proprietary about it. I am wonderful to both her and Hunter, just as much as if I'd cut him out like a paper doll. And I insist on a good deal of respect for him, but I shan't do anything horrid to him. The New York Times has had *two* editorials in ten days about our July issue. Isn't that wonderful? I don't believe any other magazine in America has had such an experience. Sunday before last it was about Ernest Boyd's paper, and last Tuesday it was Gerald Johnson's. I'm enclosing the last one. It says we are "full of the cleverest sort of modernity, Southern, Northern and foreign." Did you like the Johnson paper? It is terrible here—paper-hangers, furnace men and somebody pounding on the roof. It is just like being in hell, without the excitement and prestige of being there. Alice and I argue all day long about whether I shall or shall not wear clothes in my room. It is not my custom to, in summer, and they put their heads in my door every hour or so, to look at the radiator, or the paint, or something, when they could do perfectly well without. Carl sent the Bow-Boy, and I've just finished it. I can't decide whether it is quite brilliant or rubbish. And I can't decide about the very last sentence, can you? But he *does* know a lot. Of course I want to see you. You needn't be cross about Mrs. Jones or Lustre Ware. I've had a *terrible* time. I went out with the Tompkins today in their new car. It is a seven-passenger Marmon, and Nellie drives it. Mary still feels unable to move without her family. Give my love to Dorothy. Write me *soon*.

Emily.

Amélie has had to dismiss Marie, the Czecho-Slovakian maid— I don't know why. She is in great distress about it—quite prostrated.

[68]   [August, 1923]

I know you have been moving and are terribly busy, and I hate to bother you, but did you get the Garden Book? Your last letter was written several days after I mailed it, and as you hadn't got it then it made me uneasy about it. And I want to see about it before I go, if you didn't get it. But if you are moving, just get your secretary to let me know, because I know you haven't time. The last Reviewer got wonderful publicity. Besides the two editorials in the Times, there were good notices in the Herald, the Evening Post, the Baltimore News, and in several of the Virginia papers. That last is very unusual. Lustre Ware has ended very well. It has given me more publicity in Virginia than seven years of legitimate, hard work could have done. They are still talking about it, but most of what they say is quite nice. And all the men say it is brilliant—business men and people who don't usually read my things. The Evening Post said in the notice they gave The Reviewer that The Presbyterian Child would soon be ready. I told Mr. Benét that it would be a very gorgeous little book, and he put it in the paper. Have you read The Blind Bow-Boy yet, and do you like it? I should think it might be suppressed on the strength of the very last sentence. It isn't like anything I have read, except Valmouth.[1] *Are* there any people like that in New York? I've never met them. I've never seen anyone at all like them at the Algonquin, or uptown, or in Greenwich Village. I sent the Century my first thing, and Glenn Frank must have been away. Carl Van Doren didn't take it, but he wrote me an extremely nice letter and told me what was wrong, but said part of it was "admirable," and asked for something else, and said he had been "following my work in The Reviewer with interest." So I'll send him something else, because I didn't get a rejection slip anyway. This was my first venture outside the Smart Set. Everything is finished here now and the workmen have gone, and everything is nice and clean and quiet. Mary Tompkins thinks all the time, and *she* was *never* meant to think. *You* started her, I think, and some day you will be responsible for a wrecked life and a tortured little brain. It doesn't suit her at all. Alice would send love if she knew I'm writing.

Emily.

I don't believe Hunter was faithful to the Russian while he was away. He is on the way home now. He is very thrilled about his experiences. He wrote me a horrid letter from Paris, and says I "hurt him damnably." Then he wrote Alice and apologized for having said it. She says he is in awe of me. He should be.

[1] A novel by Ronald Firbank, published in 1919.

16 East Lafayette Avenue,
Baltimore, Maryland
[September 13, 1923]

Did you get Historic Gardens of Virginia? *Please* let me know.
I wanted to see about it before I left home—that is why I wrote you
last week. Did you get my note? You see, there is a limited edition
of just a thousand copies, and I can't get any more, so I want to
trace it if you didn't get it. It is nearly four weeks since I mailed it
to you, and in your last letter, written a few days after I sent it, you
didn't mention it, so I am worried. Are you ill? Write me soon. I
have an engagement with Mr. Mencken. He is having a terrible
time—hay fever and sixty letters a day to write for the Mercury.
Hunter is in New York. Carl gave him introductions to Ronald Firbank and Gertrude Stein, and Carl got papers from both of them
for The Reviewer, which I regret. I wish Carl would use more dis-
cretion. *Please* write me, and if you are ill or anything—which I
hope you aren't—ask Dorothy or Miss McLeary[1] to let me know
about the book. I'm so sorry to write you again, but it is very important.

Emily.

Please don't be cross with me for asking again. I can't help it.

[1] Hergesheimer's secretary at this time.

[70]

You are quite right about the book—I've wasted time frightfully this summer, but I've had a great deal on my mind and it is hard to write. I *hate* to write anyway—I have always to force myself to sit down and do it, and what I am writing is rather different from what I am thinking about, which makes it all the more difficult. Yet I am unhappy when I don't write for a long time, and can't bear to contemplate an existence—married or unmarried—that doesn't get anywhere, so I suppose I *have* to write. When I look at my friends, even those with lots more money than I have—and *all* of them have more—I feel curiously sorry for them all, and think how dull their life must be. And I like fewer and fewer people—though no one suspects it—I won't play bridge anymore and even dancing, which I used to love, seems a little silly sometimes. Uncle John dances at the Country Club every Saturday evening and looks sort of pathetic, though of course I'm not as old as he is. Perhaps this mood means an overdose of Mencken. He asked me the other day to write for the Mercury, and I am thrilled. But David Bruce feels the same way, and he is younger than me. He hasn't been to a debutante party for a whole year, and they all run after him too. Ida has been ill with a heart attack which she has about once in three years, so I haven't been there, and have spent all my time in Ruxton and the Green Spring Valley and here. But all my mail is sent here. I love Maryland very much. It is the most perfect combination of North and South possible. Some of the women I know have stayed home, and practically all of the men, of course. And everyone has been absolutely wonderful to me. I have been down to small parties on the Severn, near Annapolis, and I have always thought Annapolis the most perfect place to look at that I have seen in America. You must go there sometime. Everything has been nice except one horrid experience with an old man, and he moved here from Chicago fifteen years ago, so he isn't representative. He has wads of money, like all Chicago people, and the most beautiful garden I've seen around here. David, I think, is going in for a political career, although he dabbles with writing. It should be easy for him on account of his father. There are three or four gentlemen in politics here—not at all at home—and the Governor of Maryland is a first cousin of Mr. Cabell. David is going in very heavily now for democracy—he won't be called David K. Este Bruce anymore, but just David Bruce. And he and his brother James and Richard Cleveland—son of Grover—made themselves quite celebrated at Princeton by breaking up the club system there, almost. They could have joined *any* club, and wouldn't, and kept others from doing it, which I think was very amusing of them. David always remains aloof, and pulls the *other* way, and poses fearfully a part of the time. He has read as much as Frances Newman, in all languages too, and thinks I am frightfully illiterate. But he says I am the most intelligent woman he knows. Frank Beirne has just been to Mencken's house to a meeting of the Sun, and says everything is arranged according to the rules laid down in House and Garden, which is the only magazine H. L. M. pays for. I wish he'd have me there. I long to see the females of the family. He never exhibits them. He is certainly the kindest and best and most dependable person in the world, but *so* funny with me. He simply can't get used to me, although he is improving. He says I'm the most successful magazine editor he knows, because none of the others have had my difficulties. I believe in his heart he thinks Mr. Nathan rather shoddy. He told someone here that he was "a miserable little Jew chicken chaser." I'm going to a wonderful party this afternoon. The most impressive one for years in this community; a golden wedding reception at Hampton, the Westover of Maryland, and the old Ridgely place. It has never changed hands, and has Lely and Gainsborough portraits. Baltimore people are coming back from the North for it, and people from New York, and Biddles from Philadelphia. Uncle John is a Virginian, of course, but his wife, Aunt Rosa, was a Ridgely. She says old ladies will be there who haven't deigned to go to parties for forty years, in the queerest costumes imaginable, and I think it will be great fun. The Valley crowd is largely new and Northern, and have lots of love affairs and excitements. Aunt Rosa's friends are very quaint and conservative. I scratched that out because I'd rather explain it when I see you. I'm so *very* sorry, but I have to go home next week, so I can't go to West Chester as you won't be ready until the week after. I'm as sorry as possible, because I'd adore to see you and Dower House. I hope sometime I may, but, as I said before, there are certain times when [I] have to be home. I was beginning to be very mad when you wrote me, because Mencken said you'd written him, so I knew you weren't ill. And everyone here thinks I am much nicer and more important than Mr. Mencken. I can't tell you how *very* sorry I am, because I'd like it tremendously. I'd give anything if I could go. Please send me something for The Reviewer if you can *possibly* manage it. I'm so terribly sorry about West Chester.

Emily.

I'd rather see you than anyone at all.

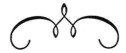

16 East Lafayette Avenue
Baltimore

[71]   [September, 1923]

This is just to tell you that it is *very* important for you to send me something if you have even a few extra, unpublished sentences, on no matter what subject, because of the emergency about the next Reviewer. If you write to me here you'd better do it now, as I'll probably go home Sunday. I don't want to be in this neighborhood the first of next [week] for one or two reasons. Oh dear, I *wish* I could talk to you—my brain is almost addled. I wish I knew if I had a *real* talent, worth working for. I have wheels in my head just now. Tell Mr. Hemphill Mencken says he is *the* civilized man of West Chester, the only one with no Babbitt qualities. I told him I thought Mr. Hemphill was nice too. He is so peaceful, and nearly everyone is so hectic. I'm afraid I shall have brain fever soon. Hampton yesterday was marvellous, almost like a French chateau. A hall bigger than any in Virginia, full of pictures of lovely ladies with harps, and gentlemen with powdered hair. And *such* furniture, and an Eighteenth Century garden with four terraces. And Ridgelys have always lived in it. There is even a little private wood. There is an old Mr. Balch[1] here from Philadelphia, part Willing, to whom I have recommended Cytherea. He is rich and fat and aristocratic, and rather nauseating at times. He says he is coming to Richmond & I wouldn't have him do it for *worlds*. He says he reads French novels because American ones are sentimental. I told him they'd changed greatly, and advised him to learn about his own community from Cytherea and the Black Pennys. He is going to. He subscribed to The Reviewer, and then got sentimental in the garden at Hampton & it was terrible. Don't tell. I haven't seen you for so long, and I want to talk to you. *Please* help me about The Reviewer. I'm quite desperate, & I haven't been able to work here. Send me *anything* at all. I'm very worried. I want to see you *very* much.

Love—

Emily.

[1] Edwin Swift Balch, whom Emily married the following year.

16 East Lafayette Avenue
Baltimore

[72]   [September, 1923]

Have you *any*thing you could give me for the October Reviewer, and do you know anybody who has? *Three* people have disappointed me, and I'm *frantic*. I need something as badly as possible. I'd rather have it from anyone you could get it from. The last issue got such wonderful publicity, and I can't bear to fall down on this one. I have never had such an experience before, but there is just an unfortunate coincidence of several people not being able to write at once. And this is an *extremely* important issue, because Mr. De Vine will have an extra number printed for Miller and Rhoads' book fair in November. Please try to help me as soon as possible.

Mr. Mencken was ever so nice—he has gone to New York now. He stayed with me four hours after lunch, which is the longest he has ever done, and said nobody could have carried The Reviewer but me. He says there will be no difficulty whatever about Knopf publishing my book. It has turned very hot and I have to go to lots of parties and can't write at all. I stayed over because Ida is sick. Are you in New York about Cytherea?[1] I think it is rude of you *never* to write to me, and I shan't write you unless you do. What are you doing? *Please* get me something now for The Reviewer.

Emily.

[1] The movie version, which was released in 1924.

I had such a wonderful time with you, and it was sweet of you
to have me before you were ready. I wish I could have pleased you
more and annoyed you less, because I do try hard to please, and only
managed to be irritating. But I had a *wonderful* time, and Dower
House is the loveliest thing I ever saw. But I can't bear for you to
think I was being horrid about Mencken, and wept large tears of
despair for the first hour in the train, until the porter came and
asked me if I had a cinder in my eye. I do greatly admire, respect
and like him, (H. L. M.) and did not intend lése majesté, although
I can't help knowing The Reviewer is better than the Smart Set,
without paying for material, either. But I realize that he is enormously important, and that I am infinitesimal, and I shall never be
disrespectful again. You see, there are some people in Baltimore
who had been telling me that I was very nice indeed, and that their
world would be gloomy without me, and it was like going from a
relaxing Turkish bath into a cold shower with electricity, when I
arrived in your extremely bracing vicinity. I hope next time you will
be able to relax, because I *can* be amusing if the other person is in the
proper mood. You have to forget though, that you were ever a
Presbyterian child, in order to acquire the proper mood. And I *don't*
think of myself all the time—consider how much I think of you,
that takes lots of time, and there are other people to be thought of
too, only not to the same extent. I think Mr. Mencken is miles superior to Baltimore, and I have said so throughout the city. I think
he is splendid and I hope he comes back to Richmond next winter,
because I don't think anyone who was angry about the Rosewell Page
review will remain angry after they have seen Mencken. He is delightful, and I am so very grateful to him. There was a letter from
him here when I got back, and he has written a beautiful paragraph
about The Reviewer in the October Smart Set. Everyone is very kind
to me and I am very humble and very grateful. To Carl too, and to
Mr. Cabell. But I am truly unhappy at the horrible thought of Mr.
Mencken or Mr. [——]—as you suggested—overhauling my letters

to you in event of any disaster. Hadn't you better burn them, or send them back to me?

I do hope I didn't worry you terribly. Please write and say you are pleased with me. I didn't mean to behave badly about H. L. M. I wish you'd bring him back here. Alice sends love to you and Dorothy. So do I.

Emily.

You haven't thanked me for the list of Father's Virginia books either. They should be useful. And it was troublesome.

[September, 1923]

I shall write you very austere letters henceforth. I'll try hard not to babble carelessly, and I shall speak only with respect of the literati. I'm truly fond of most of them anyway—they are so kind and philanthropic—and I had *no* malice in my heart last Sunday. I had a beautiful time, every minute, and I adore your house. And the champagne was wonderful, and you too. I think you look very nice indeed at home—I like your shirts. And I cannot bear to displease you, and I am a nicer person than you realize. I do hope you aren't still cross. Mr. Cabell has been here to bring me The Eagle's Shadow,[1] and I have told him about Dower House and your lovely, lovely workrooms. Poor darling, he has a terrible time and will have to spend this winter in an apartment at the Chesterfield. But he will at least be accessible, and when you come you and I must go see him frequently, and amuse him, and annoy Priscilla.[2] She *is* such a blight. Mrs. Archer Jones said yesterday that she was quite hopeless, and

[1] Cabell's novel, published in 1904, revised in 1923.
[2] Mrs. Cabell.

that she was sacrificing him to her own petty, provincial ambitions at every turn. She has not enough imagination to see that in helping him she would benefit herself, and she spends her time trying to collect young men for her daughters. That is stupid too, because young men are not collected in that way. If she made her house attractive and taught her daughters a few necessary facts they would have a good time without all that struggling, and so would Mr. Cabell. But she is innately common—I mean it in an un-snobbish sense that has nothing to do with birth or position—and she can't learn. I am extremely fond of Mr. Cabell, so the situation especially irritates me. I've told her how wonderful Dorothy was, quite innocently. Hunter asked Mr. Cabell what he thought of The Blind Bow-Boy, and he said he'd reply as Queen Victoria used to, to unseemly jokes, "We are not amused." *I* think it is amusing though. Carl told Hunter in New York that Mencken and Nathan especially liked it, and he was extremely anxious for your opinion, which he had not received. Mr. Cabell did like Peter Whiffle. Hunter dined with Ronald Firbank several times in London and Paris, and says he is of all men most miserable. He is repulsive to look at, and Hunter says that everyone who passed the two of them in the restaurants gave them amused or scornful glances, as Firbank's face showed unmistakably what he was. Like leather, Hunter says, and full of lines. He said to Hunter, "Mr. Stagg, you are courageous to be willing to be seen with me." He told Hunter that he wanted to go to New York, but was afraid, because he didn't know if there was room there for "a solitary person like me." Hunter told him that many men there would be afraid to be seen with him, and Ernest Boyd told Hunter that was unpardonable of him. But Hunter felt he ought to be frank. He adores and worships Carl as his patron saint, and Hunter said his gratitude was touching. One reason he hesitates to come to America is because he fears that Carl, his discoverer, will lose interest in him when he sees him. He says he can't *bear* for Carl to be disappointed and disillusioned about him, as he has been kinder to him than anyone in America or England has, and he loves his letters. Hunter says the fact that he is a gentleman makes his situation the more heartbreaking, and that he must have gone through hell in the English public schools. He was grateful for sympathy from even an insignificant person like Hunter. Hunter admires his books enormously and told him so. He says Firbank believes implicitly in his own genius, and has not been broken there. Firbank said that two English ladies were kind to him, and received him. Hunter says his face is *terrible*. You were so wonderful to give me something for The Reviewer. I wish you'd send me the Marriage book, and I want to see the August Adelphi too. Mr. Knopf has written of his own accord and *offered* a full page advertisement to The Reviewer for the whole next year—four issues. Isn't he a *darling?* No other publisher has even done that. Everyone is so kind, and Carl writes that he is still collecting things for me. I realize that I am a miserable worm, but I wish you didn't think so too. It would be suitable if you wrote me a nice letter and thanked me for the Virginia Gardens—you haven't done it yet. Ida is going to have a baby in January, and has just written me a rather sentimental letter about it. I had *such* a good time in West Chester, and it is sweet of you to talk to me for my own good. But they are all doing it now. Even David says he is making it a rule to teach me at least one thing every time he is with me.

Only Carl has no wish to improve me. John Powell lectures all the time, even about my painting my mouth.

You have the nicest things of anyone I know, and your books too. And your garden.

For Mr. Joseph Hergesheimer:

This is to introduce Mr. Frederick Eddy, of New York, who is an extremely good friend to The Reviewer. He is a contributor, as well as a valuable aid in getting advertisements from publishers! He also got us our Machen article last winter, and is very kind in every way. Mr. Eddy writes for Dr. Canby in the Literary Review. He is very fond of your books and Mr. Cabell's and met Mr. Cabell here last fall. So you must sign all his books and do anything else that he wants you to. He has some lovely, special paper copies of your things. Mr. Eddy specially likes you and Mr. Cabell and Walter de la Mare, so you see he is very nice and discriminating. I have told him that you talk very much better than Mr. Cabell does, so you must be sure to let him hear you do it. And show him the lovely place you write in. He is very good to us.

Emily Clark.

Prince Troubetzkoy is going to Wilmington soon to paint Mrs. Alfred du Pont. He will stay at Nemours.[1] He spent today with us and I told him to telephone you. He didn't know Wilmington was so near.

---

[1] The du Pont home.

The Presbyterian Child is most beautiful, and I have seen no lovelier writing anywhere. Mr. Cabell was here for tea Friday, and he said it was perfect, and the only book he had seen in a long time that he would not change a word of if he could. He said it was your most perfect book. I like the preface *specially*, best of all. Did you know there is a mistake in the folding of the book? In mine the preface is broken by three pages—contents, dedication and all that—that come in the middle of it. Mr. Cabell said his was all right. It is lovely. Carl has written me twice lately to say he is coming here next week "if it would still amuse me." And that he is coming with you on the fifth or sixth, unless you change your plans. But that he is coming anyway, with or without you. I don't want him without you, so for Heaven's sake come with him. He keeps clamoring, too, about gin and whiskey and his bad cold, so bring plenty with you. He tells me he is going to Dower House Friday, the day the Cabells leave. At least he told me that more than a week ago. I didn't answer until today, and I've just invited him to dinner. Of course I expect you with him, unless you only notify Mrs. Archer Jones, as you did before, and make your plans with her! I heard yesterday you were coming on the sixth, but not from you! Emma Gray, however, tells me that she is to be with you from Sunday until Tuesday. Will that interfere with your plans? I hope not. What did you do with Mr. Eddy? I don't know enough about him to recommend him for a party—I had him here to lunch alone with Mr. Cabell last year, and Mr. Cabell liked him. He is good to The Reviewer, and he collects your things. I was at Miss Ellen Glasgow's today—we've grown very fond of each other—and she is *very* distressed because she has already made her plans to go to New York this Tuesday and stay exactly two weeks, until the thirteenth. She wants to give a dinner for you and Carl. If you stay two weeks she will get back a week before you leave, but she won't see Carl then. She said Hugh Walpole had told her he was very charming and she told me to write and ask him either to put off his visit, or wait until she got back, so she could have the party while he was here too. I didn't like to ask him to put it off, but perhaps you can ask him if he'd like to go to a dinner there. I don't know if he'd like her, but I'd like him to see her house. She has such beautiful food and drinks, and she lives in the only old house in Richmond except the Archer house. And I'd like Carl to see an old Virginia house. She wants to see you too, and was very pleased when I told her you said she had the loveliest ankles in literature. I wouldn't say legs to her. And she says she will give Mr. Mencken a party too, if you bring him down. She wants him with you, not alone. I think she gives nicer and more distinguished parties than anyone. And she likes to meet writers here better than in New York. She is going to make her first visit to the Algonquin this time, and is going to the Knopfs' too. When Carl last wrote he said he'd be here only two days, so I've told him to come here to dinner either Tuesday or Wednesday evening. Mr. Cabell said he'd come whenever I wanted him to. *Please* come with Carl. Prince Troubetzkoy was here a week ago, and said he was going to Wilmington early in November to paint Mrs. Alfred du Pont and stay at Nemours. He thinks the du Ponts will be a good opening for him. He paints very fast, and wants to get to Richmond before you leave. He likes you lots. I promised to have him here with you. It has been a horrid week here about Mrs. Jones and The Reviewer. Mr. Cabell will tell you something about it if you want to know. I haven't discussed it with anyone else. She and I are on perfectly good terms personally, but she is not really truthful. I was with Emma Gray yesterday, and she said Mrs. Jones was a person that you had always to be slightly on guard with and never quite trust. But she also said that nothing Mrs. Jones might say in connection with me could possibly hurt me here, and would only hurt Mrs. Jones. Because she isn't quite our sort, and could never influence *old* Richmond! But, as I said, Mrs. Jones and I are on the friendliest terms possible, and she told me a few days ago that nothing about The Reviewer would ever affect that. But when you come, don't discuss The Reviewer with her until you've already talked to me. One nice thing happened this week though—old Mr. Edwin Balch had written that he was coming down from Philadelphia for two days, and two conventions met at the Jefferson, so he couldn't. *That* was a relief. He is coming later in

195

the fall though! Don't tell that, or anything I write you. He has been sending me his fearfully erudite books which he publishes for geographical, philosophical and historical societies, and I cannot read them. Willing Balch, the one Dulany Whiting married, is purely historical, like Armand Hallett. This one has been reading you and Mr. Cabell and Mr. Mencken since I met him. The Baltimore Evening Sun—Mencken's paper—wrote me a week ago and asked me to review books for them. I was so surprised. They've sent me three at once. Let me know about your plans as soon as possible, and be *sure* to come when Carl does, because I can't have him here alone, and there isn't enough for him to drink here anyway. So you'd both better bring things with you. I'll get Mrs. Sale to open Tuckahoe anyway, whether Carl gets to Miss Glasgow's or not, and he can see Westover if he wants to, whether Mrs. Crane is at home or not. She is David's cousin, and I think he said something to Carl about going there. Do you still want a place for Miss McLeary? Love to Dorothy and you—

Emily.

Miss Ellett says ask you if you will talk to the Little Theatre League the evening of November sixth and please telegraph me *at once* if you can or cannot. Of course you cannot! But I promised to ask you. Mrs. Cabell told Alice the other day that "James was even more trouble than the pigs." *Their* pigs are temperamental, not phlegmatic.

Something quite miraculous has happened to me, so I must tell you. You have borne with, and doubtless been bored by, the sorrows of The Reviewer during the last few months to such an extent that I owe it to you to tell you that they are over. An amazingly philanthropic person in the North has bought the remaining three thousand dollars worth of stock, half of the whole magazine, and put it in my name. Nothing like this has ever happened to us before, and it seems incredible. I am now in a position to deal with the situation with no threats of debt from irate business managers. But the money has come from the North, not the South! If the history of The Reviewer is written some day as Virginiana it will be a scream. I met this person when I was away last summer, and he subscribed at once, and adored the magazine and the whole idea of it. He has been down here lately, heard of the fearful stew we were in and made the magnificent gesture I've just told you of. He has, fortunately, plenty of money. It is more stock than any one person has taken—more than twice as much as even Mary Street took, so it is rather demoralizing, but exceedingly nice for me. Only three people in Richmond know of it, or will know of it, until we've had a directors' meeting. So that's enough of The Reviewer just now. I don't expect ever to speak of it again except from a politely literary standpoint. As a problem it no longer exists.

How does the book go, and when did it change from Bale Hundred[1] to Balisand? And what does Balisand mean? Did you know Dr. McIlwaine was rushing Miss Julia Sully? Miss Sully is an ex-belle, and is too wonderful. She says that although she has ceased to be physically attractive to men her mental charms remain, and that she has always found it impossible to have a friendship with a man that did not become sentimental. Frances Newman is coming here soon to spend Christmas with the Pattersons. She is going to New York in January, and back to Atlanta for the rest of the winter. She

---

[1] The tentative title which Hergesheimer later changed to *Balisand*. This is his Virginia novel, the idea of which he had toyed with earlier. Published in 1924, it became his favorite among his novels because it expressed his Federalist political and social views.

is translating now, instead of writing a book, and is wearing purple all the time. She has lavender note paper and lavender nightgowns. It should suit her rather well. I may have her for a party when she comes here. I am celebrating the recent miracle by writing again, which is by far the most amazing celebration. Also I am gradually being propelled toward Mah Jong. I don't play games, but this seems unavoidable. I wonder if you ever got the Virginia books that I gave you in the list of Father's. Emma Gray tells me you may stop in Richmond in January. Does that mean Balisand will be finished then? The High Place[2] is amazing, I think. The most perfect writing, to me, that Mr. Cabell has ever done; the most beautiful and the ugliest. One sentence, especially, is the ugliest I've ever read in any language. I took Mildred Hackett out to see Mr. Cabell last week, and she talked about you on the way out. She was here Tuesday afternoon and left for Philadelphia Wednesday. I'm enchanted with Jennifer Lorn.[3] I'd rather have written it, I think, than any book I've ever read by a woman. And I'd rather see Elinor Wylie than anyone in New York. Carl wrote that I would specially love the book—I am quite fond of him again—so I read it and he is right. I do. Her poetry has never interested me much. It is not only that she has written of the darling Eighteenth Century, but she has so brilliantly managed to suggest the style without really imitating it. I told you when you were here that I liked a simple manner. The Eighteenth-Century manner is just the sort I mean, and of course that's not a simple century. But the manner is exactly right. This book sounds so deliciously like Macaulay's Essays on Clive and Warren Hastings, and Burke's Speech on the Conciliation of the Colonies. And she has taken their manner and used it in absurd and beautiful ways of her own. I adore the book and I'd like to tell her what a wonderful time she has given me. But it would be silly, when I've never met her. Is she old or young, and why, or why did she marry Mr. Benét? I used to try in my youth to write like Addison in the Sir Roger de Coverley papers, and I've never got over wanting to do it. An unseemly ambition for a modern young woman, but a

[2] Cabell's novel, published in 1923.
[3] Elinor Wylie's novel, published in 1923.

quite authentic one. I'd almost be willing to be dead now in order to have lived then. Mr. Cabell has given Doran a paragraph to advertise the book, although he tired of it before the end. I didn't. Did you notice that the Oriental part sounds beautifully like the translation of the Arabian Nights made at that time? And the "wicked passivity of the apple" in the French part—there is not a sentence, it seems to me, that could be changed. I've written Susan Boogher[4] in New York, as I don't know her West Chester address. Margery Latimer's[4] Reviewers were sent to the University of Wisconsin, but if that is wrong, and you let me know, I'll send her others. We are using her second paper, and Miss Emmerling's[4] in January. Several people have said they liked Miss Latimer's first paper. So do I. I've written Mr. Knopf about the advertising, myself, since I've grown more influential, and he was very nice and is sending it for January. I wish the Baltimore Sun would give me Jennifer Lorn to review. I've more to say about it than anybody will ever listen to. I don't like Love Days;[5] it annoyed me from beginning to end. I don't know why. Mildred Hackett is very nice, I think. Sometime when I'm passing I'll stop and spend the day with her. Alice is going to the country Sunday for a week or ten days, and I shall have to collect some people to have lunch and dinner with me now and then. Emma Gray's two children and nurse are sick, and she has been having quite a domestic period indoors with them. Ida's baby is to arrive in January, and I truly hope it will be the last. As soon as possible I'm going to Baltimore for a little while—it is queer that Carl likes Richmond better, but he insists he does. To me, Baltimore is just right. I've written to Gertrude Carver too, by the way, and sent her a magazine. Did you like the Stettheimer portrait? Burton Rascoe had something about it, but nothing interesting. Dick Carrington has, unfortunately, read The Blind Bow-Boy, and is shocked to the core of his being, baffled too! Billy hasn't read it. I think the only

<hr>

[4] Susan Meriwether Boogher (who had published stories in The Saturday Evening Post), Margery Latimer (a student at the University of Wisconsin, whom Hergesheimer met on his Western tour), and Margaret Emmerling (another student he encountered at Wisconsin) were all suggested by Hergesheimer as possible contributors to The Reviewer.

[5] The novel by Ettie Stettheimer, written under the pseudonym Henrie Waste.

two people here who have it had better hide their copies. Mr. Cabell showed me a picture taken at a Hunt Club in West Chester. You looked more dignified than he did. Mrs. Knopf looked utterly abandoned. Isn't it nice about the money? Does Richard Bale die? And I *do* want to know what Balisand means.

Emily Clark.

Give my love to Dorothy.

I have tried hard to behave with decorum, but I've been in an automobile accident this week, and it has upset my poise. I'm not smashed or scarred, only laid up and rather battered. It was very *horrid*, and a woman in the car had hysterics, which was the horridest part of it. I can't bear screaming. I told you about The Reviewer as soon as I was at liberty, because I was bursting with it, although everybody I met told me they'd heard from you, and I had not, which naturally infuriated me. Then, I thought that of course you'd say you were glad—because nothing like this has ever happened to us before, we've been offered still more money but I'm not willing for it to be accepted until we see how this works—but you said *nothing* whatever. *Then*, Emma Gray told me you had said, at Delia Carrington's, that you were rather bored with The Reviewer just now, and that you'd asked her if she was going to continue her interest in it, and she said yes. I could scarcely believe my ears—it was almost as severe a shock as the automobile collision—because though I knew you were very cross with me and the magazine when you were here I didn't dream you'd tell other people so, specially Mr. Jones. And I minded *horribly*, because of course your opinion counts with Richmond people. I mind it too, apart from that. It isn't at all correct for me to mention this, but if I don't, while I'm laid up at least, it would have an ingrowing effect, so it is much better to speak of it. So perhaps you are still bored with it, and that is why you have said nothing. Even the money isn't very amusing if you have stopped being friends with The Reviewer, because you were its best friend. I wonder if you are now. I'm sending a clipping from Hunter's column yesterday about one of The Reviewer's discoveries, because you and Carl so outrageously accused us of having made none. Mrs. Peterkin is only one of many. I've apologized very nicely to Carl for dashing out of the room and leaving him. It was because I'd been so frightfully harassed by Mrs. Jones and Mr. De Vine; just think, that is all over now. And Carl—in his way!—has made up for the grilling he gave me, for he has been nicer, in every way, than he has ever been before. I do like him now. So does Alice. Although he has written me one thing so utterly ribald that I can never let her know, and he is very amusing about golden panthers. I've sent my negro prostitute story—it is very chaste, not a vulgar line in it—to Mencken, because Miss Amy Lowell has something about a Chinese concubine in the next Reviewer, and the combination would be, I fear, far too much for Richmond. I'm writing hard, now that my troubles are over, and I can write this week in bed. I've written one sentence that is the nicest I ever made, and Mr. Cabell said Saturday that I had my own style now. I've stayed drunk or drugged these last three days as much as I'm allowed to, but I'm not allowed to as much as I'd like. I've always been quite sure that I could die with the most complete nonchalance, but the other day, when I thought I really might, I discovered that I wasn't the least bit keen about it. I did *not* have hysterics though, although I feel quite churned up still. But yesterday lots of stockings came, which was very cheering. One from Ida, with gold clocks that shine, who had just heard that I'd been absorbed in business cares and was being a recluse, saying "Lest you forget that your legs are as much admired as your brains." It was quite thoughtful of her when she has so much on her mind. We have acquired lots of apple brandy. I wrote Carl a note about Jennifer Lorn, and he read it aloud to Elinor Wylie and W. L. George. He says they both survived. The Sun has written for a list of books that

I'd like to review, and I put Jennifer first. They wanted me to take Amélie's two new plays, but I refused because I adore her and I don't adore her books. She wrote yesterday that they were going to New York the middle of January. Miss Glasgow wants me to call her Ellen, and I cannot do it, although she is much younger than Amélie. Mr. Cabell thinks it doesn't matter who you marry and I'm wondering if that may not be true, and if it isn't sensible to do it for Continental reasons just as he did. Ida did that, and is much better off now than Emma Gray and Delia, who married for attraction, and are both married to fools. But I don't believe Delia knows the difference, and Emma Gray has a much more amiable disposition than Ida's. I think Delia is really in love. I believe the practical way is best, but that may be because I have time to theorize when I'm in bed. I'd probably never have the courage to do it. But I do think I ought to travel a lot and hear more music and have a great many contacts, because Carl says everyone writes better for doing that, and I don't want always to write about Virginia. And you and Carl told me too that the best way was to expect nothing—you both gave me a very rough lesson about that. But I thought it was just a punishment for I don't know exactly what, and that afterwards you'd be just the same again, as Carl has been. But instead you vanish into space, and I hear dreadful echoes of you from other people, and I don't know whether you are friends with me still or not. Do you ever intend to communicate with me again? Besides, I *do* think you should remember that if my head was turned, all of you helped turn it, and I got far more publicity than I deserved in a very short time. I assure you it is not turned now—I am living in a world of which I expect nothing, except hard work for a little reputation. And if I decide that money is necessary I know too that I'd have to pay for that. So I'm bored with being called a prostitute! Speaking of them, Hunter is through with his Russian, having given me all the details. He is the most infantile creature imaginable. Carl thinks he has *great* talent and is *extremely* fond of him. But he hasn't much driving force. Mencken thinks him a lightweight. Please put this letter where Mr. Mencken and Mr. [———] will not see it when you die. Why were you so cross suddenly? After being so nice before. Anyway it is nice not to be dead, and especially nice not to be scarred. I have a *ton* of cigarettes and smoke all the time. Tell me about Balisand. I want to know what it means.

Emily Clark.

I will tell you more about The Reviewer money when I see you, if you are still interested.

I have found out, though, that I can be dignified when I'm going to die, no matter how much I dislike it, and *that* is something. It was a nice description of Dower House in the Francis Jammes story. What *is* the matter with you? ...

[79]   [December 30, 1923]

I've just written to thank Dorothy for the stockings, and you too. They are lovely. She says Balisand is going beautifully, and I'm so glad. Will it be out next fall? I'm hoping to get to the country soon, but I don't know exactly when. Christmas here has been very satisfactory, and there have been some nice parties. A most lovely Mah Jong set was given me in a lacquer cabinet—one of the best I've seen, and it *is* nice to handle. But I don't believe I have a real passion for games. Carl has written something about the Sabbath Glee Club[1] for the January Reviewer, and used Miss Sally's name on it. She is very much pleased. In Burton Rascoe's column he called the Glee Club "a negro prayer meeting." Mrs. Cabell has had a number of her teeth removed, and is telling everyone about it with her usual engaging candour—also it will, beyond doubt, be detailed

[1] This was the glee club whose performance at Ellen Glasgow's home was described in Letter 58.

in semi-mythological form in Mr. Cabell's next book. Margaret Freeman is back from Paris, looking better than I've ever seen her. She came here to a tea a few days ago and made the eyes of Emma Gray and Delia start from their sockets with tales of strange, new, ultra-chic life in Paris. A Lesbian lady tried to pick Margaret up in a café. Everyone was enthralled. Frances Newman, who could have enlightened them further, left before that topic was started. She could have told them about England. It was entirely a female tea, and the six who stayed late sat on the floor in a circle at Margaret's feet and fired questions at her. She has been moving in a very advanced circle, and is eager to tell all she has learned. She is enormously pleased because some people thought she was Russian instead of American. Isn't it queer that Americans would rather be thought *anything* than American? I took Frances Newman to Ellen Glasgow's party yesterday because she wanted very much to see her, and she was ecstatic over the house and Miss Glasgow—although I now say Ellen!—together. She said she wished some of the New York writers with wild apartments and wilder clothes could see it. It stays very warm here. I'm going to a New Year picnic Wednesday, and to a party given by your little Helena Caperton, who is back from England after being presented at Court. I feel quite ill from a surfeit of candy and cigarettes and Coty perfume—my Christmas presents ran to that, in many cases. I've just had an amusing Baltimore letter about Carl's visit there, and I bought a new dress yesterday, the most extravagant one I ever had. That is all the news I can think of except that the Jones' [*sic*] have a yellow streak. I'm quite through with nouveaux riches—even as necessary conveniences. I've learned that certain inconvenient inherited standards are more necessary than anything. But *that* is *private*. Hunter called Mrs. Jones "Mrs. Poe" the other day by mistake. Poor, put-upon Poe! I had a melodramatic scene with John Powell yesterday. He is the only person I know who can be melodramatic in these drab days, and it is stimulating. I hope the New Year will be the best possible for you and Balisand.

Emily Clark.

June 26, 1924

Dear Joe,

Thank you very much indeed for The Tailor[1]—it was extremely nice of you to let us have it, and I like it immensely. Would you like us to print the date of writing, as we did with Old Bolly[2] in October? Miss McLeary said it was written some years ago, but didn't mention the date. This will be in the July Reviewer and the manuscript will be returned to you as soon as it is used. It is a very great help indeed to The Reviewer to have it.

I was glad to see the catalogue from Drake[3] too. I'd never seen The Reviewer advertised that way, and I told Mr. Cabell. We have still some of that issue left, but I won't let it be known.

With many thanks,
Emily.

[1] A brief story by Hergesheimer, published in *The Reviewer,* July, 1924.
[2] Hergesheimer's sketch, published in the issue of October, 1923.
[3] James F. Drake, Inc., of New York, dealer in rare books and autographs.

[81] July 26, 1924

Dear Joe,

I've just seen this in the paper—are you making a picture with them? Hunter wrote me something about The Three Black Pennys, and Mr. Mencken wrote that he heard you were going to California. Carl too says you have lots of movie people with you. Is it just the Pennys or another picture too? I'm so glad to hear you are personally directing it. All the directors seem to be so hopeless. And I hope there is someone who looks enough like a lady to play Mariana.

Phoebe Gilkyson[1] said you and Mr. Barthelmess had been to see her—I hope that doesn't mean he is in the Pennys. He was charming as Tol'able David, but had no distinction as Charles Abbott and I can't think of any part he could have in the Black Pennys. It ought to be a wonderful picture if you direct it, but I should think it would be frightfully difficult to cast.[2] I wonder if you know Jack Holt—I don't know how much ability he has, but he ought to have a good manner. His mother was a Marshall of Virginia, and his father an Episcopal clergyman. I read the first of Balisand in the Post yesterday and it looks very nice in print—but I won't read any more until the book comes. Alfred[3] sent his advertising copy for The Reviewer cover yesterday and it was just Balisand and The Tattooed Countess,[4] but he didn't give Balisand's date of publication. If the book has not been set up get him to change the mimosa blooms from white to *pink at once*—they are *always pink* and are in blossom now. I grew up among them in Halifax and I told you in April they were definitely pink but you must have forgotten. The Reviewer is on the press and I'll send you some as soon as they are ready. I'm so very glad to have The Tailor as a lead, especially as I may not edit but one more issue after this. But I haven't said this to anyone, so please don't mention it. Carl apparently wants me to go on with it forever, but I'd much rather write a book now. As far as I can see, his principal argument in favor of The Reviewer is that it is a means of meeting visiting English authors. But in my experience anyone can meet them who will feed them well and drive them around. But I don't know anything definite about The Reviewer yet to tell even to Hunter. Frances Newman is here with her short story translations[5] to take to Huebsch—I don't know why you think her so malicious.

[1] Mrs. Hamilton Gilkyson, Jr., of Mont Clare, Pennsylvania, who reviewed books for the Philadelphia *North American*. She had an essay in the July, 1924, issue of *The Reviewer*.

[2] This venture came to nothing. *The Three Black Pennys* was not made into a movie.

[3] Alfred A. Knopf.

[4] The new novel by Van Vechten (1924).

[5] The foreign-language stories translated by Frances Newman for inclusion in her anthology *The Short Story's Mutations* (1925).

She is so extremely open in her likes and dislikes, and that is not malice.

Carl told me, just before I left New York, that you told him the name of the Philadelphian[6] that I spoke to you about here. And I also decided to speak of this matter, without name, to two or three other persons who are interested in The Reviewer, with which, unfortunately, my own personal affairs are inextricably involved. He (Carl) especially asked that I should not tell you he learned the name from you. I am doing so now at this late period because it has occurred to me that this might be one of Carl's fantastic tales intended only to annoy. If I am right in thinking that perhaps you didn't give Carl a name but that *he* gave it to *you*, it misrepresents me. Margaret Freeman is the only person to whom I told the name, and I have recently found, to my deep regret, that she told Hunter Stagg. I'm sure you will understand my asking you not to speak of this letter to Carl, as he was so insistent about my not mentioning the matter to you. I'm doing it because it worries me not to have things straight. And of course the less that is said about it the better. It was necessary to get a few opinions from The Reviewer's special friends about the life or death of the magazine in such new conditions. But fortunately—and marvellously!—my affairs are not known in Richmond even now. Which, considering the excessive interest which everyone here takes in everyone else, is rather a triumph. I've now acquired diamonds as well as pearls, and that too is not known, even to the select literary friends of The Reviewer here or away.

Wild Oranges[7] is being shown here today, and Alice and I are going to see it as we were down in Asheville when it opened in February. Nothing much happens except my work, and that we are looking at some old furniture with Mr. Ahern. Frances wants me to ask Ernest Boyd to review her translations for the next Reviewer— she is much impressed with his learning.

Affectionately,

Emily.

---

[6] Edwin Swift Balch, whom Emily married on November 1, 1924.

[7] The movie version of Hergesheimer's novel, published in 1919.

Dear Joe,

I've quite definitely decided within the last few days not to edit another issue of The Reviewer after the next one—October. I hadn't entirely decided it until now. I shan't tell the directors or *anyone* in Richmond until the October issue is out. That will give them three months to find another editor if they and the stockholders and Hunter Stagg decide to continue the magazine. But that, of course, isn't my affair. I shall get out the next issue more promptly than the others have been appearing, as I want to be entirely free in October to go wherever I like. All of my affairs are arranged. Mr. Cabell has already written something for my last Reviewer, and Mencken is going to, too, as soon as his sore foot and hay fever permit. I would have asked you to send me something too, even though you did for July, except that you said you were so terribly busy. And if Miss Mc-Leary is attached to your picture of course she has no time to look up old papers. But I'm ever so sorry—I'd *adore* to have you if you found it at all possible, because you and Mr. Cabell and Mr. Mencken have been The Reviewer's best friends and I'd like to have all of you in it together and retire as brilliantly as possible. It is a relief in every way to have settled everything, and I'm sure you'll think it sensible about The Reviewer because it is what you advised in the circumstances. Mr. Cabell and Mr. Mencken approve too. Mr. Mencken wants me to write, and says I'll "roast in hell with Darwin and Ingersoll" if I don't. Carl will probably be annoyed when I tell him, because he urged me to continue in *any* circumstances, but I know now that this way is best. It (The Reviewer) is a phase that is past, so far as I'm concerned. But I'm so very glad I didn't stop The Reviewer in the Poe-Jones embroilment last fall. Because they would have had the honour of extinguishing the magazine. I couldn't permit that. So I proved that I could get more money for it than they could supply, as well as contributors and friends. I shall leave it with a fair circulation, money in bank and no quarrels on its hands. That is more than can be said for other "little" magazines. It is so much better to leave it of my own free will, with a legitimate reason, and to leave it with an opportunity to continue if it wants to. The magazine has never failed, you see, financially or literarily, and it can return everybody's subscription cheques if it expires before the year is out. That is not a bad job, considering the history of enterprises of this sort, and I am very pleased. If I'd let it die at any of the periods when the other editors and Mr. Cabell would have been willing to let it go, it would have gone out in a mess, under compulsion. And I couldn't have stood that. Hunter hasn't returned yet, so I don't know what he'll say or if he'll try to carry it on. But I've an impression, and so has Margaret Freeman, that he has given up all idea of either having a literary career or making any money, and intends just to enjoy himself and write book reviews for the Times-Dispatch. He is thirty now, and tells me that, so far, he feels no urge toward anything. It may be lack of vitality. He doesn't expect to write a book and he doesn't want to bother with making a living until his parents die. Margaret has just been home and keeps worrying about his future, but I think she is extremely silly. But I don't want anything about The Reviewer known in Richmond until October. Mencken said the last issue was one of the best we've had, and specially liked your paper. So did Edwin—it is the first of your short things he has read, and he liked it very much. Mencken didn't dislike anything in the last number except Hunter's reviews, which, he says, are always sophomoric (although I think they are quite good usually), and Phoebe Gilkyson's essay, which, he said, was "idle fluff, Agnes Repplier boiled down." But *that* is a secret. I think Phoebe's mind is very good, although her manner is undistinguished. A trifle loose and messy, just like her clothes and earrings. But I like Phoebe. I can never understand why mind and manner aren't inevitable accompaniments of each other. But, oh dear, they often are not. I don't know what the literary ladies will say if The Reviewer really goes out. Gertrude Carver writes me ardent letters about it and says I must be sure to let her know next time I'm in Philadelphia. So I've promised to see to it that she knows, when next I arrive there! But she may not be as eager when I arrive without any Reviewer.

This is just to let you know that everything of mine is quite settled—at the risk of disturbing you when you are busy. I hope the picture goes well. I think it would have been polite if you had let me know who had the six main parts. But then you have been neither polite nor friendly for sometime—in fact, quite decidedly not. I wish you could be in this last Reviewer.

Emily.

I'm so glad too that I've worked with a magazine, because I learned more about people than I could ever have learned in that length of time without it. And my writing will probably be more horrid, and therefore more chic, for having been an editor. I've given up the plan I mentioned to you of financing The Reviewer after I leave it, as Hunter suggested. Of course the magazine will have the money that is still in the bank, but beyond that I shan't do anything. I'd rather do some quite different things now, and I'm sure I'll be able to think of plenty of amusing things.

If you *should* have anything, be sure to send it. I could make this issue quite thick.

[83]   September 3, 1924

Dear Joe,

I am sorry to annoy, but I want something for The Reviewer within the next week if possible. Haven't you something old that you can send? I don't feel at all badly about it, because this is the very last time that The Reviewer or I can ever disturb your peace again. And when you next see me I may be so dignified that you won't be able to realize that I once edited a little magazine which was the pet charity of the literati. So I shall be a raging pestilence this month if I feel like it. It is very important to get everything together now, for the magazine must go to press next week to be ready by the first of October. And I'm obliged to finish *everything* this month—The Reviewer and two papers for the Mercury if possible. And besides that, a perfectly *appalling* list, the Social Registers and club lists from Richmond and Baltimore and Philadelphia, besides the names of people who aren't in cities. I'll probably forget lots. I do think it would be very fitting for you to be in my last Reviewer with Mr. Cabell and Mr. Mencken. Besides that, I want you to have Balisand sent to Hunter as soon as possible, as I want it reviewed in this issue. The Tattooed Countess, you see, is already out, and I want Balisand in this Reviewer as I don't know if they will publish another. The review copies should be ready now. Hunter has arrived with lurid tales of life in West Chester. People there seem to be as much interested in each other's affairs as they are in Richmond. I hope Philadelphia is more disengaged but I don't know. Hunter fell madly in love in New England and has, as usual, furnished me with all the details. He is quite over with Margaret now. He said you might ask Emma Gray to be in the Pennys. Is she going to do it, and will she work on Long Island? Were the mosquitoes bad at Cape May? Hunter likes the McKenna girl too, but has a grande passion besides. Please see about Balisand as *soon* as you can—I want The Reviewer out before I go away. Isn't it time I saw it? Balisand, I mean. I have always felt I should have a specially nice copy because my Presbyterian Child had a flaw in it. A tall paper copy would not, I think, be inappropriate; first, because the Presbyterian Child is flawed, second, because I have none of your tall paper copies, third, because the novel is about Virginia, and *finally* because—as Vanity Fair would say—I am retiring from The Reviewer. After this month I shall fall into a well of silence and you will not be troubled again, but—if you will attend to all of this—I shall endeavor at some future time to make suitable acknowledgment.

Emily Clark.

INDEX

Abdullah, Achmed: on contemporaries, 66, 67, 74; apartment of, 119; mentioned, xxiii, 77, 78, 128
"Absentee Father": 68
"Adam and Little Eva": 46
Adams, Franklin Pierce: 103
Adelphi, The: 178, 192
Ahern, Mr.: 207
Aïde, Hamilton: xviii
"Aiken Paper, An": 17
Akins, Zöe: 54
Algonquin Hotel: Emily at, 111, 118, 182; mentioned, 31, 128, 148, 182, 195
"Allegory of the Young Intellectuals": 173
Allen, Hervey: xxiii
Allison, James: and *Reviewer*, 20; and Emily, 36, 102; mentioned, 21, 59, 90
American Mercury, The: xii, 183, 184, 211
Anderson, Henry: as *Reviewer* director, 49, 52, 77; Emily's story about, 138, 146, 167, 169, 172, 177; mentioned, 151
Anderson, Margaret: xiii
Anderson, Sherwood: 52, 113, 135, 165
Arrow of Gold, The: 165
Asbury, Herbert: xii
Asquith, Margot: 13, 36, 169
Astor, Nancy: 12, 13, 60, 96, 126
Atherton, Gertrude: 154, 157
"Atlanta": 173
Atlantic: 40, 151

Babbitt: 88, 187
Back to Methuselah: 16
Baskt, Léon: 130, 137
Balch, Edwin Swift: marriage of, to Emily, xix, 187, 195; mentioned, 207, 209
Balch, Willing: 196
Balfour, Arthur: xviii, 13
Balisand: 197, 198, 200, 203, 204, 206
Bankhead, Tallulah: 112

Baptists: 11, 93
Barnes, Djuna: 148
Barren Ground: xiv
Barrister Lodge estate: 171
Barrymore, Ethel: 12
Barrymore, John: 12, 137
Barthelmess, Richard: 111, 114, 144, 162, 163, 206
Battle, Martha Bagby (Mrs. Gordon): 115
Baugh, Hansel: xxiii, 46
Beard, Mr.: 146, 149
"Beauty—and Mary Blair": 9
Beer, Thomas: 128
Begbie, Harold: 41 n. 9
Beirne, Frank: 48, 79, 185
Beirne, Rosamund Randall: Emily visits, 67, 75, 79, 83; mentioned, 77, 80, 172
Belasco, David: 66, 74, 119
Bellamann, Henry: xxiii
Benét, William Rose: 51, 95, 181, 198
Benjamin Franklin: xvii
Bennett, Jesse Lee: xxiii
Bennett, John: xxiii, 63, 73
Berry Hill estate: 171
Bible Belt: xi
Bierstadt, Edward: 16, 36, 73, 132
Bishop, John Peale: 120
Björkman, Edwin: xxiii, 52, 55, 156
Black, Harry: 82, 131, 132
Blind Bow Boy, The: 125, 149, 172, 177, 180, 181, 191, 199
"Blue Ice": 150
Blue Teapot: 128
Bodenheim, Maxwell: xxiii
"Booboise": xi, 51
Boocock, Murray: 73
Boogher, Susan: 199
Bookman: 26, 55, 75, 76, 96, 106, 132, 135, 137, 159
Bookman's Day Book: xvi
Book of Prefaces, A: 35
Borgia, Lucrezia: 36, 169
Bosher, Kate Langley: 58, 126

213

Van Doren, Carl: 178, 182
Valentine, Edward: 152
Valentino, Rudolph, 163
Vanity Fair: 5, 17, 211
van Loon, Hendrick: 80, 88
Van Vechten, Carl: on contemporaries,
xi, 46, 54, 116, 135, 168, 202; and
Emily, xix, 84–85, 93, 101, 108, 112,
117, 141, 146, 151, 189, 192, 194,
195, 198, 201; writing of, xx, 66, 88,
130, 149, 154, 172, 176, 180, 191;
characteristics of, xxi, 53, 61, 70, 96,
99, 118, 119, 121, 157; and *Reviewer*,
xxii, 25, 39, 89, 97, 106, 126, 150,
152, 177, 183, 203, 206, 208; and
Hergesheimer, 48, 55, 124, 138, 178,
205, 207; mentioned, xxiii, 94, 98,
107, 115, 120, 173, 174, 196, 199, 204
Van Vechten, Mrs. Carl. SEE Marinoff,
Fania
Van Vechten, Ralph: and *Reviewer*, 53,
57, 67, 78; and Emily, 61, 75
Victoria, Queen: 191
Villon, François: 36
"Violets in the Sahara": 61
Virginia State Library: 152
Volstead Act: xi

Wallace, Maxwell: 102
Wall Street: xii
"Walnut": 149
Walpole, Hugh: and *Reviewer*, 43, 46,
48, 68, 158; and Richmond, 57, 77, 98,
99, 139, 146, 148, 150, 151, 152, 153;
and Hergesheimer, 86, 97, 106, 110,
137, 172; and Emily, 96, 154, 166,
194; mentioned, 116, 124, 135, 149,
176, 194
War Between the States: 94, 95
Ward, Mrs. Channing: 44, 129
Washburn, Beatrice: 73
Waste, Henri: 135, 199 n.

Waters, Ethel: xxi
Watkins, Bessie: 112
Wave: xvi
Weaver, John Van Alystyn: 69
West, Frank: 30
Westley, Helen: 117, 118
Westmoreland Club: 166, 167
Westover estate: 34, 62, 87, 92, 94, 111,
126, 152, 171, 185, 196
Wharton, Edith: xx, 81
What Maisie Knew: 86
White, Mrs.: 112
"White Angora": 123, 133, 146, 149,
161
Whiting, Dulany: 196
Whiting, Eleanor: 80, 82
Whitty, James H.: 152
Wilde, Oscar: xviii, 13
Wild Oranges: 207
Wiley, Hugh: 130, 149
Williams, Mrs. John Skelton: 178
Williamson, Miss: 59
Wilson, Edmund, Jr.: 120, 145
Wilson, Woodrow: 132
Winfree, Mr.: 39
Winnington-Ingram, Bishop: 96
Woman's Club of Richmond: 58, 92
Woodlawn estate: 178
World (New York): xxiii
Wright, Mrs.: 137
Writers' Club of Richmond: 3, 5, 8, 91,
106, 126
Wylie, Elinor: xxi, 198, 201

Yale Review: 63, 178
Yale University: 140
Yellow Book, The: xviii, 13
Young Intellectuals: 52, 84, 86, 88, 119,
145
Youth and the Bright Medusa: 3
"Youth and Wings": 178